THE AUDIO HANDBOOK

THE AUDIO HANDBOOK

GORDON J. KING
T.ENG.(C.E.I.), R.TECH.ENG., A.M.I.E.R.E., F.I.S.T.C., F.C.S.T.E.,
M.I.P.R.E., M.A.E.S.

LONDON
NEWNES–BUTTERWORTHS

THE BUTTERWORTH GROUP

ENGLAND
Butterworth & Co (Publishers) Ltd
London: 88 Kingsway, WC2B 6AB

AUSTRALIA
Butterworths Pty Ltd
Sydney: 586 Pacific Highway, NSW 2067
Melbourne: 343 Little Collins Street, 3000
Brisbane: 240 Queen Street, 4000

CANADA
Butterworth & Co (Canada) Ltd
Scarborough: 2265 Midland Avenue, Ontario M1P 4S1

NEW ZEALAND
Butterworths of New Zealand Ltd
Wellington: 26–28 Waring Taylor Street, 1

SOUTH AFRICA
Butterworth & Co (South Africa) (Pty) Ltd
Durban: 152–154 Gale Street

First published in 1975 by
Newnes-Butterworths, an imprint
of the Butterworth Group

© Gordon J. King, 1975

ISBN 0 408 00150 X

Filmset by Thomson Litho, East Kilbride, Scotland

Printed in England by J. W. Arrowsmith Ltd., Bristol.

Foreword

by Donald Aldous
Technical Editor, *Hi-Fi News & Record Review*

Do you know the Zanzibar Fallacy? Octogenarian Percy Wilson, the first and most distinguished British reviewer of hi-fi equipment, likes to tell this story: "On the Isle of Zanzibar, there is a town clock at one end and a cannon at the other. Each day, at noon, the clock strikes twelve and the cannon is fired. When a visitor enquired of the keepers of the clock, how the time was set, he was told, 'By the sound of the cannon'. When he asked how the noon time was checked, he was told, 'By the striking of the clock'."

Many of the audio articles and discussions today on hi-fi equipment are of this kind, but Gordon King has always been aware of the dangers of opinions and information based on mistaken logic or lack of observed facts. Continually adding to and upgrading his test equipment, standards and knowledge, Gordon King is in the direct line of the great reviewers. Totally professional in his approach, and in the preparation of material for the Press— as those of us who work with him will know—he retains the enthusiasm of the amateur 'in love' with his hobby.

Towards the end of the war years, Gordon served in India with a Special Communications Unit, and he likes to reminisce on some experiments with a design of 20 watt amplifier using transmitter modulation transformers as output transformers and transmitting valves as power amplifiers. Other areas he devoted time to included the see-saw phase-splitter and primitive wire recorders and disc recorders for sending home Forces' messages.

On returning to civilian life, like many veteran audiophiles, he constructed Williamson amplifiers, and later joined a company directly concerned with the design and manufacture of audio equipment, and making gramophone records.

The full impact of Gordon King's work, both as a development engineer and as a technical writer in the fields of audio, radio and television, is now known throughout the world. This present book I regard as his most important to date on audio. I enjoyed reading it immensely and it cannot but add to his reputation.

Contents

Introduction

A BRIEF HISTORY of this current volume would not be amiss. Back in 1959 I wrote a book called *The Practical Hi-Fi Handbook*. This was published by Odhams Books and was very well accepted, requiring several reprints to satisfy the UK requirements. There was also a Spanish edition. The book was revised and extended in 1969 to take in transistor equipment, tape recording and video-tape recording and was published by Newnes-Butterworths under the new title *The Hi-Fi and Tape Recorder Handbook*.

Such has been the advances in the world of high quality audio reproduction that this third design has been demanded. This time, however, the book has been completely rewritten and no longer resembles the earlier volumes, and the generic term 'audio' has been used in the title. At one time equipment with the label 'hi-fi' was several planes higher in design detail and hence in potential quality of reproduction. This is still true to varying degrees even today, but the art of solidstate electronics has evolved such that the distinction between 'basic' audio equipment and equipment carrying the hi-fi tag is diminishing, and from the electronics side, anyway, it appears that before very long there will not be all that much difference between the important parameters of the two classes of equipment.

There will always be a call for the 'super' class of equipment, of course, designed for the enthusiast satisfied only with extra high power at barely measurable levels of harmonic and intermodulation distortion and with facilities and features well in advance of the economics of the basic class.

Electronics aside, some of the greatest differences lie in the signal sources feeding the amplifiers and the loudspeakers fed by them. High quality record playing units with minimal rumble turntables of constant speed and low wow and flutter, with low-tracking magnetic cartridges and partnering low inertia, low bearing friction arms cost money. The same is true of top-flight loudspeaker systems capable of yielding domestic scene sound pressure peaks towards 100 dB at low distortion and with extended frequency response, particularly at the bass end, and minimal coloration.

Tape machines are other items where quality is more reflected by price, and this is particularly true of the latest cassette machines incorporating noise reducing artifices like Dolby B. The low linear velocity of cassette tapes demands

1

highly sophisticated tape transport mechanisms if speed inconstancy and wow and flutter are to be reduced to an acceptable 'hi-fi' level, while highly accurate transducer head engineering is a prerequisite for extended frequency response and minimal crosstalk. The microgaps essential for extended high-frequency response are more prone to wear and distortion by the passage of the tape past the heads than those of some of the earlier reel-to-reel machines, and for this reason more costly head designs—some composed of glass-ferrite—are incorporated in the better class machines. All these features cost more money than the partnering electronic circuits, some of which in replay machines only are not unduly complex. Dolby B, essential for an acceptable signal/noise ratio at the lower tape velocities, is a more complicated circuit addition, though, as also is that of any of the other recently developed noise reducing systems.

Dolby B, for example, together with the relatively recent high energy (such as CrO_2) tapes, have significantly improved the dynamic range potential of the cassette as a programme signal source, even at the dramatically low velocity of 4.76 cm/sec. The Philips system, which provides stereo (mono compatible) in two-channel pairs (four tracks in all), is the existing 'standard', and most serious cassette machines are correspondingly engineered.

For 'four-channel stereo' or quadraphony both the disc and the standard 6.3 mm ($\frac{1}{4}$ in) tape (cartridge housed) are in current application. At the time of writing no definite four-channel standard has evolved for the cassette, though a two-channel matrix arrangement, using the two-channel pairs of the standard cassette tape would be feasible. This would then be rather similar to the matrix four-channel disc. A four-channel cassette deck has been made by JVC and H-K.

In addition to this type of disc, however, there is also the so-called 'carrier' disc where the rear information constitutes the modulation of a subcarrier recorded in the single groove, which also accommodates the front left and right information in the conventional way. This type of disc is often referred to as four-channel discrete because the four channels are handled from start to finish in essential isolation (i.e. the JVC CD-4 system, where C stands for compatible—meaning that the disc will play in stereo on a stereo system—D stands for discrete, and the 4, of course, indicating four channels).

The number of channels involved in the passage of the information from microphone to loudspeakers, via the recording medium, is commonly given in terms of 4-4-4 for the discrete system and 4-2-4 for the matrix system. The first 4 means that the signals are in four channels to start with (i.e. four microphones). The second number tells how many isolated channels there are in the recording process. In the discrete system, of course, there are four and in the matrix system only two. The third indicates the number of replay channels (i.e. how many separate amplifiers and loudspeakers are used). On this basis, therefore, a two-channel stereo system could be designated 2-2-2.

Pseudo-quadraphony, sometimes called 'surround sound' or 'ambiophony' is designated 2-2-4, which implies that the four loudspeakers obtain their signals from the two-channel source, which was also transmitted or recorded in two channels. The signals for the rear loudspeakers are, in fact, derived from the differential of the left and right stereo signals, so the system is not true four-channel. However, since concert hall ambience is responsible for some of the antiphase or differential components between the left and right channels, the rear loudspeakers respond to this and enhancement of the stereo reproduction is sometimes experienced.

The radio tuner as a programme source is assuming greater importance, particularly now that the audio quality is being improved by the pulse code modulation links between studio centres and the v.h.f./f.m. transmitters, which is also resulting in the stereo service of the BBC being extended over the country. In fact, with a well programmed 'live' transmission the quality of the audio signal from a good f.m. stereo tuner is above that obtainable from any other contemporary source—except, perhaps, from microphones direct!

While the gulf between the detailed electronics of the true hi-fi tuner and the basic counterpart is still quite wide, a well designed f.m.-only basic type with inbuilt decoder is nevertheless capable of providing a very acceptable programme signal when operating under good reception conditions. As with amplifiers, the more expensive models include facilities and features which may not be fundamental to the signal quality. For example, one might pay extra for a.m. bands, for elaborate tuning mechanisms and enclosures, for switchable filters and other technical features which themselves are not directly responsible for the quality of the resultant audio signal.

On the other hand, acceptable reception under adverse conditions, as for example when the aerial signal is weak or when it is required to tune a weak signal which is located close in frequency to a much more powerful one, requires a tuner in which the various circuits have been deliberately tailored to take account of such reception difficulties, and these, of course, have to be paid for.

Since *The Practical Hi-Fi Handbook* was written in 1959, therefore, the standard of basically acceptable quality reproduction has been elevated by innovation and development in almost all associated areas of the art. Apart from television sound and the small transistor radio, stereo reproduction is now the norm. In fact, hi-fi and stereo are often regarded as synonymous in this audio age; but stereo does not change by some magic mediocre quality audio into hi-fi.

From two channels we are now graduating to four; but the practice here is little more advanced than was stereo when *The Practical Hi-Fi Handbook* was launched. Technically, however, developments abound, though there is still some way to go before universal four-channel standards can be expected. In spite of this, both the hardware (the mechanics and electronics) and the software (discs and tapes) are available for those wishing to join the early pioneers.

What is happening, therefore, is that hi-fi in the strict term is embracing new areas and that audio which a decade or two back would have been regarded as hi-fi is now almost 'domestic quality'.

In writing this new book emphasis has been removed from the topic of servicing (since from the audio aspects this is covered in my companion volumes *Radio and Audio Servicing Handbook* and *F.M. Radio Servicing Handbook*, both by the same publisher as this book) and applied more to the new arts and the sciences relating to them, thereby making it a book of wider appeal not only to the service technician and hi-fi dealer, but also to the audiophile and music

3

lover desirous of keeping abreast of the changing face of home audio reproduction.

In conclusion, I should like to acknowledge the encouragement given by
colleagues throughout the audio industry from those concerned with making
the records to those whose job it is to design the electronics, including the
editors of the hi-fi and audio magazines in which area I work. Special thanks
are offered to my friend Donald Aldous for his helpful suggestions, for reading
the proofs and for contributing the Foreword.

Brixham, Devon   Gordon J. King

CHAPTER 1

Audio Fundamentals

EQUIPMENT DESIGNED for high quality sound reproduction differs from the basically 'domestic' type of equipment in that extra special attention is given to a large number of small points of detail. This is what costs the extra money. Minor changes, either as the result of alteration in value of a component or components or unskilled servicing, will disturb the critical design balance and in some way or other impair the quality of reproduction. Distortion, for example, may increase or the frequency response may suffer.

The service technician insensitive to the hi-fi equation may not be aware of these shortcomings; but the hi-fi perfectionist, whose equipment it is, will certainly notice a difference. The technician is thus obliged to employ accurate audio test equipment to judge the standard of the equipment before and after repair or adjustment. Listening tests waste time and lead to frustration. It is the technician's job to ensure that the equipment matches the parameters of its specification.

Experience has shown that hi-fi types fall into three main categories. There is the music lover whose primary desire is to play his favourite records with the least apparent distortion. This type is generally the least technically exacting since fair quality reproduction is adequate to re-create in his mind the atmosphere of the concert hall—slight distortion and other minor shortcomings—thus go unnoticed.

Then there is the technical perfectionist whose senses are sharply focused on the various technical parameters of the equipment. This type may not possess a highly developed aesthetic interest in music, but he is often able to judge with uncanny accuracy whether there is more distortion than there should be; whether extra damping would improve the bass delivery of the loudspeakers; whether there is a droop or peak in the overall frequency response; and similar technical matters. He secures satisfaction from listening to loud reproduction at low distortion, and when *he* says that the distortion, etc. is higher than it should be it is prudent for the technician not to disagree with him—until he can prove otherwise more objectively, of course!

The third type is a mixture of the previous two, and here is represented the large majority of hi-fi enthusiasts and audiophiles. This type is an enthusiast because he is both technically interested and at the same time a true music lover.

The audio technician, therefore, should be aware of these three shades of enthusiast. The technician should desirably have an interest in music and attend live concerts if only to acquaint himself with the real thing! The technician practising in the high quality audio field needs to be something of a psychologist as well as an engineer, and it is just as well to know one's subjects. Sound as it is heard is a purely subjective function, so from here let us proceed.

SOUND

The source of any sound is always in some state of vibration. This is clearly demonstrated by the piano string, the tuning fork, the cone of a loudspeaker unit, etc. The vibration may be so slight or so rapid as not to be visible, while it may be large and relatively slow as to be clearly visible, as in the case of a very loud mains hum emanating from the loudspeaker. There is no future in removing the vibration in the latter case by glueing the speech coil to the magnetic pole pieces—a condition once observed by the author when investigating a system for lack of output! When questioned, the owner was true in principle by commenting 'but I got rid of the terrible hum which was being caused by this cone thing vibrating' (a true story, incidentally).

With organ pipes and other wind instruments the source is air vibration. The vibration can often be experienced by placing a finger over the pipe, etc. or on the string or loudspeaker cone. It is surprising how sensitive the finger can be in detecting vibration. In fact, some engineers check for slight mains hum—which may be inaudible—by placing a finger lightly on the cone.

A sounding source causes the surrounding air to be alternately compressed and rarefied in sympathy with the vibrations. A pulse of high pressure is thus followed by a pulse of low pressure and so on.

LONGITUDINAL WAVES

Sound waves in air are known as *longitudinal* waves, which implies that the molecules of the air travel to and fro in a path which is parallel to the direction of the wave propagation, and that each molecule executes the same motion as the one before it but a small interval of time later.

Waves associated with the electromagnetic family—radio, light, etc.—are known as *transverse* waves because the particles of the medium travel in a path perpendicular to, instead of parallel to, the propagation of the wave.

SOUND VELOCITY

The speed at which a sound wave travels—called the velocity of propagation—depends on the physical properties of the medium, the relationship when the medium is a gas being

$$c = \sqrt{\frac{\gamma p}{\rho}} \qquad (1.1)$$

6

where c is the velocity, γ the ratio of specific heats (which is a constant and about 1.4 for atmospheric air), p the pressure (which is nominally 10^6 dynes/cm^2 corresponding to 1 bar or, in SI units, to 10^5 newtons/m^2 and ρ the density (which for air is close to 1.2 kg/m^3).

The velocity through atmospheric air at sea level and 20 °C is close to 344 m/s (1 130 ft/s). The velocity in a given gas medium and at constant temperature is thus dependent on density and 'compressibility', but because the density is proportional to the pressure, the velocity is independent of pressure over a wide range, but changing temperature changes the velocity.

Velocity is also related to the frequency f and the wavelength λ of the sound by

$$c = \lambda f \tag{1.2}$$

so that the wavelength can be found by dividing the velocity by the frequency. For example, the wavelength of a sound of 50 Hz (the mains frequency) is 6.88 m (22 ft 7 in). At 20 Hz the wavelength is 17.2 m (56 ft 4 in), while at 5 kHz it is 6.9 cm (2.7 in). Thus the wavelength diminishes as the frequency increases. A knowledge of the wavelength can be useful when investigating for standing waves (eigentones) in the listening room, as well as for other aspects of the audio art.

To summarise, therefore, any gas, such as air, consists of a large number of molecules moving rapidly at random. A pressure is thus experienced by an object within the gas of a value dependent on the number of molecules per unit volume and on their kinetic energy; in other words, on the barometric pressure of the gas (air) and on its temperature.

SOUND PRESSURE

The normal atmospheric pressure is about 10^6 dynes/cm^2, which in contemporary term corresponds to 1 bar or to 10^5 pascals (Pa), equivalent to 10^5 N/m^2 in SI units. Sound waves cause variations within this normal pressure over the range from about 20 μPa (micro indicating one-millionth) to 60 Pa—from the quietest sounds round the threshold of hearing to sounds of intensity into the threshold of pain.

A sound wave is thus characterised by an oscillatory (depending upon the nature of the sound) variation in the air pressure above and below the prevailing atmospheric pressure and by a corresponding to and fro velocity of the gas molecules about the random gaseous velocity. The *power* propagated by a sound wave is the product of the sound particle velocity about the random velocity and the acoustical pressure about the normal atmospheric pressure.

SOUND POWER

The mean power per unit area can thus be expressed as

$$W_a = pu \tag{1.3}$$

where p is the r.m.s. gas pressure and u the r.m.s. particle velocity. From the electrical point of view, p can be regarded as the analogue of voltage and u as the analogue of current, their product giving the power.

7

AUDIO FUNDAMENTALS

The specific radiation impedance Z is given by

$$Z = \rho c \tag{1.4}$$

where c is the velocity of propagation and ρ the gas density. Thus W_a can also be expressed as

$$W_a = Zu^2 \tag{1.5}$$

or as

$$W_a = \frac{p^2}{Z} \tag{1.6}$$

Z is often given as 40.7 acoustical ohms in c.g.s. units or 407 acoustical ohms in SI units, so by using the appropriate value in, say, expression 1.6 it can be calculated that a sound pressure of $20\,\mu$bars (2 Pa) gives W_a a value of 9.828 ergs/cm^2 or $98\,280 \times 10^{-7}$ joule/m^2, equal to 98 280 ergs/m^2. Taking these respectively as 10 ergs/cm^2 and $100\,000$ ergs/m^2, and since 1 watt is equal to 10^7 ergs (1 joule) per second, we derive unit powers of $1\,\mu$W/cm^2 and $10\,$mW/m^2.

SPHERICAL WAVES

When the wavefront is at right-angles to the direction of propagation the waves are called plane. Under most practical conditions, however, the wavefront expands non-uniformly, such that in unrestricted free space, the waves radiate outwards as an expanding sphere (spherical waves). The *power* per unit area then falls inversely as the square of the distance and the *pressure* inversely as the distance.

The mean power W_a per unit area due to a spherical wave is given by

$$W_a = \rho c u^2 \frac{2\pi^2 r^4}{\lambda^2 d^2} \tag{1.7}$$

while the r.m.s. pressure p (when the distance is greater than the wavelength) is given by

$$p = \rho c u \frac{\sqrt{(2)}\pi r^2}{\lambda d} \tag{1.8}$$

where in both expressions ρ is the gas density, c the sound velocity, u the r.m.s. particle velocity, r the radius of the wavefront, d the distance from source and λ the wavelength.

AMPLITUDE OF SOUND WAVE

The loudness of a sound is governed by the amplitude of the wave and hence on the energy carried by it to the ear, since sound is ultimately perceived by our faculty of hearing.

The r.m.s. amplitude of a plane wave is given by

$$a = \frac{u}{2\pi f} \quad \text{or} \quad \frac{p}{\rho c 2\pi f} \tag{1.9}$$

8

and of a spherical wave by

$$a = \frac{u}{2\pi f} \frac{\sqrt{(2)}\pi r^2}{\lambda d} \qquad (1.10)$$

when the distance is greater than the wavelength, where a is the amplitude, u the r.m.s. particle velocity, f the frequency, r the radius of wavefront, d the distance and λ the wavelength.

CHARACTERISTICS OF SOUND

The pitch of a sound is determined by the frequency and hence wavelength, while the quality or timbre, which distinguishes between notes of the same pitch sounded by different instruments, is determined by the harmonic composition of the sound, which can be regarded for the present as subsidiary vibrations whose frequencies are multiples of the fundamental vibration.

As the frequency is reduced, the note eventually becomes resolved into the separate impulses of which it is composed. As the frequency is increased, the note becomes very shrill, and around 15 kHz it tends to fade into a very high-pitched hiss.

The high-frequency limit of audibility is related to age. With young people it is around 20 kHz, falling possibly to 6 kHz or less in old age. Some young people are uncomfortably conscious of the line timebase whistle of television receivers, while older people are not at all disturbed. The squeak of a mouse is commonly inaudible to people in their fifties yet dramatically apparent to the younger person.

TRANSIENTS

Nevertheless, a person whose hearing is failing at the high-frequency end of the spectrum due to normal age is still able to appreciate music containing harmonic components extending above his cutoff frequency. It is thus still necessary for audio equipment used by such a person to be capable of responding to high audio frequencies. One reason for this is that parts of music waveforms consist of steep, rapidly occurring wavefronts, called *transients*. These can be resolved into a large number of harmonic components, so attenuating the high-frequency response has the effect of reducing the rate of rise of the wavefronts and of diminishing the amplitude of the transients. Since transients are responsible for the 'attack' of music reproduction, impairing these such that their acceleration and amplitude are reduced is obvious equally to persons with and without extended high-frequency hearing response.

THE DECIBEL

The pressure and energy (power) of a sound wave are often expressed as a decibel (dB) unit, so we must now see what is meant by this.

The dB expresses the ratio of two powers logarithmically—ten times the common logarithmic ratio in fact, so mathematically we have

$$dB = 10 \log_{10}(W/W_o) \qquad (1.11)$$

9

where (W/W_o) is the ratio of the two powers concerned. Because the dB value implies a *ratio*, the reference power W_o must always be stated or at least clearly understood.

Now, since sound power is proportional to the sound pressure *squared*, the number of decibels between two pressures is given by

$$dB = 10 \log_{10}(p/p_o)^2 \qquad (1.12)$$
$$= 20 \log_{10}(p/p_o)$$

where (p/p_o) is the ratio of the two pressures, the implication again being that the reference pressure p_o must be stated or understood.

By international agreement, the reference sound pressure is 0.0002 dyne/cm² or 0.0002 microbar, and the SI equivalent is 20 micronewtons per sq. m $(20 \, \mu N/m^2)$ which corresponds, again by international agreement, to 20 micropascal whose symbol is μPa. Thus 0 dB, the reference level, corresponds to $20 \, \mu$Pa or 0·0002 microbar, which is the sound pressure approximating to the threshold of hearing.

When the pressure of a sound wave exceeds about 120 dB a tickling sensation and ultimate pain is experienced by a listener. 120 dB corresponds to a pressure ratio of 10^6:1, which means, then, that the pressure at this level is 200 μb (20 Pa). Thus, from the practical point of view the human ear is able to accommodate a pressure range from 0.0002 (20 μPa) to 200 μb (20 Pa) for the softest sounds (threshold of hearing) to the loudest sounds (approaching the threshold of pain). In actual fact, the upper limit is more like 130 dB, corresponding to a sound pressure of just over 600 μb (60 Pa), but then the sound experience is so intense as to be really painful and damaging.

Table 1.1 gives some examples of sounds, their pressures in μb and the dB equivalents.

PER UNIT SOUND POWER

We have seen (expressions 1.3 and 1.7) that power is propagated by a sound wave as a function of the sound pressure and particle velocity. At 0 dB (0.0002 μb pressure) the power is 10^{-12} W/m², which has international acceptance. Thus at 100 dB the mean power per m² is 10^{-2} watt (10 mW). At 120 dB the power is 1 W/m² and at 130 dB 10 W/m². Thus from the threshold of hearing (0 dB) to 120 dB the power or energy range is a massive 10^{12}:1, which is also shown in Table 1.1. The pressure range is 10^6:1, as we have seen.

All this may give thought as to why such high power amplifiers are used for domestic sound reproduction. The reason for the need for high electrical power will become apparent later.

THE DECIBEL AND RATIOS OF ELECTRICAL UNITS

Before we leave the subject of decibels, mention must be made of the fact that they are used also to represent ratios of power, voltage and current in electrical circuits.

For electrical power ratios expression (1.11) is applicable and for voltage ratios expression (1.12) is applicable, but then the ratio is (V/V_o), where V_o is the reference voltage. Expression (1.12) is also applicable to current ratios, the ratio then being (I/I_o), where I_o is the reference current.

However, it is important that the resistance R in which current I or voltage V operates is common to both sides of the ratio in the expressions. When R

Table 1.1. EXAMPLES OF SOUNDS, THEIR PRESSURES, RELATIVE ENERGIES AND DECIBEL EQUIVALENTS

Noise	Decibels	Relative energy	Pressure microbars	Typical examples
	120	1 000 000 000 000	200	
Deafening	110	100 000 000 000		Jet aircraft at 150 m (500 ft) Inside boiler-making factory 'Pop' music group Motor horn at 5 m (16 ft)
————	100	10 000 000 000	20	
Very loud	90	1 000 000 000		Inside tube train Busy street Workshop Small car at 7.5 m (24 ft)
————	80	100 000 000	2	
Loud	70	10 000 000		Noisy office Inside small car Large shop Radio set—full volume
————	60	1 000 000	0.2	
Moderate	50	100 000		Normal conversation at 1 m (3 ft) Urban house Quiet office Rural house
————	40	10 000	0.02	
Faint	30	1 000		Public library Quiet conversation Rustle of paper Whisper
————	20	100	0.002	
Very faint	10	10		Quiet church Still night in the country Sound-proof room Threshold of hearing
	0	1	0.0002	

differs from side to side, the following expressions should be used

$$dB = 20 \log_{10}(V/V_o) + 10 \log_{10}(R/R_o) \qquad (1.13)$$

$$dB + 20 \log_{10}(I/I_o) + 10 \log_{10}(R/R_o) \qquad (1.14)$$

where R_o is the resistance of the circuit referring to the reference voltage or current and R is the resistance of the circuit in which the other side of the ratio is measured.

11

When the dB number is known, the power, current or voltage ratio can be found from

$$(W/W_o) = \text{antilog dB}/10 \qquad (1.15)$$

$$(I/I_o) = \text{antilog dB}/20 \qquad (1.16)$$

$$(V/V_o) = \text{antilog dB}/20 \qquad (1.17)$$

where dB is the decibel *number*.

To save the toil of calculation dB tables have been evolved, samples of which are given in Tables 1.2 and 1.3. Figures not given in these can easily be calculated. For example, when two dB numbers are added their ratios are multiplied.

Table 1.2. CONVERSION OF DECIBELS TO POWER AND VOLTAGE/CURRENT RATIOS

dB	Power Ratio	Voltage Ratio	dB	Power Ratio	Voltage Ratio
1	1.26	1.12	15	31.6	5.62
2	1.58	1.26	20	100	10
3	2.0	1.41	30	1 000	31.6
4	2.51	1.58	40	10^4	10^2
5	3.16	1.78	50	10^5	316
6	3.98	2.0	60	10^6	10^3
7	5.01	2.24	70	10^7	3 160
8	6.31	2.51	80	10^8	10^4
9	7.94	2.82	90	10^9	31 600
10	10	3.16	100	10^{10}	10^5

Table 1.3. CONVERSION OF POWER RATIOS TO DECIBELS

Power Ratio	dB	Power Ratio	dB	Power Ratio	dB	Power Ratio	dB
1.0	0.000	3.3	5.185	5.6	7.482	7.9	8.976
1.1	0.414	3.4	5.315	5.7	7.559	8.0	9.031
1.2	0.792	3.5	5.441	5.8	7.634	8.1	9.085
1.3	1.139	3.6	5.563	5.9	7.709	8.2	9.138
1.4	1.461	3.7	5.682	6.0	7.782	8.3	9.191
1.5	1.761	3.8	5.798	6.1	7.835	8.4	9.243
1.6	2.041	3.9	5.911	6.2	7.924	8.5	9.294
1.7	2.304	4.0	6.021	6.3	7.993	8.6	9.345
1.8	2.553	4.1	6.128	6.4	8.062	8.7	9.395
1.9	2.788	4.2	6.232	6.5	8.129	8.8	9.445
2.0	3.010	4.3	6.335	6.6	8.195	8.9	9.494
2.1	3.222	4.4	6.435	6.7	8.261	9.0	9.542
2.2	3.424	4.5	6.532	6.8	8.325	9.1	9.590
2.3	3.617	4.6	6.628	6.9	8.388	9.2	9.638
2.4	3.802	4.7	6.721	7.0	8.451	9.3	9.685
2.5	3.979	4.8	6.812	7.1	8.513	9.4	9.731
2.6	4.150	4.9	6.902	7.2	8.573	9.5	9.777
2.7	4.314	5.0	6.990	7.3	8.633	9.6	9.823
2.8	4.472	5.1	7.076	7.4	8.692	9.7	9.868
2.9	4.624	5.2	7.160	7.5	8.751	9.8	9.912
3.0	4.771	5.3	7.243	7.6	8.808	9.9	9.956
3.1	4.914	5.4	7.324	7.7	8.865	10.0	10.000
3.2	5.051	5.5	7.404	7.8	8.921		

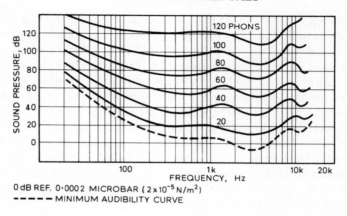

FIG. 1.1. *Curves of equal loudness (after Robinson and Dadson)*

LOUDNESS

Loudness is the subjective effect that a sound wave has on a listener; that is, a listener's auditory perception to the strength of the sound. Loudness is mostly a function of the sound pressure acting on the ear drum, though, resulting from the complex properties of the human ear, other factors are involved. The unit of loudness is the *phon*. It refers to a subjective comparison between the sound under consideration and a reference 1 kHz sinusoidal progressive essentially plane sound wave arriving directly from the front of the listener. The loudness level in phons is numerically equal to the sound pressure level of the 1 kHz reference sound when the two are *judged* to be equally loud.

The ear is not equally sensitive to all frequencies, it being towards maximum around 3 kHz and showing gain over the range 500 Hz–5 kHz. The curves in Fig. 1.1 indicate how the sensitivity of the ear changes over the range 20 Hz–15 kHz for pure tone at different sound pressure levels. At low sound pressure levels the fall in low-frequency sensitivity is greater than at higher levels. The curves also reveal a fall in high-frequency sensitivity. The gain in sensitivity around 3 kHz is accredited to cavity resonance of the outer ear.

The curves are based on the result of work carried out at the National Physical Laboratory by Robinson and Dadson, and form the basis of British Standard 3383:1961. With increasing age the sensitivity of the ear diminishes progressively from about 2 kHz upwards, but the curves in Fig. 1.1 refer to the 20 year age group. The Robinson and Dadson curves differ from the earlier Fletcher and Munson (1933) and Churcher and King (1937) curves. It will be seen that the minimum audibility curve is about 4 dB up at 1 kHz, cutting the 0 dB line at about 2 kHz. With the Fletcher and Munson curves the 0 phon curve is placed at 0 dB at 1 kHz (see, for example, page 45 of the *Hi-Fi and Tape Recorder Handbook*). The threshold of hearing is still, nevertheless, often referred to as 0 dB sound pressure.

13

We have seen, therefore, that the loudness of a sound is related to its pitch or frequency as well as to its amplitude or intensity (i.e., sound pressure). These factors have encouraged the introduction of the so-called 'loudness' control, which functions to increase the bass output, and sometimes the treble output to a lesser degree as well, as the gain of the amplifier is reduced. Rarely, however, is this sort of control accurately tailored to the curves of equal loudness, and because the bass and, perhaps, treble lift is coupled to the setting of the control, the precise lift introduced will depend on the level of the programme signal applied to the amplifier! Moreover, it is argued that such electronic 'equalisation' is incompatible with realism and hence hi-fi. It is true, of course, that any required degree of equalisation can be introduced at the bass and treble ends of the spectrum by the tone controls, and many enthusiasts prefer to use these rather than the 'loudness' control or switch.

DYNAMIC RANGE

A fundamental characteristic of music is its dynamic range. That is, the range between the softest and loudest sounds. Tests have shown that a large orchestra is capable of a dynamic range of 70 dB, corresponding to a sound pressure range of 3162:1 or an energy range of 10^7:1. From the threshold of hearing this would be accommodated by a sound pressure at the listener rising to about 0.63 μb on peaks. Under concert listening conditions, however, the ambient noise is far above 0 dB, so in order for the whole dynamic range to be assimilated by a listener the softest sounds must obviously be above the ambient noise level to avoid their masking.

If it is assumed that the peak (fff) level of a concert orchestra is 100 dB at the listening position and the dynamic range 70 dB, then the softest sounds (ppp) will be at a level of 30 dB ($100-70$ dB).

NOISE LEVELS AND CURVES

A sound level meter (s.l.m.) measuring the ambient noise level during a pause in the music would almost certainly indicate a level in advance of 30 dB, but this is because sounds at all frequencies over the measuring spectrum would contribute to the reading. To find the noise level at particular frequencies in the spectrum the sound has to be filtered into discrete channels. By using octave filters, for example, spectral noise masking curves can be constructed for different *total* noise levels. The nature of such curves, of course, reflects the frequency composition of the total noise, but for ambient noise (which is rather like white noise) the curves are strongly similar in character.

Two such curves are given in Fig. 1.2 for total noise levels of 43 and 33 dB.

Now, if we take a threshold of audibility curve, such as based on the minimum audibility curve of Robinson and Dadson (Fig. 1.1), a noise masking curve as in Fig. 1.2 can be applied directly to it, as shown in Fig. 1.3, which refers to a

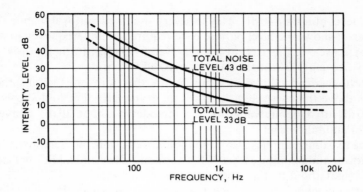

FIG. 1.2. *Masking levels for noise in rooms of 43 and 33 dB total noise*

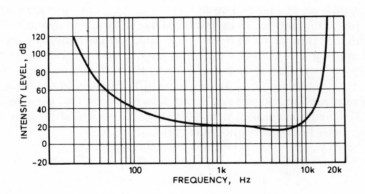

FIG. 1.3. *Audibility curve for a total room noise level of about 40 dB*

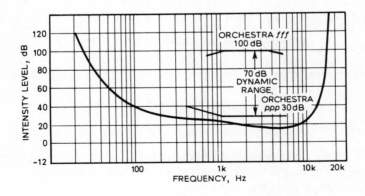

FIG. 1.4. *Audibility curve for a total auditorium noise level of about 42 dB, showing that at the listening position the full 70 dB of orchestra dynamic range is achieved well above the threshold of audibility referred to 100 dB peaks*

15

total noise level of about 40 dB. This is a very useful curve for dynamic range studies since it shows the level of pure tone required at any frequency to avoid masking by noise—in this case at a *total* level of 40 dB. In other words, pure tone at any frequency below the curve is masked by noise.

The softest sounds produced by an orchestra, therefore, must be of sufficient level to be above the curve. Fig. 1.4 gives an example of this, and shows that the full 70 dB of dynamic range is accommodated about 10 dB above the threshold of audibility level.

The same reasoning applies also to sound reproduction, but here we have the relatively lower ambient noise level of the domestic scene and additional factors of noise brought about by the reproducing equipment itself.

The total ambient noise of a quiet listening room is about 35 dB (see Table 1.1), but when the amplifier is under power and the volume control advanced for a realistic reproducing level background hum and hiss (albeit, of very low intensity) contribute to the overall noise level. The noise level is further increased by the noise produced by the pickup stylus tracing the groove of a gramophone record and sometimes by the noise produced by the turntable unit as well.

Thus with the reproducing equipment operating but not delivering sound or music the ambient noise level of the room might well rise from the nominal 35 dB to about 42 dB. Recent tests conducted by the author have proved this to be the case. Now, the room accounting for 35 dB of noise and the total noise with the equipment operating being 42 dB does not mean that the noise contribution of the equipment is a mere 7 dB (42 − 35 dB). Sound pressure levels in decibels *cannot* be added or subtracted arithmetically.

A formula which can be used to solve problems like this is

$$Y = \left[10 \log_{10} \left(1 + \log_{10}^{-1} \frac{X}{10} \right) \right] - X \qquad (1.18)$$

where X is the *dB difference* between the two dB levels and Y a dB value to be added to the *larger* of the two dB values to give the total noise.

It is upon this formula that the scales of the nomograph in Fig. 1.5 are based. This saves considerable tedious calculation, and it works as follows. Subtract the second largest sound pressure dB level from the largest level and locate this

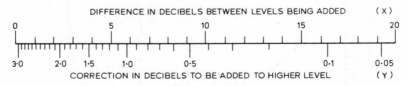

FIG. 1.5. *Nomograph for combining dB levels (see text for full explanation)*

on scale X. At the corresponding point on scale Y a correction dB value is given which needs to be added to the largest of the two dB values being considered to give the total dB pressure level.

As an example, take 35 dB and 41 dB. The difference is 6 dB which we find on scale X. Under this a correction close to 1 dB is given on scale Y. This we

16

add to 41 dB (the largest of the two values) and thus obtain a value close to 42 dB, which is the total sound pressure. This example corresponds to the noise levels previously considered and shows that the equipment produces about 41 dB of noise on its own, since the room noise of 35 dB and the equipment noise of 41 dB give an answer close to 42 dB.

It is here assumed that the total equipment noise is of a random nature, and this is reasonably true provided the mechanical noise and amplifier hum are at negligible levels, which is generally the case with high quality reproducing equipment.

The nomograph is useful for other similar applications in electrical circuits, for example. It is also possible to find the sum of more than two levels. The two largest are processed as already explained and the other levels are then processed one at a time. When the difference in levels is greater than 10 to 15 dB, the amount to be added becomes insignificant and can usually be ignored.

REPRODUCED DYNAMIC RANGE

From the reproducing point of view we are interested only in the total noise in the room, so an audibility curve based on a total noise level of 42 dB, as in the example, can be constructed and used as a basis for reproduced dynamic range assessment.

Now, although a large orchestra might have a peak dynamic range of 70 dB or so, such a wide range is barely reproducible in the present state of the art. The amplifier might possess a volume range potential of this order (sometimes more) but to allow the recording or modulation signals to operate above the intrinsic noise yielded by the system as a whole it is necessary for recording and transmitting engineers to apply some degree of peak limiting to the programme signal to avoid overloading and consequent cutter/groove damage or over-modulation.

The effective 'noise threshold' of the programme signal is often of a lower order than the total noise in the listening room. Thus the lower limit of the reproducible dynamic range is established essentially by the total room noise. Having established that it then becomes possible to calculate the least power required from the amplifier and loudspeakers to provide the maximum reproducible dynamic range, which in the present state of the art is around 60 dB, corresponding to a power range of $10^6:1$ or a sound pressure range of $10^3:1$.

In Fig. 1.6(a) is given an audibility curve corresponding to a total room noise level of about 42 dB (i.e. 35 dB ambient room noise and 41 dB of equipment noise) above which is a shaded area corresponding approximately to the spectral range of a recorded concert of 60 dB dynamic range. Thus, provided the amplifier/loudspeaker partnership is capable of yielding r.m.s. peaks of about 96 dB, the full 60 dB of available dynamic range will be reproduced without overload distortion on the one hand or loss due to noise on the other. A room of total noise level below that detailed will permit the same dynamic range fully to be accommodated at a r.m.s. peak level below 96 dB, while a greater total noise level will require a r.m.s. peak level in advance of 96 dB for the full dynamic range.

17

Since the operating audio system itself accounts for a high proportion of the total room noise, small differences in ambient noise level will not make very much difference to the total noise. For example, assuming about 41 dB system noise, a room noise of 40 dB (5 dB up on the previous example) will put the total noise up only by about 1.5 dB to about 43.5 dB, so the threshold of audibility curve would be only slightly different from that in Fig. 1.6(a).

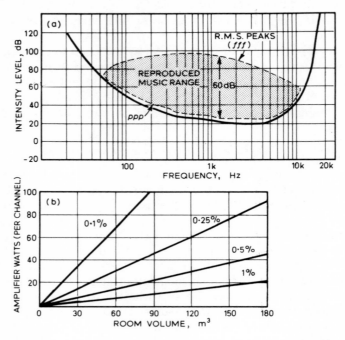

FIG. 1.6. (a) *Audibility curve based on approximately 35 dB of ambient room noise and 41 dB of equipment noise. The noise below the curve is masked by reproduced music over a 60 dB dynamic range within r.m.s. (fff) peaks of about 96 dB. (b) Stereo per-channel amplifier power versus room volume required for 96 dB reverberant field sound intensity for different loudspeaker efficiencies, based on average reverberation time (see text). For 100 dB reverberant field sound intensity the power needs to be increased by a factor of 2.5 times*

The question, then, is how much power do we need to handle a r.m.s. peak of 96 dB without running into overload and hence distortion? The answer is somewhat complex since it involves a number of factors. The actual mean acoustical power per unit area is incredibly small as we have already seen. At 100 dB sound pressure level, for example, it is a mere $10 \, \text{mW/m}^2$. A sound pressure level of 96 dB is 4 dB down from this, which corresponds to a power ratio a trifle over 2.5:1. Thus at this level the power is about $4 \, \text{mW/m}^2$. This sadly fails to indicate the amount of acoustical power that the loudspeakers need to radiate into the room. Clearly, the properties of the room itself must enter the equation, but before we approach this subject let us consider a sounding loudspeaker operating under free-field conditions. Free-field conditions mean in the open air or in an anechoic chamber—anechoic signifying 'without reverberation'.

FREE-FIELD RADIATION

Under such conditions, therefore, the sound is radiated from the source in all directions as an expanding sphere (for the present excluding beaming effects due to loudspeaker directivity, which is true of the lower frequencies). It is this effect which produces the inverse distance law, the pressure falling inversely as the distance from the source increases. In other words, the level decreases by 6 dB each time the distance is doubled or increases by 6 dB each time it is halved.

Thus, if we measure 96 dB at a distance of 1 metre, then the level at 2 metres would be by 96 dB–6 dB, or 90 dB. The pressure at 96 dB is $12 \mu b$, so at 2 metres it would be 6 dB down from this, which is $6 \mu b$ (we are dealing with sound *pressure*, remember).

With power it is different. At 1 m (where the pressure is 96 dB) it is $4 \, \text{mW/m}^2$, as we have seen. At 2 m it is 6 dB down from this, but because we are now dealing with a power ratio the power is not half, as with pressure, but a quarter of the 1 m value, which is $1 \, \text{mW/m}^2$. It is this which yields the inverse distance squared law, the power falling inversely as the *square* of the distance.

POWER EMISSION AT SOURCE

If we assume spherical free space with an omnidirectional source radiating freely outwards from the centre, and knowing the power per unit area at a specific radius r, say at 1 m, we can refer back to the source mathematically to discover the sound power actually emitted.

The area of a sphere is $4\pi r^2$, so at 1 m radius the unit area is $\frac{1}{4}\pi \, \text{m}^2$ (Fig. 1.7). Source power emission can thus be calculated from

$$W_s = 4\pi W_a d^2 \tag{1.19}$$

where W_s is the source emission in acoustical watts, W_a the mean power in W/m^2 and d the distance from the source in metres.

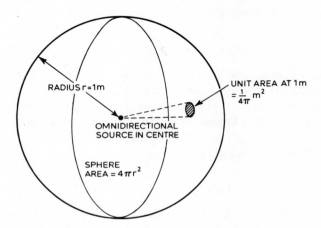

FIG. 1.7. *Model illustrating power per unit area (see text for details)*

Taking 96 dB intensity at 1 m, corresponding as we have seen to unit area power of 4×10^{-3} W/m^2, we obtain an answer very close to 0.05 W (50 mW) for W_a. At 2 m W_a would have to be close to 0.2 W (200 mW) for the same (96 dB) intensity.

An alternative expression, again assuming spherical free-space emission, is

$$P = \frac{4\pi d^2 p^2}{Z} \tag{1.20}$$

where P is the sound power emitted in ergs/s or 10^{-7} W, d the distance from source in cm and Z the specific radiation impedance (see expression 1.4).

By accepting some rounding off and approximation, a little simplification is achieved by

$$W_s \simeq 0.000\,333\,p^2 d^2 \tag{1.21}$$

where W_s is the source power emission in acoustical watts, p sound pressure in microbars and d distance in metres. Thus at 1 metre for a sound pressure of 12 μb (96 dB as in the previous example) the power emission is approximately 48 mW—not too far removed from the answer obtained by the alternative approach!

Differences can arise over the values chosen for ρ and c in the Z factor.

The pressure resulting from a given acoustical emission at a given distance from the source can be found from the simplified expression

$$p \simeq \frac{\sqrt{W_s}}{0.0182d} \tag{1.22}$$

where the symbols are the same as those in expression (1.21).

LOUDSPEAKER EFFICIENCY

Under true free-field conditions, therefore, and assuming an omnidirectional source, an intensity of 96 dB at 1 metre requires an acoustical emission of about 50 mW. It is now possible to discover the efficiency of a loudspeaker system from

$$\text{Eff. \%} = \frac{W_s}{W_e} \times 100 \tag{1.23}$$

where W_s is the acoustical power in watts radiated by the loudspeaker and W_e the electrical power in watts to the loudspeaker. For example, if 5 W input is needed for 50 mW output then the efficiency is obviously 1%.

A knowledge of loudspeaker efficiency is necessary in order to calculate the power requirements of the amplifier for non-clipping full dynamic range operation in a room of specified parameters.

DIN 45–500 LOUDSPEAKER STANDARD

Unfortunately, not many manufacturers specify the efficiency of their loudspeakers very clearly. One or two are adopting the DIN scheme (DIN 45-500), which calls for a minimum sound pressure output of 12 μb average level over

20

the band 100 Hz–4 kHz when measurement is made on axis at a distance of 1 metre under *hemispherical* free-space conditions. The electrical input power to yield this output level is called the 'operating power', the standard requiring the manufacturer to specify this.

Specially filtered noise signal is used for the test and the noise power taken by the loudspeaker is assessed either by comparison with the noise power taken by a resistor of value equal to the nominal impedance of the loudspeaker (V_n^2/R) or by the use of r.m.s. responsive current and volt meters ($V_n \times I_n$).

Although tested in free space (i.e., in the open air or anechoic chamber), hemispherical implies that the radiation is in the form of half a sphere in front of the loudspeaker—no emission from the rear. Under this condition, therefore, the acoustical emission required for a given intensity at a given distance is less than for spherical free-space conditions. For instance, the 4π in expressions (1.19) and (1.20) becomes 2π. The loudspeaker is thus considered as a small source in an infinite baffle.

For the lower omnidirectional frequencies this puts the acoustical emission at about 24 to 25 mW for an intensity of 96 dB ($12 \mu b$) at a distance of 1 metre.

As the frequency is raised beaming and directivity effects come into play, but the error is not much more than 1 dB at 500 Hz with a cone 25 cm (10 in) in diameter.

Based on the DIN method of measurement, quite a few of the acoustical suspension (sometimes called 'infinite baffle') loudspeakers barely approach 1% efficiency. Some tested by the author have been less than 0.5%. With the small systems efficiency is exchanged for bandwidth. Horns are the most efficient, rising towards 30–40% over their bandwidth.

We can now begin to see why large power amplifiers are required for hi-fi-scaled loudness in the listening room; but so far we have considered the loudspeaker operating under free-field conditions. We must now bring it into the listening room!

POWER REQUIRED INDOORS

When a loudspeaker is operated in a room the direct radiation is supplemented by sound reflected from the various surfaces of the room. For a given electrical input, therefore, a listener would normally experience a greater loudness in a room than he would from the same loudspeaker operated similarly under free-field conditions (i.e. out of doors).

The sound intensity due to the direct sound decreases with distance and it is also affected by loudspeaker 'beaming', but beyond a certain distance from the source a good deal of the sound reaching the ears of a listener is from the so-called reverberant field. When the intensity of the reflected sound equals that of the direct sound 3 dB is added to the direct radiation (see, for example, the nomograph in Fig. 1.5). However, one usually listens to domestic sound reproduction beyond this distance and hence in the reverberant field well into the room.

The room thus tends to 'magnify' the sound, but this is affected by the volume of the room, its reflective characteristics and by the total sound absorption of the room. Large items of 'soft' furniture and thick carpets make good sound absorbers, while hard walls, ceiling and floor make good reflectors. Outdoors, away from reflective surfaces and objects, there is maximum absorption. Indoors, even in a highly furnished room, there is obviously less absorption because there will be some reflective surfaces around, unless the room is designed deliberately for anechoic properties.

Different parts of the room will have different *coefficients* of absorption depending on the material of which they are made, and the value of the coefficient, which is referred to unity for 100% absorbency, depends to some degree on the frequency of the sound—the absorption generally being greater at high frequencies. A coefficient of 0.5, for example, implies that half the incident sound energy is absorbed and half is reflected. A thick cushion may have a coefficient of this value.

The *unit* of absorption (derived before the advent of SI metric units, but here modified) corresponds to $0.0929\,\text{m}^2$ of surface which is 100% absorptive. Thus a carpet of $9.29\,\text{m}^2$ of 0.1 absorption coefficient would have a value of $9.29/0.0929 \times 0.1 = 10\,\text{sabins}$.

These considerations are also appropriate in the soundproofing of a room, but this science falls outside the scope of this book.

REVERBERATION TIME

When a sound is started in a room it does not arrive at maximum intensity immediately and, conversely, when it is stopped it does not collapse immediately to zero. Time is taken for it to build up to maximum intensity and to fall from maximum intensity to zero. This stems from the multiplicity of 'echoes' from the reflecting surfaces. The time that elapses from the cessation of a sound to the moment it reaches one-millionth of its original energy (i.e. when it has fallen by 60 dB) is called the *reverberation time*.

For the reproduction of music the reverberation time should not be too large otherwise the 'definition' will be impaired owing to the commencement of a new component of sound before those preceding have died away sufficiently. Experience indicates that a time not greatly in excess of 0.4 s is desirable. The reverberation time of a concert hall may be longer than this, but this is of no moment from the reproducing point of view since the information is contained in the signal. It is the aim of hi-fi reproduction, of course, to reproduce the whole of the original, *including* the reverberation, which should not be unduly modified by the listening room.

Reverberation time increases with volume of the room and decreases with absorbency such that

$$T = \frac{V}{0.567\,S} \tag{1.24}$$

where T is the reverberation time in seconds, V the volume in m^3 and S the total absorbency is sabins. It was shown earlier that S is the product of the surface area and the coefficient of absorbency, so by calculating the value for each area and adding them together the total value for the room, including the items in it, can be obtained.

For example, a room of total surface area 111.45 m² (1200 ft²), including walls, ceiling, floor (possibly carpeted), furniture, etc., and 0.2 coefficient of absorbency, signifying that 20% of the sound is absorbed and 80% reflected, would have a total absorbency of almost 240 sabins (111.45/0.0929 × 0.2). Thus by using expression 1.24 it can be discovered that a room of 56.63 m³ (2000 ft³) volume and of such total absorbency would have a reverberation time close to 0.41 second.

Reverberation time and room volume thus figure in expressions dealing with the acoustical power requirements of rooms. Frequency also comes into it, such that the 'room gain' is not constant with frequency. Indeed, at some frequencies there could be 20 dB gain and at others zero or even negative gain! Owing to the many variable factors involved it is possible only to approximate power requirements.

Simplified and approximate expressions have been evolved, but correlation between them is sometimes lacking. However, two derived by the author may be of practical use. For the 96 dB r.m.s. peaks in Fig. 1.6(a) the power can be approximated by

$$W_s \simeq \frac{V}{620} \tag{1.25}$$

where W_s is the acoustical power emission in r.m.s. peak watts and V the room volume in m³.

For 100 dB r.m.s. peaks the formula becomes

$$W_s \simeq \frac{V}{248} \tag{1.26}$$

where the symbols are the same as those above. Both are based on an average reverberation time of 0.3–0.4 s. Since the value of the absorption coefficient depends to some extent on the frequency of the sound, it follows that the reverberation time is also frequency dependent.

Expression (1.25) shows that in a room of some 62 m³ an acoustical power of about 100 mW is required for the conditions outlined in Fig. 1.6(a). Thus if the loudspeaker is 1% efficient an amplifier of at least 10 W would be needed to avoid r.m.s. peak clipping.

With a stereo system the two channels working together modify the power requirement. If the two channels carry exactly the same signal at the same power, then each would need to operate at only 5 W to yield the 100 mW and hence 96 dB room intensity on r.m.s. peaks. However, because the information and power in the two channels differ on a stereo signal, each channel needs to be about 50% more powerful than half the total required power, so that an amplifier of at least 7.5 W per channel would be required, see Fig. 1.6(b).

In practice one would not run right to the limit of clipping, so an amplifier of 10–15 W per channel would be employed, and if one wished to reproduce r.m.s. peaks of 100 dB intensity in a room of similar parameters the amplifier would have to be about 2.5 times more powerful, and loudspeakers capable of handling this power would have to partner it.

Moreover, loudspeakers of lesser efficiency would call for even more scaling-up of amplifier power.

Thus, although the acoustical powers are very small, quite large amplifier powers are required to produce them.

When measuring r.m.s. peaks with a sound level meter account must be taken of the instrument's inability to respond sufficiently quickly for a correct reading. Tests made by the author suggest that the peak dynamic range of music is some 10 dB greater than indicated by a sound level meter, with short, sharp peaks sometimes being even greater. This means that if a sound level meter reads 80 dB during *fff* peaks, the reproduction contains r.m.s. peaks of 90 dB or, perhaps, more.

Although air is the chief medium for the transmission of sound waves, all other material substances can also transmit them. For example, if a faint tapping or scratching is arranged to be made at one end of a long table the noise is audible to a listener at the other end by placing an ear to the table, thereby proving that the sound waves have passed through the wood. The velocity of propagation, however, differs from air, it being significantly greater in liquids. For ordinary water it is around 1420 m/s and for distilled water about 1485 m/s, depending on temperature.

BEATS AND RESONANCE

When one is slowly overtaking a heavy goods vehicle in a car a drumming or beating sound is often heard, which changes in frequency as one accelerates to overtake. When this phenomenon is first experienced one may incorrectly conclude that the car's back axle is in trouble. This is unlikely since the beat is probably caused by the interaction of the sounds from the two vehicles, the beat frequency being equal to the difference in frequency of the two sounds.

Such beats are also produced in electrical circuits, encouraged by non-linearity, and the spurious tones so created in an amplifier, for example, is known as intermodulation distortion. This distortion is responsible for an uncomfortable stridence or 'harshness' in the reproduction.

Resonance crops up a great deal in audio work. If an audio generator is connected to the input of an amplifier driving loudspeakers and the generator is tuned slowly over the audio spectrum, it will be found that at various frequencies different objects in the room will start vibrating vigorously in sympathy with the sound. When the sound is of a frequency corresponding to the natural frequency of an object, the object will vibrate in sympathy. This is called resonance.

The resonance frequency of material objects is a function of their mass and compliance (compliance being the reciprocal of stiffness) and is expressed mathematically as

$$f_0 = \frac{1}{2\pi\sqrt{MC}} \qquad (1.27)$$

where f_0 is the frequency at resonance, M the mass and C the compliance.

24

NOTE ABOUT UNITS

Although SI (International System) units have been introduced elsewhere in this chapter, in some areas of electromechanics, particularly pertaining to gramophone pickups, the microscopic values that may be involved sometimes render the former c.g.s. units more convenient. Moreover, at the time of writing many manufacturers still insist on specifying the parameters of their products in c.g.s. units, so to avoid confusion these units are retained in this book where appropriate (with the equivalent SI units sometimes given in parenthesis) and where they are likely to correlate more closely with the units used by the manufacturers.

The equivalent SI units should be known, of course, and those of major concern here and in some of the subsequent chapters are time, length, force, mass and compliance which, in the c.g.s. system, correspond respectively to the second (s), the centimetre (cm), the dyne, the gram (g) and to cm/dyne. In the SI system time is still seconds, length is the metre (m), force the newton (N), equal to 10^5 dynes, mass the kilogram (kg) and compliance in m/N. Other SI units are pascal (Pa) for pressure, equal to N/m^2, joule (J) for energy, equal to 10^7 ergs, weber (Wb) for magnetic flux and tesla (T) for magnetic flux density, equal to Wb/m^2.

Returning now to expression 1.27, a typical audio resonance results from the effective mass of the pickup arm and the compliance of the partnering cartridge. For example, an effective mass of 10 g (10×10^{-3} kg) and a cartridge compliance of 20×10^{-6} cm/dyne (20×10^{-3} m/N) resonates at about 11.25 Hz. If the mass is high and a high compliance cartridge is used in the arm the resulting very low frequency resonance can affect the tracking.

Loudspeakers, too, are subject to resonances—the units as well as the enclosures and their combination.

The power of resonance is illustrated by the traditional order 'break step' given to a company of soldiers about to cross a flimsy bridge. If the troops' normal rhythmic step happened to coincide with the bridge's natural resonance vibrations of large amplitude would occur which could well destroy the bridge!

Air, too, can resonate in an enclosure (room as well as loudspeaker cabinet). This is how wind instruments work. A well-known air resonator is that due to Helmholtz which was developed some hundred years ago for harmonic analysis. The original consists of a .brass spherical shell going into a taper at one side for the ear and opening into a mouth at the other side for the air.

This sort of device resonates at the frequency to which it is tuned, and when sound waves are applied it picks out and effectively 'amplifies' only that component to which it is tuned. The resonance frequency is a function of the air volume and mouth area. The reflex loudspeaker works on a similar principle.

Heavy mechanical damping of the object, resulting from its design and firmness, greatly reduces the intensity of the resonance. Loudspeaker enclosures are usually designed so as to minimise the natural resonances, and damping is sometimes applied to pickup arms.

Resonances also occur in electrical circuits, but here the elements involved are capacitance C and inductance L, with resistance for the damping. The expression is the same as that of (1.27), M and C being changed to inductance and capacitance, which are the electrical analogues, with L in henries and C in farads.

Sound 'magnification' can also result from *forced vibration*. For example, a tuning fork pressed against a wooden table top will sound louder than in free space. This is because the vibration is communicated to a greater quantity of air, and may not be due essentially to resonance.

ROOM RESONANCES

Room air resonates within the wall, ceiling and floor boundaries, the frequency being a function of the dimensions. Basically, the effect is that the sound waves are bounced to and fro many times before decaying to a non-disturbing value (see under *Reverberation Time*, previously). At some frequencies the sound reflections are phase coincident. This happens when the spacing between the reflecting surfaces is a multiple of half the sound wavelength. A standing-wave resonance is then produced, so that an observer moving about in the sound field will experience successive nodes and antinodes as he moves along the line of wave incidence. The sound intensity thus varies with the pressure change. This is observed when a continuous tone is produced in the room.

Such resonances are often called *eigentones*, the major ones occurring at those frequencies where the spacings of the boundaries correspond to half a wavelength. A 2.44 m (8 ft) ceiling will thus incite a major eigentone around 70 Hz relative to the floor, but owing to the heavy damping due to plaster and carpets, this resonance is often pretty well tamed.

Hard walls, which absorb little of the incident sound energy, are usually more troublesome. Hard walls spaced by 6 m (about 20 ft) will give rise to a strong eigentone around 30 Hz. A big problem occurs when the room is cube shaped and of relatively small dimensions. As mentioned, apart from the fundamental eigentones, others present themselves at harmonic frequencies, the number of standing waves in the room then being greater. Small rooms tend to put the lower-frequency eigentones fairly close together, which has the effect of giving unnatural lift to music in the mid-bass region. Room diagonals can also affect the distribution of eigentones, and suggestions for optimum room dimensions have been given in the literature over the years. Based on unity height, one is 1.25 width and 1.6 length for a small room and 1.6 width and 2.5 length for a large room.

In rooms prone to eigentone disturbances, alleviation can be obtained by the use of acoustical tiles, drapes, etc. on the offending surfaces. These absorb sound of higher frequency, anyway, so that less is reflected for eigentone formation.

Sound waves are also diffracted, which has some analogy with radio and optical diffraction of electromagnetic waves. For example, if a sound wave comes up against an obstacle of size approximating to its wavelength, the wave will fail to be completely reflected back along the line of incidence, but instead will be re-radiated in all directions. This causes interaction with the incident wave and resulting diffraction due to pressure changes.

EFFECT OF WIND ON SOUND WAVES

Wind also affects wave propagation as shown in Fig. 1.8. The effect is that the velocity of the *medium* is superimposed on the velocity of the sound. The sound waves are tilted downwards when the wind is in the direction of the sound and conversely when the wind is against the sound.

This is not strictly a refractive effect although the net result is similar. Refraction, however, does occur when the wave passes from one medium to another (as with light), its direction of propagation then being changed. During

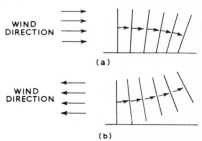

WIND DIRECTION

(a)

WIND DIRECTION

(b)

FIG. 1.8. *Showing how sound waves are inclined downwards when the wind is in the direction of the sound (a), and are given an opposite tilt when the wind is against the sound (b). Refraction due to temperature variation of the air can give a similar effect*

a hot summer's afternoon, for instance, sound waves may be tilted skywards owing to the air temperature being greater at lower than at higher levels. The converse occurs when the lower air is at a lower temperature than the upper air.

HARMONICS

Vibrating bodies often execute a simple harmonic motion and thus a sound of pure tone. When the vibration is composed of a combination of motions so-called overtones are produced which may or may not be harmonically related in frequency to the fundamental. The sine wave in Fig. 1.9 represents a simple harmonic motion, such as produced by a tuning fork vibrating on a resonator which enormously boosts the fundamental frequency relative to overtones at 6.27 and 17.55 times the fundamental frequency, characteristic of vibrating metal bars fixed at one end.

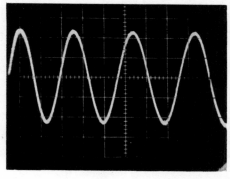

FIG. 1.9. *Simple harmonic motion such as executed by a tuning fork can be represented by a sine wave*

Overtones or harmonics are responsible for the difference in quality between the sounds produced by the various instruments of an orchestra. The human voice is also rich in harmonics, and because these differ between people it is possible to identify a person by his voice.

High quality audio amplifiers must be capable of responding fully to all the high-order harmonics, and themselves must not be responsible for the introduction of harmonics of significant amplitude which are not present in the original sound.

Fig. 1.10 at (a) shows two sine waves, one being twice the frequency of the other. The higher frequency one is the second harmonic of the lower frequency

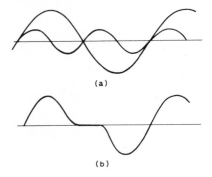

(a)

(b)

FIG. 1.10. *The two sine waves at (a), one of twice the frequency of the other, are compounded at (b). Here the sound is no longer 'pure' but has a high second harmonic content*

one. At (b) the graphic sum of the two is given, obtained by adding the ordinates of one to those of the other. A waveform such as this produced by an amplifier to which is applied pure sine wave signal would signify very dramatically that the amplifier is suffering from severe second harmonic distortion!

The addition of higher harmonics change the waveshape, a square wave, for example, resulting from the addition of odd harmonics and a sawtooth wave from the addition of odd and even harmonics; but the resulting shape is also influenced by the relative phasing of the separate waves.

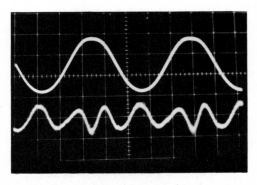

FIG. 1.11. *Oscillogram of sine wave signal from the output of an amplifier. The bottom trace is the distortion in the sine wave after high amplification and removal of the fundamental*

Certain harmonics sound more discordant than others, higher-order odd harmonics being particularly fatiguing.

Harmonic distortion cannot be seen on an oscilloscope display of the output of a high quality amplifier when a pure sine wave signal is applied to the input (not unless there is something radically wrong with the amplifier, of course!). To detect the small amplitude distortion which emanates from such equipment the output signal has to be passed through an instrument which removes the fundamental and leaves only the highly amplified harmonics. The oscillogram in Fig. 1.11 shows on the top trace the output signal, on which distortion is not apparent, and on the bottom trace the distortion actually present on the signal, which in this case is predominantly third harmonic.

Having now dealt with the very important audio fundamentals we can now progress to other topics.

CHAPTER 2

Requirements for Hi-Fi

A PRIMARY REQUIREMENT for hi-fi reproduction lies in the ability of the amplifier/ loudspeaker partnership to yield sufficient acoustical power to reproduce in the listening room the full dynamic range of the programme material without clipping and hence distorting *fff* peaks on the one hand and without masking by noise *ppp* swings on the other hand.

State-of-art programme material can be expected to encompass a dynamic range approaching 60 dB. Thus so far as the amplifier is concerned this should not itself produce a noise signal −60 dB higher in level than the rated channel power of the amplifier. Amplifier noise is commonly measured over the full spectrum with the volume control at maximum and the input loaded into a low value resistance, and hum and noise ratios exceeding 60 dB are not unusual on most sources when referred to the rated power of the channel.

In practice the volume control is never set at maximum, a setting of about 1 o'clock (−20 dB) being more typical for optimum dynamic range reproduction of 'normalised' programme signal level, which means that the full noise energy of the preamplifier stages is not fed to the power amplifiers; since the volume control is commonly placed between the preamplifiers and power amplifier, the noise contribution of the preamplifiers is reduced by the volume control (Fig. 2.1).

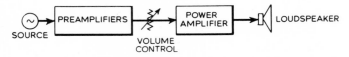

FIG. 2.1. *The disposition of the volume control is commonly between preamplifiers and power amplifier, which means that the noise contribution of the preamplifiers to the total output noise is diminished as the control is turned down (see text). The DIN 45–500 measurement of s/n ratio takes account of this (see page 44).*

The intrinsic noise of the power amplifier is always fed to the loudspeaker, of course, and the attenuated preamplifier noise adds in vector sum (see the nomograph in Fig. 1.5). The net result is that the effective signal/noise ratio is better under normal operating conditions than with the volume control set at maximum. However, the resistance or impedance of the connected source can modify (impair) this. Moreover, some amplifiers might not have the configuration of Fig. 2.1.

The minimum rated power of the amplifier should be geared to the efficiency of the loudspeakers and the parameters of the listening room and referred to the r.m.s. peaks of the music at the required level of reproduction, as explained in Chapter 1.

For a smallish room and about 1% loudspeaker efficiencies under reasonably quiet conditions an amplifier of 7.5 to 10 W per channel of signal/noise ratio not less than about 60 dB should make realisable the full intrinsic dynamic range of contemporary programme material, but with little spare margin at the *fff* end.

For greater r.m.s. peak music levels, larger rooms and less sensitive loud-speakers amplifiers of 100 W per channel may not be powerful enough to avoid peak clipping! It is sad that loudspeaker manufacturers do not issue more information on the efficiency of their wares. The DIN 45-500 specification in this respect goes some way in providing the 'bridging' information as long as the specification conforms with the DIN method! One manufacturer, for example, is quoting sensitivity at the time of writing referred to 95 dB at 1 metre under anechoic conditions and seemingly based on steady-state signal of 400 Hz only.

The DIN method can be translated fairly easily to per cent efficiency (Chapter 1) since the test conditions are clearly defined, but since amplifiers are rated in *watts* of power a direct efficiency parameter based on an average output over a specified bandwidth would be more useful and meaningful. The parameter of sound *pressure* is more compatible with voltage (not power) delivered by the amplifier across the load.

HARMONIC DISTORTION

Total harmonic distortion should be less than 0.5% over the dynamic range, and so far as the amplifier alone is concerned a more realistic state-of-the-art value is not greater than 0.1% at 1 kHz. The distortion should not rise dramatically at the low and high frequencies, but it is difficult to design such that there is no increase in distortion at low bass and high treble.

Total harmonic distortion is commonly measured with a *distortion factor meter* which means that all the harmonics within the test bandwidth *and the noise* contribute to the readout, giving an overall value colloquially referred to as total harmonic distortion (THD) when *distortion factor* is meant.

As the power at which the distortion factor is measured is reduced so the noise components contribute more to the readout, so that at a very low power the actual THD contributes very little to the readout, the meter then reading mostly noise. This is illustrated by the oscillograms in Fig. 2.2, where (*a*) shows the distortion residual at high power and (*b*) the residual at low power. The second-beam sine wave trace in each case corresponds to the unfiltered fundamental signal across the amplifier's load. It is obvious, therefore, that the high noise content at (*b*) will contribute significantly to the readout.

Like two or more noise signals, noise and distortion add in quadrature, so that when the noise level can be measured it is possible to calculate it out to yield a true THD assessment.

Distortion factor D_f can be expressed thus

$$D_f = \frac{\sqrt{(N^2 + D^2)}}{S} \tag{2.1}$$

where N is the noise voltage, D the r.m.s. sum of the harmonic voltage components and S the total r.m.s. signal voltage. The true THD, designated D/S, is thus given by

$$D/S = \sqrt{[D_f^2 - (N/S)^2]} \tag{2.2}$$

where the symbols are the same as in (2.1).

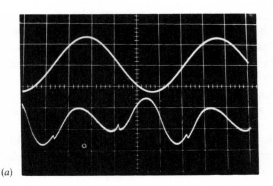

(a)

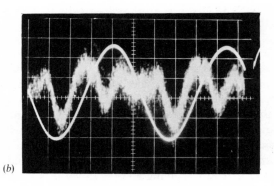

(b)

FIG. 2.2 *Noise-free distortion factor residual (a) and noise-laden residual (b), which also reveals mild output stage transfer characteristic discontinuity (see also Figure 2.3)*

It is possible to measure each separate distortion harmonic by using a wave analyser, and since this instrument tunes each one individually within a very narrow 'window' bandwidth of a few Hz, noise is not troublesome down to very small distortion percentages. The main disadvantage of this scheme, though, is that one is obliged to calculate THD from:

$$\% \, \text{THD} = \frac{\sqrt{(E_2^2 + E_3^2 + E_4^2 + \cdots)}}{\sqrt{(E_1^2 + E_2^2 + E_3^2 + E_4^2 + \cdots)}} \times 100 \tag{2.3}$$

where E_1 is the voltage of the fundamental and E_2, E_3 etc. are the voltages of the second, third, etc. harmonics.

Moreover, a wave analyser is generally significantly more costly than a distortion factor meter.

INTERMODULATION DISTORTION

Intermodulation distortion (IMD) of a top-flight hi-fi amplifier should not be much greater than the THD. Like THD, IMD is a function of amplifier non-linearity, but since the distortion components result from the presence of two or more signals passing through the system simultaneously, they can be of a singularly discordant nature and thus contribute more to listener fatigue than simple THD.

IMD is responsible for sum and difference signals not present in the original signal, and when there are two signals f_1 and f_2 the percentage IMD, referred to f_2, is given by

$$\% \, \text{IMD} = \frac{\sqrt{[(E_{f2-f1}+E_{f2+f1})^2+(E_{f2-2f1}+E_{f2+2f1})^2+(E_{f2-3f1}+E_{f2+3f1})^2+\cdots]}}{E_{f2}} \qquad (2.4)$$

where E_{f2-f1}, for example, is the voltage of the intermodulation component at frequency f_2-f_1, measured at the output. Signal f_1 is often about 100 Hz and signal f_2 5 kHz in amplitude ratio of $f_1 : f_2 = 4{:}1$.

Quasi-class B amplifiers with push-pull output transistor pair transfer characteristic discontinuity tend to exhibit more IMD than THD, as well as being less subjectively palatable due to the resulting high-order harmonics, some of which are disgustingly dissonant.

Such distortion, however, is revealed on an oscilloscope display of the distortion factor residual as peaks or discontinuity in the distortion waveform corresponding to the 'zero' or switching points between the positive and negative half cycles of sine wave signal. This effect in mild form is shown on the residual of the oscillogram in Fig. 2.2(a) and more seriously in Fig. 2.3.

Since a distortion factor meter is unable to respond to fast-occurring peaks such as those shown in Fig. 2.3, the readout may appear to be perfectly

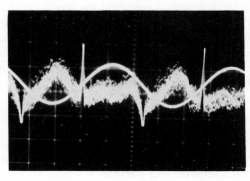

FIG. 2.3. *Severe discontinuity or crossover distortion shown on the noisy distortion factor residual*

satisfactory in spite of the heavy switching distortion, colloquially termed *crossover distortion*, so full appraisal of the distortion characteristics of an amplifier demands distortion factor residual study or, at least, IMD measurements in addition to distortion factor or THD distortion measurements.

DAMPING FACTOR

The amplifier should present to the connected loudspeaker a very low value of source resistance to provide high electromagnetic damping at low frequencies as well as high. The damping factor F_d is expressed as

$$F_d = \frac{R_L}{R_s} \qquad (2.5)$$

where R_s is the amplifier's output source resistance (which is, in fact, assumed to be substantially resistive) and R_L the nominal resistance of the connected load. A good few amplifiers, especially those incorporating direct coupling from the power amplifier to the loudspeaker, boast a damping factor of 40 or more at low-frequency as well as at high-frequency which, referred to 8 ohms R_L, implies an R_s of 0.2 ohms or less. A very low R_s in parallel with the loudspeaker inhibits overshoot and rings on transient type signal, and this is particularly desirable at the loudspeaker's bass resonance frequency where, without such damping, the cone can oscillate vigorously when triggered by a transient, an effect which is responsible for 'overhang' and 'boomy' bass, particularly when the acoustical damping of the loudspeaker could be better.

NEGATIVE FEEDBACK DAMPING

The low R_s results from negative feedback so that the damping on the loudspeaker is different from that which would result by connecting a very low value resistor across it which, of course, would merely bypass all the amplifier's power from the loudspeaker and possibly damage the amplifier or, at least, precipitate fuse failure or protective cut-out action.

With negative feedback damping the amplifier's input signal is effectively the difference between the source voltage and the voltage across the loudspeaker. Now, since the latter is largely dependent on the cone velocity the negative feedback tends to make the loudspeaker voltage proportional to the source voltage. A damping effect is thus applied to the cone movement. For example, with zero input any spurious movement of the cone will send a voltage to the input of the amplifier, via the negative feedback loop, such that the output stage will exert power to halt the movement.

POSITIVE FEEDBACK

The low R_s results from negative *voltage* feedback, the basic scheme of which is shown in Fig. 2.4. Negative *current* feedback increases R_s, the converse of the requirement for a high damping factor. Positive feedback means that the phase of the signal fed back is coincident with the phase of the source or input signal. This is regenerative feedback which results in sustained oscillation. Negative feedback is called degenerative feedback. This decreases the gain of the amplifier since the signal fed back is out of phase with the source or input signal.

Negative feedback not only 'stabilises' an amplifier, but it also reduces distortion and improves the frequency response and power response. Referring to Fig. 2.4, the *gain with feedback G* can be written as

$$G = \frac{A}{(1 + AB)} \qquad (2.6)$$

where A is the gain without feedback and B the fraction of the output voltage fed back. Factor $(1 + AB)$ is sometimes called the 'gain reduction factor', and may be expressed in decibels.

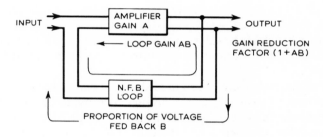

FIG. 2.4. *Basic negative voltage feedback*

As an example, an amplifier of $A = 180$ and $B = \frac{1}{20}$, giving $AB = 9$, would have a gain reduction factor of $(1 + AB) = 10$, thereby making $G = 18$. In other words, the feedback would reduce the gain by 10 times, which is the same as saying that the amplifier has 20 dB of feedback. Thus to obtain the original output signal the input signal would have to be increased by 20 dB.

The term 'loop gain' often appears in relation to feedback. It refers to the factor AB.

Negative feedback reduces the distortion in the same ratio as it reduces gain, so that an amplifier yielding, say, 10% distortion without feedback would produce approximately 1% distortion with 20 dB of feedback. Of course, the distortion produced by the circuits outside the negative feedback loop would not be reduced.

Although by itself positive feedback is regenerative, used under controlled conditions in conjunction with negative feedback it can provide a further reduction in overall distortion and also facilitate variable damping control.

The positive feedback effectively increases the loop gain in the negative feedback circuit, thereby reducing the distortion proportionally. The scheme is of maximum use in circuits of limited gain, and was sometimes adopted when low gain triodes were employed in amplifiers.

The diagram in Fig. 2.5 shows how a positive *current* feedback loop can be incorporated with a negative voltage feedback loop to provide variable damping factor control without the control affecting the overall gain of the amplifier. It is noteworthy that while negative voltage feedback decreases R_s and negative

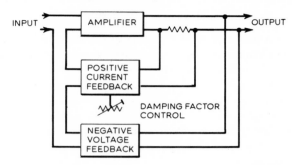

FIG. 2.5. *Negative voltage feedback and positive current feedback combined to provide variable damping factor control*

current feedback increases it, the converse effects occur with positive feedback. Thus a decrease in R_s also results from the positive current feedback loop in Fig. 2.5.

The amount of positive current feedback is adjustable by the control, so that R_s and hence F_d can be set by the user to provide the best damping for the loudspeaker. The circuit can be engineered to provide a swing of R_s from a positive value, through zero (where $R_s = R_L$), to a negative value. There is a limit, of course, to how negative R_s can be made, for when $-R_s > R_L$ the amplifier turns into an oscillator!

There is reason to believe that some loudspeaker systems sound better when R_s is slightly negative, which might be due to the negative source tending to cancel some of the impedance components of the loudspeaker and its circuit.

OPTIMUM DAMPING

Optimum loudspeaker damping occurs when R_s is of such a value for the least overshoot at the loudspeaker. A simple method for its determination is given

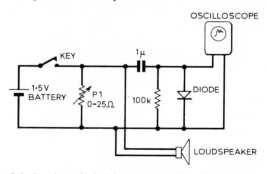

FIG. 2.6. *Simple method of determining loudspeaker damping*

in Fig. 2.6. When the key is depressed the transient resulting from battery current deflects the loudspeaker cone and the oscilloscope displays the waveform. The idea is to adjust P1 for the least overshoot shown on the trace while the key is operated in quick succession. The value of P1 at the optimum setting is then measured with a low-reading ohmmeter, the value of which corresponds to the 'best' R_s. However, as already mentioned, under dynamic conditions in a practical system a slightly negative R_s might be desirable.

It will be appreciated that R_s has in series with it the resistance of the loudspeaker connecting cable, which on a moderate-to-long run could be significantly greater than R_s! Thus, the maximum damping would seemingly be limited by the cable resistance, and from this aspect there would appear to be little future in a very low amplifier R_s. To some extent this is true, but under practical conditions improvement is often noticed when an amplifier of very low or negative R_s is partnered with a loudspeaker whose tendency is for bass transient overhang.

The resistive and reactive components of the loudspeaker system, including components of the frequency divider when used, also appear in R_s circuit, and for this reason series connected loudspeaker systems should be avoided— parallel connection being preferred in the interests of damping.

The damping factor of any amplifier is given by

$$F_d = \frac{V_1}{V_2 - V_1} \tag{2.7}$$

where V_2 is the signal voltage across the output terminals of the amplifier with no load connected and V_1 the voltage when a load, to which the damping factor is referred, is connected.

Owing to the high value of negative feedback used in transistor hi-fi amplifiers of contemporary design, an essentially constant-voltage output characteristic is achieved. Thus the difference between V_2 and V_1 is generally very small, the differential requiring digital readout for accurate measurement. It is also essential to avoid the resistance of the leads carrying the load current from reflecting a greater differential from that due to R_s alone!

A negative R_s is signified by $V_1 > V_2$, and some amplifiers are designed deliberately so that $V_1 = V_2$ towards the bass end, changing to $V_1 > V_2$ at lower frequencies. The amplifiers of the Armstrong '600' series, for example, tend to behave in this manner, thereby ensuring good bass control of the loudspeaker.

While it is often desirable to measure R_s over the audio spectrum, the measurement at low-frequency is essential. BS3860:1965 stipulates a frequency of 50 Hz with the amplifier delivering one-quarter of its rated output power, but recent experience has shown 40 Hz to be a better frequency.

FREQUENCY RESPONSE

It is not difficult to achieve an essentially 'flat' frequency response from at least 30 Hz to 20 kHz. Indeed, recent high f_T (gain-bandwidth product measured in common-emitter mode) transistors tend to make possible a response overall or of individual stages of the preamplifiers extending into the radio-frequency spectrum. Response curtailment is thus necessary to avoid breakthrough of radio and television signals and to minimise the response of the preamplifiers to impulsive (i.e. electrical) interference.

Further tailoring from the audio aspect is also desirable. In fact, a deliberate gaussian roll-off (6 dB/octave) at the preamplifier output at around 25 kHz can improve the transient intermodulation performance of an amplifier provided the high-frequency response of the power amplifier, including the negative feedback loop, is in advance of this (see under Transient Distortion).

BASS RESPONSE AND DIRECT COUPLING

Some designers prefer deliberately to roll-off the bass around 30 Hz, while others favour a response which is virtually 'flat' to d.c. to avoid undue 'differentiation' of low repetition frequency square waves. This relates to the

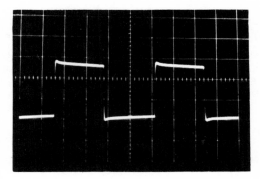

FIG. 2.7. *Low-frequency square wave suffering minimal differentiation*

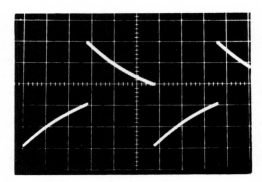

FIG. 2.8. *Low-frequency square wave suffering significant differentiation resulting from low-frequency cutoff*

trend, current at the time of writing, of direct coupling from the power amplifier to the loudspeaker. There is little doubt that a low-frequency square wave reproduced by a loudspeaker 'sounds' more as one would expect when the deviation from 'flat' is minimal (Fig. 2.7). Differentiation (Fig. 2.8) is produced by low-frequency cutoff, the sound then being of a different nature.

However, there is little agreement as to how music reproduction is affected by an extended low-frequency response. From the practical point of view, it is commonly necessary to introduce infrabass roll-off at least to attenuate rumble and other infrasonic noises which are often present on the programme signal. This is achieved by fixed high-pass filtering alone or by such filtering in addition to a switchable 'rumble' or low-frequency filter.

Programme signals rarely contain 'real' information much below 30 Hz, anyway, so the case for a greatly extended bass response is not very strong from this aspect.

POWER RESPONSE

Power response has no real bearing on frequency response. It refers to the power amplifier, and there are two ways of defining it. One is the range between low and high terminal frequencies where the power output is 3 dB below the

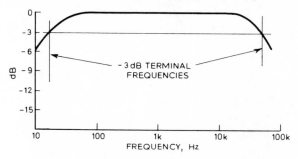

FIG. 2.9. *Half-power bandwidth*

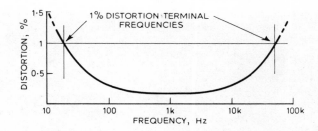

FIG. 2.10. *Power bandwidth defined between terminal frequencies of 1% distortion at 1 kHz rated power or (DIN 45–500) at any power down to 20 dB from the rated power*

rated power output at 1 kHz (Fig. 2.9). This, however, fails to take account of the distortion at the terminal frequencies, which can be dramatically high relative to the distortion at 1 kHz. The test is conducted with an input signal whose amplitude is constant over the frequency range.

The other one refers the terminal frequencies to a specific value of harmonic distortion at the rated output and, in the case of DIN 45-500 (see later), also at powers down to 20 dB below the rated power (Fig. 2.10). The DIN specification is 1% maximum distortion over the range 40 Hz–12.5 kHz.

Good transient response requires the power output to be maintained at frequencies significantly in advance of those which are audible, and this is achieved by high f_T transistors operating in a negative feedback circuit. Some high-frequency tailoring is often necessary for feedback phase correction.

RISE TIME

The time it takes the voltage at the output of an amplifier to rise from 10 to 90% of its final value (Fig. 2.11) when a perfect step waveform is applied to the

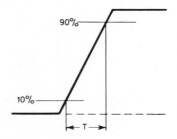

FIG. 2.11. Definition of rise time

input is known as the amplifier's rise time, and is related to the upper frequency response in terms of

$$f_{-3dB} = \frac{0.35}{T} \tag{2.8}$$

where f_{-3dB} is the upper frequency limit at which the response is 3 dB below

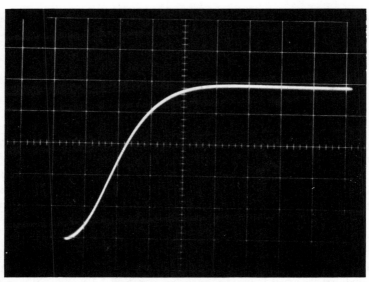

FIG. 2.12. Rise time oscilloscope display. Each horizontal (time) division corresponds to 2 μs, so the rise time of the display is approximately 5 μs

the mid-frequency response (i.e. the high terminal frequency in Fig. 2.9), assuming a gaussian upper-frequency roll-off characteristic, and T is the rise time.

Extended high-frequency response is thus required to ensure that the rise time of the amplifier is not less than that of transient-type programme signal components. Although a perfect step-wave (i.e. one of zero rise time) cannot, of course, be produced, a good evaluation of amplifier rise time is possible by using the leading side of a square wave for the input signal and measuring the time on a calibrated oscilloscope connected across the output load and hence displaying the waveform.

The error is small when the rise time of the test signal is well in advance of that of the amplifier. A rise time trace is given in Fig. 2.12. The horizontal (X axis) divisions correspond to $2\,\mu s$, which makes the rise time close to $5\,\mu s$.

Clearly, then, if components of the programme signal rise more swiftly at the input of an amplifier than the amplifier is able to respond they will fail to be reproduced correctly. They will be attenuated and possibly distorted, and the

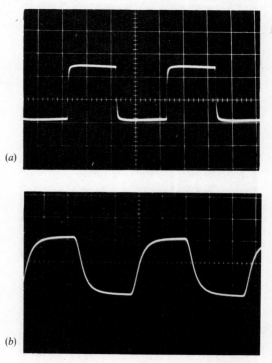

(a)

(b)

FIG. 2.13. *10 kHz square waves, (a) through amplifier of extended high-frequency response and (b) through amplifier of limited high-frequency response*

effect on the reproduction will be lack of music 'attack' and impaired high-frequency definition.

A straightforward high-frequency square-wave test also gives a fair indication of amplifier high-frequency performance. For example, the 10 kHz square waves in Fig. 2.13 show at (*a*) extended high-frequency response and at (*b*) more limited high-frequency response. These waveforms also indicate the correlation between the rise time and fall time.

TRANSIENT DISTORTION

Any mutilation of a transient-type signal during its passage through an amplifier comes under the heading of transient distortion. Transient distortion can

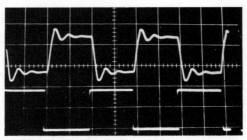

FIG. 2.14. *Rings on 10 kHz square were due to reactive output loading of amplifier. The bottom trace shows the nature of the input signal*

thus arise from too early treble roll-off but, of course, the nature of the signal to be handled by the amplifier must be considered. For example, the most

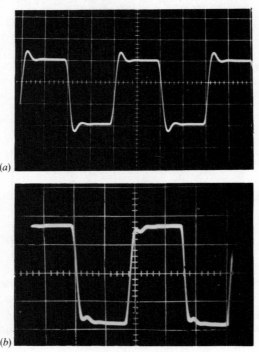

FIG. 2.15. *Minimal overshoot (a) and better transient control (b). Both at 10 kHz and with amplifier load comprising 8 ohms in parallel with 2 μF*

perfect audio amplifier would probably distort the transients of video-type signals!

Rather severe transient distortion of audio amplifiers is encouraged by ill-designed filters and couplings and by the amplifier (even some otherwise very good ones) driving into a reactive rather than a pure resistive load. The waveforms in Fig. 2.13 were obtained from a resistive load, but by adding reactance in the form of a $2\,\mu F$ capacitor across the resistance (usually of 4 or 8 ohms) the effect shown in Fig. 2.14 is not uncommonly produced. This shows that the amplifier produces a quickly damped oscillation at the conclusion of the leading and trailing sides. Overshoot or 'rings' of this magnitude appear to detract little from the quality of reproduction, but more prolonged 'rings' certainly affect the tonal character of music. More recent design techniques are tending to reduce the effect, so that some amplifiers exhibit no overshoot at all (or very little—Fig. 2.15) under the conditions of loading mentioned. No amplifier worthy of the hi-fi label should exhibit rings or overshoot into a load of pure resistance.

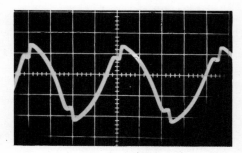

FIG. 2.16.

The oscillogram in Fig. 2.16 shows how a low-pass (high-frequency) filter can affect a 10 kHz square wave.

TRANSIENT INTERMODULATION DISTORTION

Transient intermodulation distortion is aggravated when the high-frequency cutoff of the preamplifier stages is higher than the *open-loop* cutoff frequency of the power amplifier. The effect is then that the feedback is inoperative during the open-loop rise time of the power amplifier, so that when the power amplifier receives an input signal containing frequency components in excess of the open-loop cutoff frequency, the input stages of the power amplifier are driven into overload. Owing to the integrating effect of the feedback loop, the overload condition tends to hold for a longer period than the open-loop rise time of the power amplifier, the overall result being bursts of 100% intermodulation distortion.

The mechanism involved is different from that which causes overshoot and rings on a square wave and the solution in part (also see page 124) lies in ensuring that the rise time of the power amplifier *without* feedback is greater

43

than that of the preamplifier. Designers are becoming more aware of this problem and are adopting power transistors of high f_T and applying deliberate upper-frequency roll-off (around 20 kHz or so) at the preamplifier. It will be appreciated that although the f_T of the power transistors may be several MHz the cutoff frequency is well below this in the common-emitter mode (also see Chapters 4 and 5).

Although many parameters of hi-fi amplifiers are tested with a load of 'pure' resistance, the loudspeakers they drive are far from being resistive over a substantial part of the audio spectrum. It is thus the author's considered opinion that tests of transient performance and distortion should be undertaken with a load which more closely simulates a loudspeaker. The same argument can also be applied to the signal input side—that is, the test signals should be derived

Table 2.1

Parameter	DIN evaluation	Comment
Amplifier output power	At least 10 W mono and 2×6 W stereo	Barely adequate even for the small system and relatively efficient loudspeakers. A *minimum* of 10×10 W would be better, though larger systems in bigger rooms operating insensitive loudspeakers can require 100×100 W for full dynamic range without peak clipping.
Loudspeaker sound pressure	96 dB (12 μb) at 1 metre on axis over the band 100 Hz–4 kHz (average level) under hemispherical free-space conditions. Power input for this condition to be stated.	Expression generally useful but would be more convenient in terms of electrical efficiency. Low-frequency expression inadequate for extended bass reproduction.
Power amplifier distortion/bandwidth	1% maximum from full power down to -20 dB over frequency range 40 Hz–12.5 kHz.	Inadequate. 0.5% maximum over range 40 Hz–15 kHz at all powers from rated down better.
Amplifier IMD	3% maximum with signals of 250 Hz and 8 kHz, 4:1 amplitude ratio.	Rather high. 1% better all powers from rated.
Amplifier frequency response	40 Hz–16 kHz ± 1.5 dB 'flat' inputs and ± 2 dB equalised inputs at 6 dB below rated power.	40 Hz–20 kHz ± 1 dB would be better.
Signal/noise ratio (integrated and power amplifiers)	At least 50 dB unweighted ref. 100 mW mono (50 mW per channel stereo) up to 20 W rating, increased proportionally (in dB) above 20 W rating.*	Reasonable for stated test conditions.
Signal/noise ratio (preamplifiers)	At least 50 dB, ref. nominal input signal level.	60 dB would be more realistic.

*Measured with gain controls set for stated output with 5 mV applied to pickup input and 500 mV to tuner, tape recorder, etc. input, with respective terminations of 47 k in parallel with 250 pF and 2.2 k, and with quasi p-p meter (ref. DIN 45–405).

from circuits which simulate the real sources instead of, which is now common practice, deriving the signals from a resistive source of some 600 ohms.

There would appear to be strong reasons to believe that the lack of correlation between how an amplifier 'sounds' and its measured parameters has more than a little to do with the source and load circuits employed for the tests!

It is obviously impossible in the relatively short compass of this chapter to investigate the parameters of all the items of equipment which constitute a complete hi-fi system, but those which have been looked at represent the primary ones which reflect the more important requirements for hi-fi reproduction.

The *minimum* requirements* for hi-fi equipment is expressed in the German DIN 45-500 'standard'. Although this is now somewhat dated (in terms of state-of-art techniques), some of the parameters referred to in this chapter are given in DIN terms in Table 2.1 along with appropriate comment.

<h3 style="text-align:center">NOTES ON POWER OUTPUT</h3>

There are several ways of measuring the rated output and power capacity of an amplifier. However, the power references in this chapter assume average continuous wave power (W_{av}), based on a sine wave test signal and resistive load, such that

$$W_{av} = VI \tag{2.9}$$

where V is the r.m.s. voltage across the load and I the r.m.s. current through it. Average power can thus be calculated from

$$W_{av} = \frac{V^2}{R} \tag{2.10}$$

or from

$$W_{av} = I^2 R \tag{2.11}$$

where R is the value of the load in ohms.

Expression (2.10) is that most commonly used, and the signal across the load is usually displayed on an oscilloscope, the power capacity at any frequency then being the power at the point of displayed sinewave peak clipping or at a distortion factor level of 1%, at a stated mains input voltage. The rated power, on the other hand, usually refers to a maximum value of distortion of less than 1% at any frequency or over a range of frequencies.

The misnomer 'r.m.s. power' is commonly found in amplifier specifications when the test is made as per expression (2.10), for instance, and when *average power* is meant. The erroneous term 'r.m.s. power' has stemmed from the need to distinguish the *peak power* rating of an amplifier, which past specification writers have sometimes used to give the impression to the untutored that the amplifier is twice as powerful as a competitor's, from the 'real' or average power, and also from the fact that it is the r.m.s. *voltage* across the load which is used in the calculation!

*Also incorporating uniform measuring methods. Not meant to establish as high as obtainable by existing state-of-art techniques. Evolved 1963–66 and partially revised 1972. Updating in progress.

REQUIREMENTS FOR HI-FI

PEAK POWER

The peak voltage of a sine wave is $\sqrt{2}$ of the r.m.s. voltage, so the peak power (W_{peak}) can be expressed as

$$W_{peak} = \frac{V^2 \sqrt{2}^2}{R} \qquad (2.12)$$

where V is the r.m.s. voltage across resistive load R in ohms, which shows that the peak power is exactly double the average power.

REAL R.M.S. POWER

While it is possible to calculate the r.m.s. value of the power, it has no comparable significance to the r.m.s. values of the voltage and current. Its calculation requires the instantaneous power to be squared and then integrated and the square root taken of the result.

R.M.S. power can thus be expressed as

$$W_{r.m.s.} = \frac{V^2 \sqrt{2}^2}{2R} \sqrt{1.5} \qquad (2.13)$$

$$\simeq 1.225 W_{av}$$

This means, then, that an amplifier which is measured for power in accordance with expression (2.10) has a *real* r.m.s. power approximately 22.5% greater than the average power, so if the specification writer is claiming, say, 10 watts per channel 'r.m.s.' he is effectively under-rating the amplifier to the extent of about 2.25 watts per channel!

DIN 45-500 requires the amplifier to sustain a 1 kHz sine wave signal at the rated power for at least 10 minutes. BS3860:1965 requires the rated power to be produced for not less than 30 seconds, after which the level of harmonic distortion to be measured to determine whether or not its value exceeds that specified. The IHF (Institute of High Fidelity—American) continuous output specification (1HF-A-201:1966, clause 3.1.1) is similar to that of British Standard.

MUSIC OUTPUT (POWER)

This is another IHF parameter (IHF-A-201:1966, clause 3.1.2) and refers to the largest output obtainable with a sine wave signal for a short period of time (simulating programme signal) at a reference distortion. Two test methods are described under clauses 3.1.2.1 and 3.1.2.2.

With a stereo amplifier both channels are driven together with the simulated programme signal and it is the total of the powers of the two channels which is specified. Since the signal is not *continuous* sine wave. but interrupted sine wave, the total power output is generally some 20 to 40% above that obtained from average power continuous wave measurement, depending on load and supply regulation.

It will be appreciated that a greater demand is put upon the power supply regulation and the thermal properties of the power transistor heat sinks when

46

the test is made in terms of average continuous wave power, which is partly the reason why the power yield under this test condition is generally less than obtained under music power test conditions.

However, the power output of most amplifiers is now tested in terms of average continuous wave power, even though it may be expressed as 'r.m.s. power'. The most searching test occurs when both channels of a stereo amplifier (or the four channels of a quadraphonic amplifier) are driven simultaneously, the per-channel power then commonly being less than the per-channel power with only one channel driven, depending on the power supply regulation and heat sink efficiency. Some amplifiers, notably those by Harman-Kardon (American), adopt two power supplies, one for each stereo channel, which ensure that the per-channel output remains substantially the same with just one or with both channels driven together. A well regulated single power supply feeding both channels of a stereo amplifier provides a similar performance.

The above reasoning, of course, refers to amplifiers with class B or quasi-class B power amplifiers, the input power of which increases in sympathy with increasing audio output power. Since contemporary transistor amplifiers yield an essentially constant-voltage output, the power increases as the load resistance is reduced. The power parameter must thus be qualified in terms of load resistance.

The American Federal Trade Commission (FTC) has recently ruled that advertising must clearly disclose the minimum sine wave continuous average power with all channels driven to the rated per channel power at the specified load value.

SLEWING RATE

This term, hitherto associated with operational amplifiers, is percolating into hi-fi to denote rate of change per unit of time of the amplifier's output voltage when the input is a voltage step of very small time. It refers to the *maximum frequency* at which the amplifier can deliver a voltage corresponding to its rated *full power*.

Maximum slope of a sine wave E_o This can be equated in terms of slewing rate (SR) equals $d(E_o \sin \omega_p t)/dt$, which is equal to $E_o \omega_p \cos \omega_p t$, and from this we can evaluate (at $w = 0$) thus:

$$SR = E_o \omega_p = E_o 2\pi f_p \qquad \text{or} \qquad f_p = SR/E_o 2\pi \qquad (2.14)$$

where E_o is the *peak* output voltage and f_p the highest frequency at which the *full power* is maintained.

In other words, the maximum frequency at which full power can be obtained is a function of the amplifier's slewing rate, which is different from rise time. For example, an amplifier of 50 W rated power into 8 ohms (corresponding to 20 V r.m.s. or 28 V peak across the load) and a *full power* h.f. response of 25 kHz would have a slewing rate of 4.4 V/μs approximately.

47

CHAPTER 3

Preamplifier and Control Circuits

THE POWER AMPLIFIER is designed to deliver into its rated load a specified output power when an input signal of suitable r.m.s. value is applied to its input. The input signal is obtained from the control section, which incorporates all the preamplification required by the source signals. There are also circuits for switching the various sources, for regulating the level of the output signal, for equalising the source signals when necessary, for providing variable response and for filtering. It is thus the job of the control section to deliver to the power amplifier the correct level of signal from any programme source. Excluding the action of the tone controls and filters, the level of the output signal should be substantially constant from low bass to high treble in accordance with the 'hi-fi expression', see Chapter 2.

Moreover, the control section must be designed to introduce the least possible distortion to the programme signals (usually little more than 0.05% harmonic, depending on source input) and the least possible noise, while also being tailored to offer a high rejection ratio to spurious signals, such as impulsive interference and radio and television signals.

The control section must contain two channels of identical characteristics for stereo and four such channels for 'discrete' quadraphony, with maximum electrical isolation between them. These channels are followed through the power amplifier section, also in isolation, to the appropriate number of loudspeakers. Ganged switches and potentiometers are often adopted so that common controls can be used for the two or four channels. A balance control (or controls) is then employed for gain equalisation. The alternative is the use of separate controls for each channel, which is not too bad with two-channel stereo, but rather involved (from the operating point of view) when there are four channels. A balance control is not then required, since the two volume controls can be adjusted differentially to provide the correct gain balance. However, although separate left and right channel volume controls may be used, the tone controls, source and filter switches, etc. are invariably ganged, though there are some amplifiers equipped with separate left and right channel bass and treble controls.

Equalisation in the main refers to the magnetic pickup source (this having a rising bass characteristic to complement the RIAA recording characteristic—

see Chapters 7 and 8). The other inputs, such as radio tuner, tape play and auxiliary, are unequalised, colloquially referred to as being 'flat'. One or two models from the Orient have an equalised *tape head* input (see Chapter 10), but this is a fading facility.

The control section also provides an output (after any equalisation, but usually before the tone controls and filters) for tape recording.

The transistor era has reduced the number of amplifiers based on physically separate control and power amplifier sections, though at the time of writing one or two reputable manufacturers (British) were still making amplifiers along those lines. The trend is toward 'integration', which has advanced beyond the integration of the amplifier control and power sections to the radio tuner, the design always being for f.m. reception with stereo facilities, and often with a.m. wavebands as well. This is called a tuner-amplifier or stereo receiver, and is fast becoming one of the most popular items of hi-fi hardware.

Integrated amplifiers and tuner-amplifiers are sometimes equipped with rear sockets and switching (or removable links) allowing the control and power amplifier sections to be split electrically (on both channels) so they can be operated independently. Such versatility can be useful when graduating from two-channel stereo to four-channel quadraphony.

MONO/STEREO MODE

The control section might also cater for a two-channel microphone with facilities for inter-source fading. There is almost always a switch which allows the combining of the signals in the left and right channels, so that a stereo signal can be reproduced in mono (i.e. signals in left channel *plus* signals in the right channel) and so that a mono signal applied to the source input of one

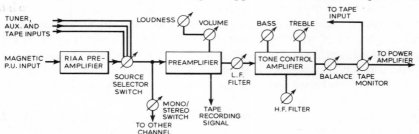

FIG. 3.1. *Block diagram of control section (see text)*

channel will drive both the left and right channel power amplifiers together. In the 'mono' mode the two stereo channels are connected in parallel at an early or late point in the control section circuitry, depending on the design philosophy.

The mono/stereo mode switch may have additional positions which provide mono from a right channel input and mono from a left channel input, as well as left *plus* right and stereo.

The block diagram in Fig. 3.1 illustrates the various aspects of the control section.

The preamplification is geared to the level of the source signals likely to be connected to the inputs, and for the various sources there is some *small* degree of 'standardisation', typical values and input impedances being set out in Table 3.1.

Table 3.1

Source input	Sensitivity (mV)	Impedance (ohms)
Magnetic pickup	2–5	47–100 k
Ceramic pickup (equalised input)	30–100	22–100 k
Ceramic pickup ('flat') input)	100–300	2M and above
Radio tuner	50–500	100 k and above
Auxiliary	100–500	50–100 k and above
Tape play	50–200	100–470 k
Microphone	1–5	47–220 k

OUTPUT FOR TAPE RECORDING

Output for tape recording ranges from about 200 mV at the rated input sensitivity to 0.1 to 2 mV per $1 \text{ k}\Omega$ of load resistance (which is the DIN parameter), a common value being about 40 mV when the load is 47 k. The feed is taken from a low impedance point in the circuit and is communicated to the tape recording socket (commonly pins 1 and 4 of a DIN socket for the left and right channels respectively) through a high value resistor (see Fig. 3.31). The feed is thus essentially constant-current, so the voltage across the load resistor (of the tape recorder) will depend on the value of the load. If, for example, the source signal e.m.f. is 1 V and the feed resistor 1 M the signal current will be $1 \mu A$. This current flowing through a load of, say, 47 k will produce a p.d. of 47 mV, which constitutes the level of the tape recording signal. In other words, for each 1 k of load resistance a signal p.d. of 1 mV is obtained. This is the DIN scheme.

One advantage is that a tape recorder of high input recording sensitivity can be presented with the correct value signal merely by shunting the input with a suitable value load. The resulting low value of resistance which then appears across the high sensitivity input ensures a good signal/noise ratio. Another is that a short at the recording output will not affect the normal operation of the control section.

Loss of treble, however, can occur if the recorder input happens to be of extra high impedance, for then the capacitance of the lead coupling the signal from the control section to the recorder might be sufficiently high to cause early treble roll-off at the ultimate rate of 6 dB/octave due to the RC combination.

Amplifiers with RCA 'phono' type sockets, as well as some with DIN sockets, derive the tape recording signal either from a preset potentiometer or from a feed circuit of significantly lower impedance than the DIN arrangement. Almost the full source e.m.f. is then presented to the recorder input. The preset arrangement allows the signal level to be adjusted to suit the input sensitivity of the recorder.

Owing to the relatively high input sensitivity required for a magnetic pickup, and because this input needs to be equalised to suit the recording characteristic, a separate RIAA preamplifier is commonly incorporated in the design, and this may contain two or three transistors in a frequency sensitive negative feedback circuit.

A typical two-transistor circuit is given in Fig. 3.2. Each stage is in common-emitter configuration with direct coupling between them and d.c. shunt feedback from Tr2 emitter to Tr1 base, via R1. The 100 μF capacitor C1 decouples the loop from the a.c. point of view.

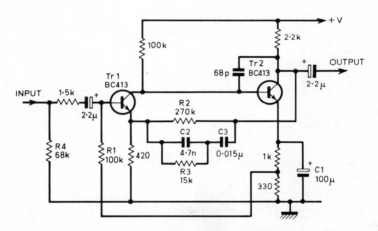

FIG. 3.2. *Magnetic pickup preamplifier with RIAA feedback equalisation as used in the Armstrong '600' series amplifiers. See text for details*

A series negative feedback path also exists from Tr2 collector to Tr1 emitter, via the network R2, R3, C2 and C3, and it is this which provides the RIAA equalisation due to frequency selective feedback. The network can be considered as consisting of two filter sections, one giving a treble-cut characteristic with a crossover frequency of 2 kHz and the other a 20 dB bass boost characteristic with a crossover frequency of 500 Hz.

This sort of circuit differs in points of detail, but there is usually a d.c. path through the loop, which in the example is through R2. The overall operating conditions of the amplifier are thus stabilised.

The equalisation must provide a response which is complementary to the velocity response of the recording characteristic (Chapters 7 and 8) so that the preamplifier delivers signals to the control section of essentially constant amplitude/frequency characteristic; that is, so that a 'flat' output over the

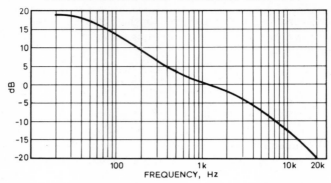

FIG. 3.3. *RIAA equalisation (replay) curve. This is the complement of the RIAA recording curve (Chapters 7 and 8)*

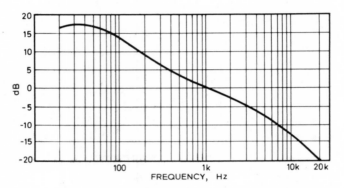

FIG. 3.4. *The measured equalisation curve of the preamplifier in Figure 3.2*

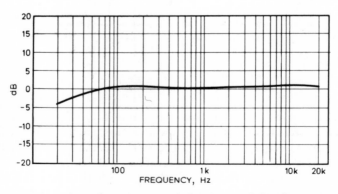

FIG. 3.5. *Deviation from RIAA when an input signal of approximately 700 ohms source resistance and simulating the velocity response of the RIAA recording characteristic is applied to the input of the preamplifier in Figure 3.2*

spectrum would be achieved from a magnetic pickup playing an RIAA-recorded frequency test record.

Fig. 3.3 shows the nature of the RIAA equalisation curve, Fig. 3.4 the curve actually plotted from the circuit in Fig. 3.2 and Fig. 3.5 the essentially 'flat' output resulting from an input signal whose response characteristic simulates the velocity response of the RIAA recording characteristic.

It must be emphasised that the curves in Figs. 3.4 and 3.5 were obtained from a resistive source of approximately 700 ohms fed to the amplifier (via a filter simulating the RIAA recording characteristic) through screened cable.

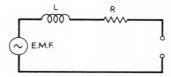

FIG. 3.6. *Approximate electrical analogue of a magnetic pickup cartridge*

Although this correctly simulates the magnetic pickup e.m.f., it does *not* simulate the electrical nature of the pickup, the approximate analogue of which is given in Fig. 3.6. In reality, the inductive element L is fairly heavily damped, and winding capacitance is also present.

This circuit is coupled to the input of an equalised preamplifier, such as that in Fig. 3.2, and since the connection is made through screened cable a capacitive element is also present. Moreover, the input of the RIAA preamplifier acts as

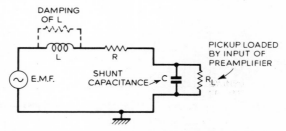

FIG. 3.7. *The electrical analogue of a magnetic pickup connected to the input of an RIAA-equalised preamplifier through screened cable*

a load for the pickup, a common value being around 47 k, which in Fig. 3.2 circuit is achieved by R4 in shunt with the input impedance of the preamplifier. We thus end up with a circuit resembling that in Fig. 3.7.

Without R_L the circuit tends to behave like an unterminated half-section low-pass filter which, depending on the values of L, C and R, might have a response something like that shown in Fig. 3.8.

However, when R_L is terminating the magnetic pickup the response is modified at the treble end as shown by A in Fig. 3.9. This, in fact, is the response obtained from the circuit in Fig. 3.2 when the RIAA-recording-characteristic-simulated e.m.f. is applied from a source of 500 mH nominal inductance and 1400 ohms resistance (i.e. the Shure V15/III cartridge in series with about 47 ohms of resistance), and when this source is connected to the input of the preamplifier through screened cable of about 150 pF capacitance, which would approximate the capacitance of the cable used to couple the pickup (per channel) to the amplifier of a hi-fi system.

It must be remembered that this reveals *only* the electrical aspect of the pickup's response. The overall response is a function of both mechanical resonances and the electrical response, the two being carefully tailored in good quality cartridges to yield a 'flat' overall output. Curve B in Fig. 3.9 shows the general nature of the treble mechanical resonance of the Shure V15/III cartridge, which is the approximate complement of A. Thus the output due to A and B together is essentially 'flat', as shown at C.

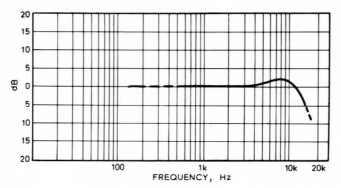

FIG. 3.8. *The nature of the electrical response, at the preamplifier output, from a magnetic cartridge connected to the input of the preamplifier through screened cable but without a load resistance or with abnormally high value load resistance*

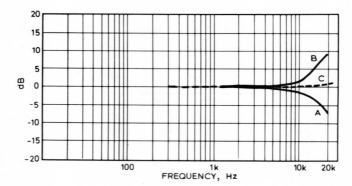

FIG. 3.9. *The electrical response of the Shure V15/III at Figure 3.2 output when cartridge connected to input through screened cable of approximately 150 pF is shown at A when the source e.m.f. simulates the velocity response of the RIAA recording characteristic. B shows the approximate mechanical response of the same cartridge, and since B is almost the complement of A, the output from a record is essentially 'flat' as shown at C*

We have seen, therefore, that the treble response of a magnetic pickup is influenced both by the loading due to the RIAA-equalised preamplifier and by the capacitance of the screened connecting leads. The majority of cartridge manufacturers arrange the electrical/mechanical parameters so that the best treble response occurs with a load of around 47 k. Hence the use of this value by amplifier designers. It is generally desirable to keep the capacitance of the connecting leads as small as possible (which means as short as possible), but the way in which the treble is affected by shunt capacitance and load resistance depends on the value of the inductive element. The optimum load for the Shure V15/III, for example, is specified as 47 k in parallel with 400 to 500 pF *total* capacitance (including input capacitance of the preamplifier); but it is also stated that loads up to about 70 k can be accommodated with almost no audible change in frequency response. Some magnetic cartridges are less obliging in this respect than the Shure V15/III.

Unfortunately, this is not always the end of the matter. Some designs of RIAA-equalised preamplifiers are mildly sensitive to the reactive signal source appearing in the negative feedback path, this modifying the feedback, particularly towards the treble end.

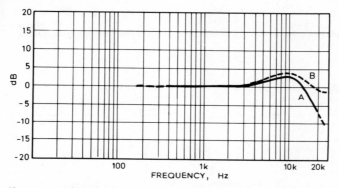

FIG. 3.10. *Showing at A how the frequency response can be affected by the reactive components of a magnetic cartridge appearing in the negative feedback path. B shows the probable response when the mechanical resonance is taken into account*

The response at A in Fig. 3.9 is perfectly respectable and, if necessary, this could be tailored to represent more accurately the complement of B merely by adjusting the value of the preamplifier's input load (i.e. by adjusting the value of R4 in Fig. 3.2).

Owing to the nature of the feedback, the input impedance of Fig. 3.2 amplifier is fairly high, which means that the load actually 'seen' by the cartridge (47 k) is defined substantially by R4.

The response given at A in Fig. 3.10 was obtained from an RIAA-equalised preamplifier of a different configuration from that in Fig. 3.2, when fed from the Shure V15/III source in the manner already described. Here the reactive components of the cartridge appearing in the negative feedback path incite mild upper-treble lift prior to the roll-off, so the response is rather like that of a low-pass filter (Fig. 3.8). Since the mechanical response fails to complement this exactly, the overall response with the cartridge playing a record would tend towards B. Error in response due to equalising can be viewed as Z_{in} change with increasing frequency. This is small in good designs, the Quad 33 for example, varying less than 5 per cent over the whole spectrum.

BUFFER STAGES

To avoid the reactive components of the cartridge from affecting the equalising feedback and to minimise the risk of overload (see later) there would appear to be some merit in isolating the pickup from the RIAA-equalised preamplifier by a 'buffer' amplifier, a technique which is adopted by Cambridge in the 'P' series amplifiers (Fig. 3.11).

A block diagram of the first stages is given in Fig. 3.12, while the circuit, including the RIAA-equalised stage, is given in Fig. 3.13. Stage A1, comprising

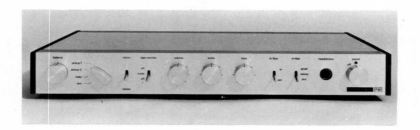

FIG. 3.11. *The Cambridge P50 amplifier in which the RIAA preamplifier stage is 'buffered' from the pickup circuit (see text)*

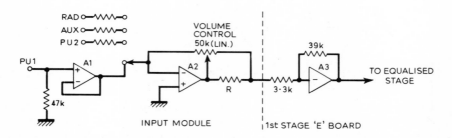

FIG. 3.12. *Block diagram of the input stages of the Cambridge 'P' series amplifiers (see text for description)*

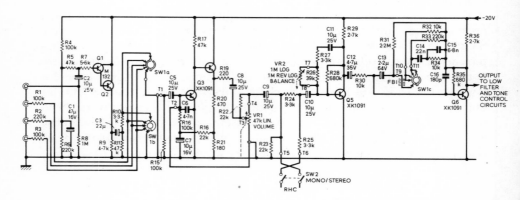

FIG. 3.13. *The input circuits of the Cambridge 'P' series amplifiers, including the RIAA-equalised preamplifier stage.*

PREAMPLIFIER AND CONTROL CIRCUITS

Q1 and Q2, is a Darlington emitter-follower which is used to buffer PU1 and to provide a low impedance to drive stage A2 at maximum gain. A2 comprises a virtual earth stage using a high gain voltage amplifier Q3 and emitter-follower Q4, with overall d.c. feedback. Here the volume control VR1 regulates the amount of negative feedback and hence controls the gain of the stage.

Signal from A2 is applied to the input of A3, also in virtual earth configuration, using transistor Q5, and the output feeds Q6 where, in the pickup position, the RIAA-equalisation is introduced.

VOLUME CONTROL ACTION

The gain control circuit associated with A2 is worthy of more detailed note since it has been carefully engineered to provide a desirable rotation/gain law for the volume control.

Referring to Fig. 3.12, it will be appreciated that with R shorted A2 gain will be controlled linearly by the volume control. If it is now assumed that R is removed A2 gain will still be controlled by the volume control, but the effective gain of A3 will also be altered as the volume control is rotated because the portion of the control potentiometer outside A2 feedback loop is in series with A3.

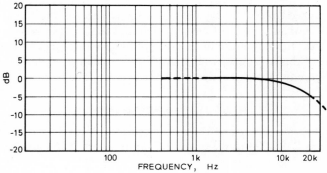

FIG. 3.14. *The electrical response at the output of the Cambridge P50 amplifier of the Shure V15/III cartridge with the cartridge connected to PU1 through screened cable of approximately 150 pF capacitance and when the source e.m.f. simulates the velocity response of the RIAA recording characteristic*

The effect is such that as the control is turned up from zero the combined gain of A2 and A3 first increases linearly and then with an approximately square law until maximum setting, the gain then being limited by the 3 k3 resistor in series with A3 input. Since practice has shown that the approximately square law reflects a too sharp volume control action, the resistance R (the 22 k R22 in Fig. 3.13) is included to modify the law and hence make the control less sharp on gain adjustment as it is rotated. With R at 22 k the gain is about − 20 dB with the control at half setting.

In the pickup positions SW1c introduces the equalising feedback network R33, C15 and R34 from Q6 collector to base, via C13. On the radio and auxiliary positions Q6 stage gain is defined by R32.

SW1a selects the source, while SW1b shorts out the sources not in use, thereby avoiding crosstalk. It will be seen that PU2 input is direct to stage A2, stage A1 being used only for PU1 where, of course, the input sensitivity is greatest.

Owing to the high input impedance of the Darlington stage A1, the load for the cartridge at PU1 is defined almost completely by R5 in Fig. 3.13. The cartridge is thus presented with an almost perfect 47 k termination without interaction from the RIAA feedback, since this is well removed from the input.

The curve in Fig. 3.14 was obtained when PU1 was fed from the Shure V15/III source in the manner already described, the treble roll-off being virtually the same as would be obtained with the cartridge connected across a 47 k resistor in shunt with the capacitance of the leads used for the measurement.

RIAA equalisation by negative feedback can be achieved in a number of ways, two of which have already been seen (Figs. 3.2 and 3.13).

ANOTHER METHOD OF EQUALISATION

Another method is arranged deliberately to exploit the natural treble roll-off of the cartridge in relation to a resistive *series* element to provide the high-frequency part of the replay characteristic (Fig. 3.3) and to introduce only bass boost to provide the low-frequency part of the characteristic.

Since this requires series resistance in the cartridge circuit, the input stage is generally arranged to have a very low input impedance by the use of collector to bass shunt feedback (emitter feedback increases the input impedance) so that a series resistor suitable for the inductance of the cartridge can be chosen. The disadvantage of this arrangement is that it is not universal, different cartridges calling for different values of series R for the correct equalisation.

THREE-TRANSISTOR CIRCUIT

Another circuit, this time using three transistors, is given in Fig. 3.15. This is from the Sonab R/P 4000 range of receivers/amplifiers. The equalisation feed-

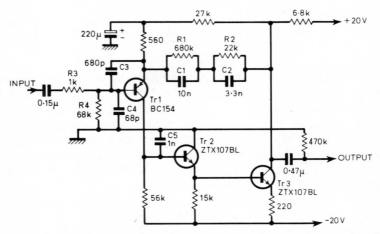

FIG. 3.15. *A three-transistor RIAA-equalised pickup preamplifier used in the Sonab P4000 amplifier and R4000 tuner-amplifier. This uses a series feedback circuit from Tr3 collector to Tr1 emitter for equalisation*

back is from Tr3 collector to Tr1 emitter, via network R1/C1 and R2/C2. An interesting aspect of this circuit is that it is 'balanced' about $+20\,$V and $-20\,$V supply lines. Direct coupling is employed overall, with Tr1 being a pnp device and Tr2 and Tr3 npn devices.

R.F. FILTERING

Owing to the high input sensitivity of magnetic pickup preamplifier stages and the wide bandwidth resulting from high f_T transistors, radio and/or television breakthrough can occur in areas of high signal field due to the base/emitter junction of an input transistor rectifying (and hence demodulating) the signal so that the resulting low-level audio information is communicated to the subsequent stages of the amplifier along with the programme signals.

Filtering in Fig. 3.15 is provided by the input resistor R3 along with capacitors C3 and C4. The value of C4 thus appears in shunt with the connected cartridge, which adds to the capacitance of the screened signal lead. However, in this design the cartridge is terminated substantially by 68 k R4. Further filtering is provided by the 1 nF capacitor C5.

In Fig. 3.2 r.f. filtering is provided by the 1 k5 input resistor and by the 68 pF capacitor across Tr2 base/collector. In strong r.f. fields, however, additional filtering in the form of a 1 nF capacitor across Tr1 base/emitter, close to the transistor, might be required, an artifice that can often be used to good effect with any other type of preamplifier when radio breakthrough is troublesome. Such filtering also helps to clear electrical interference.

Direct pick up of signal by the circuits themselves is another cause of breakthrough, and only careful screening of the low-level stages can cure this completely. The signal might also be picked up by the loudspeaker leads and injected back to the amplifier input through the negative feedback circuit (this time of the power amplifier), and breakthrough from this cause might thus demand loudspeaker circuit filtering and/or the screening of the loudspeaker cables, with the screening connected to the system's common 'earthy' circuit, though the latter is not always effective.

PICKUP INPUT SENSITIVITY SWITCHING

The input sensitivity of an RIAA-equalised pickup preamplifier stage is defined by the feedback, so by reducing the feedback the stage gain can be increased to allow full drive for the subsequent stages to be obtained from an input signal of smaller amplitude. In Fig. 3.2, for example, the feedback and hence the input sensitivity can be altered by changing the value of Tr1 emitter resistor. In the Armstrong amplifiers mentioned, the value of the emitter resistance can be changed by a switch, with low sensitivity obtaining when the value is 1k8 and high sensitivity obtaining when the 1k8 is shunted by 560 ohms, the combined value then approximating the 420 ohms marked in Fig. 3.2. Pickup input sensitivity is 10 mV low and 2.7 mV high, both referred to 1 kHz for the rated output.

PREAMPLIFIER AND CONTROL CIRCUITS
PREAMPLIFIER DYNAMIC RANGE

The pickup preamplifier (and subsequent preamplifiers) must provide at least a 60 dB signal range from noise up to clipping (Fig. 3.16) to cater for recorded programme information of such range. This is not difficult to achieve with un-equalised ('flat') preamplifiers subsequent to the input stage, but problems in this respect can arise when the input stage is, in fact, the equalised preamplifier for the magnetic pickup, since the requirement for low noise conflicts with that for maximum pre-clipping output.

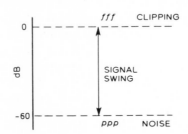

FIG. 3.16. *The preamplifier must have at least 60 dB volume range between noise and clipping for full dynamic range reproduction*

It will be realised, of course, that with negative feedback equalisation the required 20 dB of bass boost can be achieved only when the feedback at 1 kHz is greater than 20 dB. The feedback thus falls with decreasing frequency such that the gain of the preamplifier stage rises. The reducing feedback progressively diminishes the overload margin of the preamplifier, so that although a reasonable margin may exist at 1 kHz and above, the margin falls relative to the 1 kHz rated input sensitivity as the frequency reduces.

PICKUP PREAMPLIFIER OVERLOAD MARGIN

Provided the 1 kHz margin is adequate, this is matched by the reducing output of a velocity-type pickup (i.e. magnetic cartridge) with decreasing frequency—from the signal point of view, anyway. The overload margin is thus measured at 1 kHz on steady-state (i.e. sine wave) signal and is either referred to peak clipping or to a specified value of THD. For example, if the 1 kHz input sensitivity is 2 mV and peak clipping, as displayed on an oscilloscope connected to the output of the preamplifier, occurs at 20 mV, the overload margin is said to be 10:1 or 20 dB. Both signal voltages are r.m.s. values.

The maximum velocities recorded on disc records have been the subject of conjecture for many years, but from work carried out by Shure Brothers Inc. (American) it is apparent that peak velocities well into the 50 cm/s region are not uncommon on modern discs of wide dynamic range at high frequencies. Such plots, issued at the Shure 1973 Technical Seminar, are shown in Fig. 3.17, which expresses the relationship between cartridge 'trackability' (a Shure term) and recorded signal. Here it is implied that peak velocities approaching 25 cm/s at 1 kHz are a probability. Although many good quality magnetic cartridges produce an output of 1 mV r.m.s. (1.4 mV peak) per cm/s of velocity, there are some designs of significantly greater output, giving 4 mV *peak* or more per cm/s of recorded velocity. At 1 kHz, therefore, the magnetic pickup input of an amplifier could, in extreme cases and assuming the pickup could track them(!), receive music peaks of about 100 mV amplitude. To handle these without clipping, the preamplifier must thus be able to accommodate at least 70 mV r.m.s. up to the clipping point at 1 kHz.

The higher amplitude peaks at frequencies in advance of 1 kHz will then be automatically accommodated due to the greater feedback, as already mentioned. Conversely, the fall-off in overload margin (relative to 1 kHz) with decreasing frequency is matched by the decreasing peaks recorded with reducing frequency, as shown in Fig. 3.17.

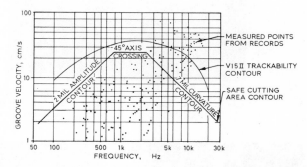

FIG. 3.17. *This Shure diagram expresses the relationship between cartridge 'trackability' (a Shure term) and recorded signal; it also shows the probability of high recorded peak velocities at high frequency (see text). The more recent Shure V15/III cartridge has a higher trackability contour than the V15/II shown. 1 mil = 0.001 in = 25.4 μm*

The circuit in Fig. 3.2 will accommodate 70 mV r.m.s. at the high sensitivity setting and 300 mV r.m.s. at the low sensitivity setting prior to clipping (which, in this design, is limited by a subsequent stage), and since the low sensitivity setting would be employed with high output cartridges the control section as a whole is immune to overload distortion.

The input overload of the Sonab three-transistor circuit in Fig. 3.15 is greater than 36 dB referred to 2 mV at 1 kHz, which is at least 126 mV r.m.s. (tests put the clipping point at about 200 mV).

The Cambridge circuit in Fig. 3.13 is a different kettle of fish, and so far as overload is concerned this is bound to score because the equalised stage is well down the chain and placed *after* the volume control. The equalised stage is thus not called upon to provide high 1 kHz gain. In fact, the gain at 1 kHz is about unity, which leaves plenty of scope for the 20 dB bass boost requirement without the circuit running out of feedback margin.

Moreover, since the pickup signal (or any other programme signal for that matter) is 'normalised' prior to arriving at the equalised stage, a very high overload margin is achieved at the normal setting of the volume control, which is well in advance of the basic requirement previously detailed. A substantial overload margin (referred to the 1 kHz input sensitivity) also holds well into bass, which makes the circuit immune to low-bass overload, such as from signals emanating from turntable rumble, record warp, etc.

Some amplifiers are equipped with an input level control, but untutored input attenuation is generally undesirable as a means of increasing the overload margin, since such attenuation can increase the source impedance (resistance) as 'seen' by the input stage and thus impair the signal/noise ratio.

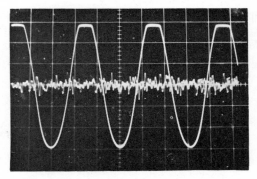

FIG. 3.18. *Oscillogram showing clipping of a sine wave due to preamplifier overload on one trace and a mildly recorded music signal from a pickup, via a similar preamplifier, on the other trace. Under this condition the overload margin is adequate*

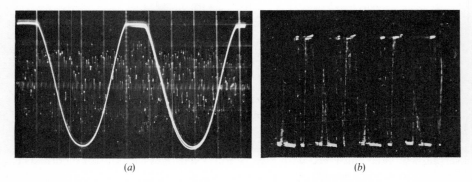

(a)   (b)

FIG. 3.19. *(a) as in Fig. 3.18 but with pickup signal from the preamplifier rising on peaks dangerously close to the clipping threshold. (b) peaks of greater amplitude would be clipped as shown, resulting in severe distortion*

Apart from transient intermodulation distortion, pickup preamplifier overload distortion is regarded by the author as a prime cause of stridence on record reproduction of high peak velocities. It is not unlike pickup mistracking distortion.

The oscillogram in Fig. 3.18 shows a preamplifier clipping a sine wave signal on one trace and a mildly recorded music signal from a pickup from a similar preamplifier on the other trace. The overload margin under this condition is thus adequate. The oscillogram in Fig. 3.19(a) shows the same setup, but this time with the pickup signal at the preamplifier output rising on peaks dangerously close to the overload threshold. Peaks of greater amplitude would thus be clipped (Fig. 3.19(b)), resulting in bad distortion.

PREAMPLIFIER AND CONTROL CIRCUITS

UNIVERSAL INPUT STAGE

Sometimes the input stage is common to all signal sources, with any equalisation required being switched in on the selected source. Such a circuit is given in Fig. 3.20. The sources are selected by S1A and the negative feedback is

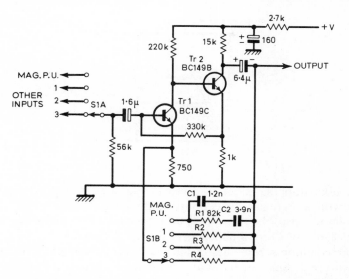

FIG. 3.20. *Circuit of 'universal' input stage. See text for description*

switched in by S1B. It will be seen that the equalising network, R1, C1 and C2, is switched into the loop on the magnetic pickup position, while resistor R2, R3 or R4 is switched into the loop on input 1, 2 or 3. The value of the resistor switched in thus defines the gain and hence the input sensitivity—the smaller the value the greater the feedback and the less the input sensitivity. Such a non-reactive loop provides a so-called 'flat' input, of course, but it is possible to switch in any type of equalising network.

INPUTS FOR PIEZO-ELECTRIC PICKUPS

Crystal and ceramic pickups do not have a velocity output. Instead, the output increases with *amplitude* of stylus deflection. This means that from an RIAA recording, which approximates constant-amplitude characteristics, the output over the spectrum is fairly 'flat'. The deviation from 'flatness' is taken care of by mechanical equalisation built into the cartridge. Thus by loading the cartridge with a high value resistance (several megohms), the signal can be applied directly to a 'flat' (unequalised) amplifier input.

The problem in transistor circuits lies in deriving such a high input impedance, and one solution is by the use of a field effect transistor, whose stage can be designed to possess a very high input impedance. Another solution is by so-called 'bootstrapping', which decreases the shunt effect of an impedance by decreasing the voltage across it. With a common-collector bipolar transistor stage the input impedance is normally high, but the maximum value is limited by the collector resistance (R_c) and the collector capacitance (C_c). By bootstrapping, the effect of R_c and C_c is virtually eliminated, so that the amplifier appears to the source as possessing a very high input impedance. A typical bias

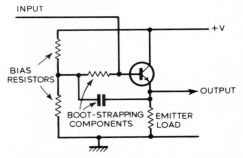

FIG. 3.21. *Simple bias network bootstrapping circuit*

network bootstrapping circuit is given in Fig. 3.21, while a double emitter-follower with collector and bias bootstrapping is given in Fig. 3.22. Both f.e.t. and bipolar transistor bootstrapping have been used for obtaining a high input impedance in transistor amplifiers over the last decade.

A more common scheme lies in the use of a low value load for the piezo-electric cartridge. Since such a source is essentially capacitive (as distinct from the essentially inductive source of a magnetic cartridge), the resistor/capacitance combination results in bass roll-off, and if a sufficiently low value is chosen for the resistor so that, together with the capacitance of the pickup, the crossover

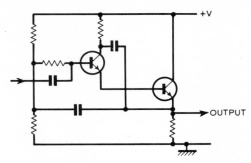

FIG. 3.22. *Double emitter-follower bootstrapping circuit*

frequency occurs around 20 kHz, or above, the signal across the resistor will have a response approximating that of a magnetic cartridge. The normal magnetic pickup equalisation can then be used to 'flatten' the response. It is, however, necessary to use a resistor suitable for the capacitance of the cartridge for the best results, and the common 47 k input impedance of the RIAA pre-amplifier is rarely low enough. Ceramic cartridges may have a capacitance from about 200 pF to about 700 pF. Crystal cartridges are somewhat higher.

Moreover, the output from a piezo-electric cartridge, even when loaded with a low value resistor, may be excessive for the magnetic pickup input which, if the overload margin is slim, could result in peak clipping of the signal (Fig. 3.19(b)). It would be undesirable to introduce input attenuation which *increases* the resistance (impedance) 'seen' by the preamplifier input since this would degrade the signal/noise ratio. In almost all cases of source coupling to transistor amplifiers, the best signal/noise ratio obtains when the impedance 'seen' by the input is as low as possible.

Manufacturers of the better class ceramic cartridges often supply details of simple padding circuits which can be connected between the cartridge and the magnetic pickup input of the amplifier (each channel needs such attention, of course) for the best loading, and the circuits in Fig. 3.23 are suitable for the

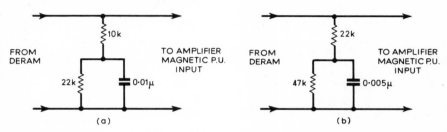

FIG. 3.23. *Circuits suitable for connecting the Decca Deram ceramic cartridge to the magnetic pickup input of an amplifier, low output (a) and higher output (b)*

Decca Deram cartridge. (*a*) produces an output approximately equal to 1 mV per cm/s, while (*b*) gives an output of approximately 4 mV per cm/s.

CAPACITIVE ATTENUATION

It is also possible to connect a high output ceramic or crystal cartridge to a relatively low impedance amplifier input, provided the input sensitivity is high enough, while exploiting the constant *amplitude* characteristic of the cartridge. This merely resolves to connecting *capacitance in parallel* with the cartridge. The greater the capacitance, the more the output is attenuated and the lower the impedance 'seen' by the input of the amplifier—which means that the signal/noise ratio is not impaired. The output signal is reduced approximately by the number of times the shunt capacitance is greater than the cartridge capacitance, and the greater the shunt capacitance that can be used, the better will be the bass response. Bass turnover frequency (f_o) is

$$f_o = \frac{10^6}{Z_{in}2\pi C} \tag{3.1}$$

where Z_{in} is the amplifier input impedance, f_o in Hz and C the total capacitance in μF.

It is also possible to secure piezo-electric equalisation by feedback, so that, in effect, the large shunt capacitance referred to above is achieved by feedback. There are other more complicated methods (see Fig. 3.47), but since it is the magnetic pickup which mostly partners a hi-fi outfit, piezo-electric cartridges are assuming lesser importance than in the past.

TONE CONTROL STAGES

The simplest tone control circuits are so-called 'passive', examples of which are given in Fig. 3.24, (a) for bass cut, (b) for bass boost, (c) for treble cut and (d) for treble boost. These basic 'blocks' are usually combined into a single tone control circuit, as shown in Fig. 3.25.

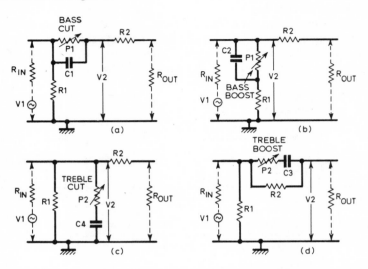

FIG. 3.24. *The elements of the passive tone control circuit in Fig. 3.25. (a) bass cut; (b) bass boost; (c) treble cut; (d) treble boost*

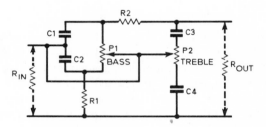

FIG. 3.25. *The elements in Fig. 3.24 combined into a single bass/treble tone control circuit. The component numbers correspond to those in Fig. 3.24 for ease of identification*

R_{in} refers to the impedance from the previous stage (source) and R_{out} refers to the impedance of the following stage (load). The circuit of Fig. 3.25 works as a 'coupling' between two stages, and since attenuation results this must be made good by amplification. For example, bass boost is secured by attenuation at the higher frequencies. In Fig. 3.24(b), discounting the effects of R_2 and R_{out}, output voltage V_2 at high frequencies is $R_1/(R_{in}+R_1)$ times input voltage V_1. When $P_1 \gg R_1$, the output voltage V_2 increases with respect to V_1 as the frequency falls. Maximum boost under the basic condition is $1+(R_{in}/R_1)$.

In Fig. 3.24(a), discounting the effect of R_1 and taking the output voltage V_2 across R_2 and R_{out} in series, maximum bass cut obtains when $P_1 \gg (R_{in}+R_2$

$+ R_{out}$), V_2 then falling at 6 dB/octave with the turnover frequency f_o occurring at

$$\frac{10^6}{2\pi C(R_{in}+R_2+R_{out})} \text{ Hz}$$

where f_o is in Hz, C in μF and the R in ohms.

In Fig. 3.24(c), discounting the effects of R_1, R_2 and R_{out}, maximum treble cut occurs when P_2 is zero, the output voltage V_2 then falling at 6 dB/octave with increasing frequency from the turnover frequency f_o which occurs at

$$\frac{10^6}{2\pi C R_{in}} \text{ Hz}$$

In Fig. 3.24(d), discounting the effect of R_1, R_2 attenuates the low frequencies while C_3 reduces the attenuation of the high frequencies. Maximum boost is given by

$$\left(1+\frac{R_2}{R_{in}+R_{out}}\right)$$

It will be appreciated from this study that the input and output impedances affect the results, as also do the components which were discounted to simplify the explanations, but which do exist in the combined circuit in Fig. 3.25. In

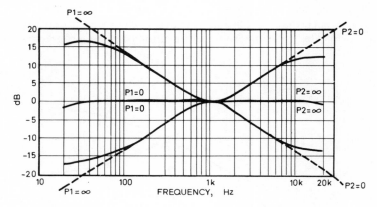

FIG. 3.26. *Tone control characteristics (see text for explanation)*

any single-stage RC circuit the response ultimately assumes a rate of 6 dB/octave, and this is shown by the broken-line extensions to the bass and treble responses in Fig. 3.26. In the practical circuit, of course, the rate is modified both at the start and conclusion of each response, so the full-line responses in Fig. 3.26 approximate the expectations from a practical circuit such as that in Fig. 3.25.

FEEDBACK TONE CONTROLS

The RC elements are usually placed in a feedback loop between the collector and base of the tone control transistor, so that the loop is made frequency dependent, as shown by the simplified diagram in Fig. 3.27, where C1 bypasses the high frequencies and C2 and C3 reject the low frequencies. The four operations of bass boost and cut and treble boost and cut can be examined in terms of separate circuit sections, as with the passive arrangement, and while the principles are basically similar, with the feedback or 'active' arrangement

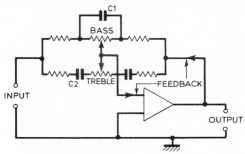

FIG. 3.27. *Basic diagram of feedback tone control circuit*

the responses are obtained by the RC elements instigating changes in feedback over the lower and upper parts of the spectrum by amounts determined by the settings of the bass and treble controls. Since both boost and cut are provided by the bass and treble controls, the reactive feedback is eliminated with the controls set to their centre positions, the overall response then being 'flat'. The control wiring is such that by rotating from centre clockwise progressive boost is provided, while by rotating from centre anticlockwise progressive cut is

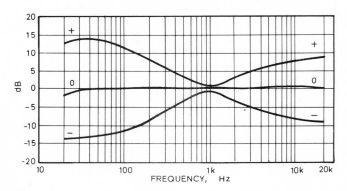

FIG. 3.28. *Tone control characteristics with less vigorous lift and cut at spectrum extremes*

provided. While the response rate is usually geared to 6 dB/octave, the responses are 'shaped' to the requirements of the designer by the impedances of the coupling circuits and by padding components.

The preference is for well tamed response characteristics, and by suitable choice of components, including padding components (i.e. the resistors either side of the bass and treble controls), the characteristics depicted in Fig. 3.28 can be obtained from the arrangement in Fig. 3.27.

Excessive boost and cut can rarely be used in practice, so by engineering for the characteristics given in Fig. 3.28, the user is provided with fully exploitable control ranges. Moreover, excessive treble boost can encourage positive feed-back and hence high-frequency oscillation at high volume control and full treble boost settings, which can seriously degrade the reproduction—though the actual oscillation may be inaudible.

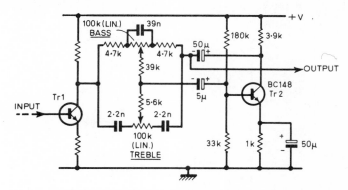

FIG. 3.29. *Full circuit of feedback tone control*

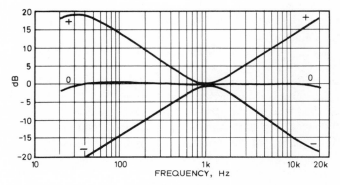

FIG. 3.30. *The characteristics of the circuit in Fig. 3.29*

A complete circuit of a feedback tone control is given in Fig. 3.29. This yields the characteristics given in Fig. 3.30, which are less well tamed than those in Fig. 3.28. Nevertheless, plots like this are not uncommon.

VOLUME CONTROL

Fig. 3.1 shows the volume control after the input preamplification and equalisation, but before the tone control circuit. This is the best position for it, since then the signal is 'normalised' before it is passed on to the tone control circuit, which can itself be designed to accommodate at low distortion a signal of level corresponding to that required for full drive of the power amplifier. The need for a suitable overload margin in those stages prior to the volume control has already been stressed.

A typical volume control circuit is given in Fig. 3.31. This follows the RIAA preamplifier stage, and Tr1 is the second transistor of such a stage. The volume control operates as a voltage divider, though sometimes it is arranged as a current divider (Fig. 3.32). It will be noticed that the output for tape recording is taken from the top of the control, via a 1 M resistor which provides the DIN constant-current arrangement already discussed (page 50). The second stage shown (Tr2) is an emitter-follower, the output signal thus being taken from the emitter.

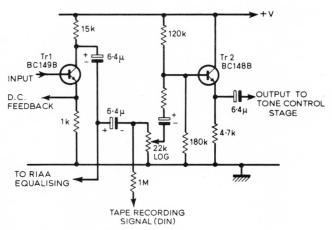

FIG. 3.31. *Voltage-divider volume control*

In some amplifiers the volume control is after a 'buffer' stage which receives signal from the output of the pickup preamplifier, and there are some designs where the control is located at the conclusion of the control section (see Fig. 3.36), possibly with a preset control (one for each channel) for signal level 'normalisation' placed at an intermediate point. In this type of circuit a logarithmic control will yield a linear relationship between angular rotation and signal output level referred to decibels.

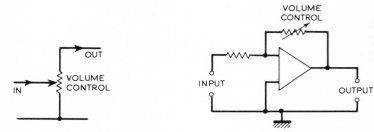

FIG. 3.32. *Alternative current-divider volume control*

FIG. 3.33. *Negative feedback volume control (also see Figs. 3.12, 3.13 and 3.35)*

The negative feedback type of control is becoming more popular, and this was described in detail for the Cambridge amplifier (Figs. 3.12 and 3.13). The block diagram of this kind of circuit (see Fig. 3.35) is given in Fig. 3.33, which is often called an 'active' volume control.

LOUDNESS CONTROL

One type of loudness control operates in the manner that as the control is rotated to reduce the gain the middle frequencies are affected more than the low and sometimes the high ones, so that the response characteristic rises at the bass and sometimes at the treble. This endeavours to compensate for the reducing sensitivity of human hearing at low and high frequencies, as the intensity of the sound is diminished (see Fig. 1.1).

A family of loudness contours is given in Fig. 3.34, where it is shown that with the control at maximum there is no compensation (the response being 'flat'), while progressively more bass, and to a less degree treble, boost occurs relative to the middle frequencies as the control is turned to increase the

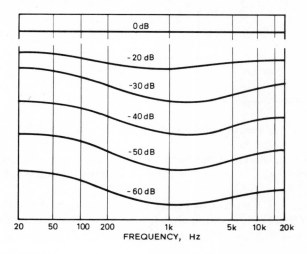

FIG. 3.34. *Family of loudness contours obtainable from the circuit in Fig. 3.35*

attenuation and thus reduce the gain. The circuit (from Sonab R4000) responsible for this is given in Fig. 3.35. This is, in fact, a feedback volume control which incorporates a loudness filter under the control of S1. With S1 in the 'linear' position the circuit works in the 'flat', uncompensated mode. The block diagram of this circuit in the linear mode is given in Fig. 3.33.

Tr1 and Tr2 form a directly coupled feedback pair, and the volume control is arranged to regulate the signal feedback. A tapping on the resistive element facilitates coupling of the loudness filter, via S1. Bass lift occurs because C2 in the feedback path reduces the gain at high frequencies, the response here being tailored by R2 and R3, and treble lift occurs because C1 in the signal path increases the input at high frequencies by a maximum amount determined by R1 in conjunction with input resistor R4. The tapping on P1 increases the filtering effects as the control is adjusted to increase the feedback and hence to reduce the gain.

With S1 in the 'linear' position, filter R1/C1 is disconnected and C2 and R3 are short-circuited.

71

Another scheme, which is based on a 'loudness' switch, is shown in Fig. 3.36. This circuit represents the final stages of the Armstrong '600' series, where Tr1 is the feedback tone control transistor and S1 is the 'loudness' switch. In the

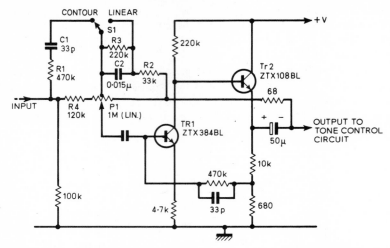

FIG. 3.35. *Negative feedback volume control with switchable loudness filter (Sonab)*

'normal' position shown, signal from Tr1 collector appears across the balance control, from whence it is fed, via the tape monitor switch S2, to the volume control.

In the 'loudness' position two filter circuits are brought into action. That comprising C1/R1 passes the higher frequencies while attenuating the lower frequencies, and that comprising R2/C2 bypasses the treble frequencies so that

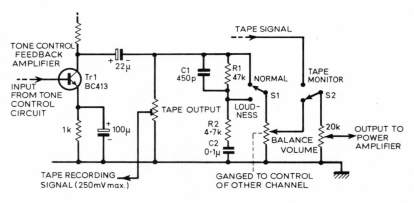

FIG. 3.36. *Final stages of the Armstrong '600' series, showing 'loudness' switch, tape output level preset, balance control, volume control and tape monitor switch*

mostly bass frequencies develop across the combination. The two filter sections together form a voltage divider, so that a signal, compensated as just mentioned, but at a significantly lower level than delivered by Tr1 collector, is passed on to the balance control and thence to the power amplifier, via the volume control.

The 'loudness' switch thus reduces the overall level of reproduction while introducing fixed amounts of bass and treble boost for low-level listening. The term 'loudness' in this case is barely compatible with the function of the circuit! Mid-frequency attenuation is approximately 20 dB, and boosts relative to 1 kHz are 10 dB at 70 Hz and 5 dB at 15 kHz.

OTHER CONTROL SECTION CIRCUITS

The Armstrong circuit brings to light some other aspects of the control section in general. The signal for tape recording is adjustable by the 100 k preset, and tape recorder signal for replay is directed straight to the power amplifier, via the volume control, through S2 in the 'monitor' position. This makes it possible to record via the control section while at the same time monitoring the signal just recorded from a separate head on the tape recorder, via a separate pre-amplifier and the power amplifier. It is also noteworthy that the volume control in this design follows the tone control stage, and that the signal for tape recording is affected by the tone controls and filters. The Cambridge 'P' series amplifiers are similar in this respect, but they differ in that the setting of the volume control also affects the level of the recording signal (tape *replay* has a preset level control) and in that the treble filter is outside the recording signal path.

In the majority of amplifiers the tape recording signal is obtained from a stage prior to the control sections (Fig. 3.31, for example).

BASS FILTERS

To avoid the effects of turntable rumble and other infrabass disturbances on gramophone record reproduction the RIAA equalisation may be designed deliberately to exhibit bass roll-off. However, since the rate of roll-off may not be very fast, and as the crossover frequency may be fairly low (about 25–30 Hz), additional low-frequency filtering is often included with a slightly higher cross-over frequency, the combined filtering then giving a more desirable greater rate of bass roll-off. Such filtering is commonly switchable and may be passive or active, the latter giving a greater rate of roll-off.

The simplest passive filter merely consists of a suitable value capacitor in series with a higher value interstage coupling capacitor, as shown in Fig. 3.37. Here Tr1 is an emitter-follower receiving signal from a previous preamplifier (sometimes the RIAA stage) and delivering signal from a relatively low impedance to the tone control stage. C1 is the normal coupling capacitor and C2 the lower value capacitor which, in conjunction with R_L (Fig. 3.37), provides the higher frequency turnover. S1 merely short-circuits C2 in the 'filter out' position. Rate of roll-off for this simple type of filter is 6 dB/octave.

For a greater rate of roll-off second-order filters are used in 'active' configurations.

A bass (i.e. high-pass) filter associated with bootstrapping is given in Fig. 3.38. Tr1 and Tr2 form a compound complementary (npn/pnp) pair with boot-strapping by C2 (see Figs. 3.21 and 3.22). The input components C1 and R1

73

constitute a simple 6 dB/octave filter of the type already described, but owing to the bootstrapping signal from C2, which is developed across R2, the effective impedance of R1 is significantly reduced. This reduces the filter effect of C1, since this now looks into a high impedance. However, as the frequency is reduced the impedance of C2 increases, which gives rise to a cumulative effect on the C1/R1 network such that there is a rapid increase in low-frequency attenuation, reaching an ultimate rate of 12 dB/octave below the turnover

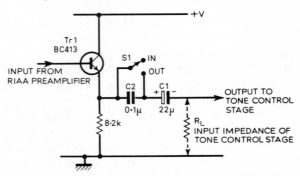

FIG. 3.37. *Simple 6 dB/octave high-pass (bass) filter, where the bass turnover frequency is determined by C2 in conjunction with the impedance into which the coupling feeds*

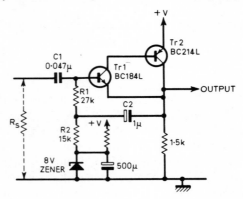

FIG. 3.38. *High-pass filter in bootstrapping circuit (see text for description, etc.)*

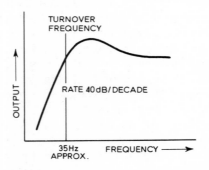

FIG. 3.39. *Nature of response of Fig. 3.38 high-pass filter circuit. The 'hump' can be eliminated and the attenuation rate increased to 18 dB/octave by a single-stage RC filter elsewhere in the circuit*

74

frequency. The nature of the response, with the turnover frequency corresponding to the values of the components shown, is given in Fig. 3.39. The hump at the turnover frequency results from phase shift in the bootstrapping circuit.

A circuit of this kind is used in the John Linsley Hood amplifier, *Hi-Fi News and Record Review*, November and December, 1972 and January and February 1973, the circuit in note being described in some detail in the February 1973 issue. It is possible to eliminate the hump and increase the attenuation rate to 18 dB/octave by single-order RC filtering elsewhere in the circuit.

The slow 6 dB/octave rate of roll-off of a simple first-order filter attenuates not only the infrabass unwanted signals but also some of the real bass information as well. A roll-off rate of at least 12 dB/octave is thus desirable. However, a rapid rate of roll-off can precipitate transient distortion as already mentioned.

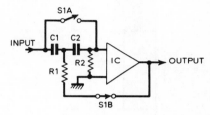

FIG. 3.40. *Active second-order high-pass (bass) filter arranged in conjunction with an integrated circuit preamplifier*

The basic elements of an active second-order filter are given in Fig. 3.40. This can be arranged in conjunction with an i.c. preamplifier stage. Poorly damped, this sort of filter also yields a substantial hump at the turnover frequency (f_o), but when the damping factor (F_d) is $1/\sqrt{2}$ there is optimum cut-off without humping. The damping factor can be evaluated from

$$F_d = \sqrt{\left(\frac{R_1}{R_2}\right)} \qquad (3.2)$$

and the turnover frequency from

$$f_o = \frac{1}{2\pi\sqrt{(R_1 R_2 C_1 C_2)}} \qquad (3.3)$$

The filter components can be switched by S1A/B.

TREBLE FILTERS

A treble filter is sometimes useful to help remove noise and excessive distortion from a programme signal. Apart from the fixed 6 dB/octave treble roll-off filter which is sometimes found in the control section for ultimate response limitation (see under Transient Distortion), the high-frequency (low-pass) filter is generally switchable, and like the low-frequency (high-pass) filter this can be either a simple first-order passive design or an active design of 12 dB/octave roll-off rate (or greater).

One or two amplifiers incorporate facilities not only for switching the turn-over frequency of this type filter, but also for adjusting the rate of roll-off (slope control or switch). To avoid attenuating wanted high-frequency programme information and increasing the rise time unduly, the f_o should be placed as high in the spectrum as possible consistent with the nature of the spurious information it is required to attenuate. A switchable or continuously variable f_o can thus be desirable.

A high rate of roll-off can encourage transient distortion (overshoot and rings) and thus affect the tonal quality of the reproduction. For general use a roll-off rate much in excess of 12 dB/octave is best avoided. However, it is possible to achieve a fast ultimate rate of roll-off with minimal tonal impairment by the use of two or more filter sections of progressively higher f_o. This

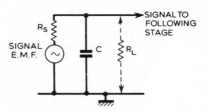

FIG. 3.41. *Simple high-frequency filter*

avoids a very fast fall-off from the turnover frequency, thereby inhibiting excessive overshoot, while building up ultimately to a faster rate of roll-off.

The simplest high-frequency filter consists merely of a capacitance in shunt with the signal path as shown in Fig. 3.41. With this f_o is a function of C and total R, such that $2\pi f_o = 1/R_T C$ (where R_T is the total R), and the ultimate rate of roll-off is 6 dB/octave. Two such networks in cascade, with suitable impedance isolation between them (i.e. in a two-stage resistance-coupled amplifier), increase the ultimate rate of roll-off to 12 dB/octave.

We have already seen that this simple network occurs when a high impedance source is coupled to a high impedance load through screened cable (owing to the capacitance of the cable). f_o is shifted outside the passband of interest by making the total R small compared with X_c (the resonance of C).

Fig. 3.42 depicts the responses of two low-pass filters, A with a 6 dB/octave rate and f_o about 5 kHz and B with a 12 dB/octave rate and f_o about 10 kHz.

The basic elements of a classic second-order active low-pass filter, engineered round an i.c. are given in Fig. 3.43. It will be noticed that this has a family resemblance to the active high-pass filter in Fig. 3.40, but in low-pass case F_d is $\sqrt{(C_1/C_2)}$, and f_o can be evaluated from

$$f_o = \frac{1}{2\pi\sqrt{C_1 C_2 R_1 R_2}} \tag{3.4}$$

S1A/B merely switches out the filter components when not required, but the

76

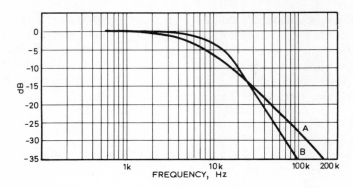

FIG. 3.42. *Low-pass filter responses. A approximately 6 dB/octave and B approximately 12 dB/octave*

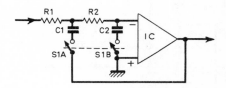

FIG. 3.43. *Basic elements of active low-pass filter (see text for description)*

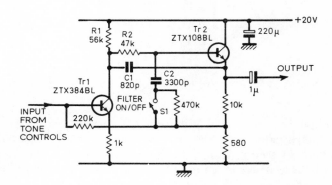

FIG. 3.44. *Active low-pass filter circuit (Sonab)*

circuit is arranged in practice so that the i.c. remains as a gain-stabilised non-filtered amplifier with S1A/B off.

Of course, the same kind of circuit can be arranged round a transistor stage, and such a circuit (Sonab) is shown in Fig. 3.44, where Tr1 is the tone control stage and Tr2 an emitter-follower into which the active low-pass filter works. In this circuit only one of the filter capacitor is switched (by S1). R1, R2, C1 and C2 correspond to the components of the same numbers in Fig. 3.43. Thus feedback is from Tr2 emitter, via C1, to the junction of R1/R2 and thence back to Tr2 base. With the circuit values given, the f_o is close to 8 kHz, and the roll-off rate is 12 dB/octave. Stage gain equals unity when R1 equals R2.

77

A circuit of a switched filter with slope (Armstrong) is given in Fig. 3.45. The filter is an active type arranged round Tr1, the tone control stage. S1 is a three-section slider switch assembly with sections A and B giving different f_o and section C changing the slope of the response. In the positions shown the filter is inactive. With either value of f_o selected, and C in the position shown, the slope is minimum. Network X is selected by section A for f_o 1, the feedback then

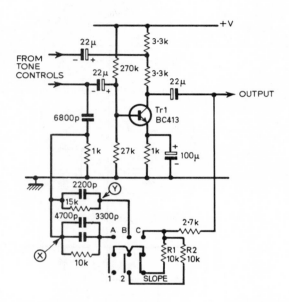

FIG. 3.45. *Active low-pass filter with switchable f_o and slope (Armstrong)*

being via R1 and R2 in parallel. With section C switched in the parallel R1/R2 is shorted, which reduces the 'damping' and increases the slope. With section B selected network section Y for f_o 2 is brought into circuit, and with section C set as shown, the feedback is again via R1/R2 parallel pair, and the slope at this f_o can be increased by operation of section C as before.

There are a variety of circuits of this kind, some having maximum slopes in excess of 12 dB/octave and some with variable slope control rather than the switched arrangement. In this case the 'damping' is made continuously variable.

While early circuits employed inductive elements for filtering, the majority now employ active circuits for providing the required rate of roll-off.

INTERMEDIATE STAGES

In addition to the equalised, tone control and filter stages already discussed, the control section may include one or two intermediate stages for gain normalisation and matching. We have already seen some of these (Figs. 3.13 and 3.31, for example). A high input impedance and low output impedance are achieved by the well known emitter-follower. The common-emitter stage is used when a moderate-to-low output impedance is required, but feedback loops are often adopted not only to achieve stabilisation against temperature variations, etc. but also to define the impedance.

The higher level stages are commonly operated from a supply line of greater voltage than the earlier, low-level stages, this being necessary to handle the higher amplitude signal without clipping.

TRANSISTOR TYPES

Noise is most troublesome in the earlier stages, particularly in the equalised pickup preamplifier stage, and such stages are designed to operate at the lowest emitter current consistent with the required overload performance. All the stages, of course, must be capable of satisfying at least the 60 dB dynamic range requirement.

For the low-level stages in particular, silicon transistors have merit in terms of gain at least, owing to the smaller leakage currents than germanium counterparts. Noise, too, is influenced by transistor type, but this also varies with frequency, transistor voltages and currents and with source resistance. Over the years low-noise transistors for audio applications have been developed, these having stable low noise even at very low frequencies.

INPUT SWITCHING

Examples of input switching have already been given (Figs. 3.1 and 3.13), also see Fig. 3.47. In most designs a rotary switch is employed which communicates the required input to the appropriate control section stage while shorting out the inputs not in use to avoid inter-signal crosstalk, which might otherwise occur due to switch capacitances, etc. (see Fig. 3.47).

The more expensive amplifier may feature inputs for two magnetic pickups, two auxiliary sources, two tape records (with a recording signal output for each), tape head and radio tuner; and there is a trend, too, towards a microphone input with separate preamplification and mixing facilities.

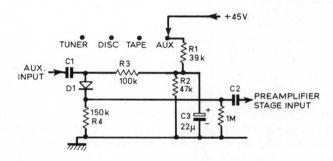

FIG. 3.46. *Gating diode source input switching (Armstrong)*

PREAMPLIFIER AND CONTROL CIRCUITS

DIODE GATING

Diodes have been used for source switching, and such an arrangement adopted by Armstrong is shown in Fig. 3.46. S1 is the selector switch whose wiper is connected to +45 V. The voltage at R1/R2 divider junction is conveyed to the anode of the gating diode D1 through R3, and since D1 cathode is returned to chassis through R4, the diode switches on and conveys the source signal to the input of the appropriate preamplifier stage through C1 and C2. The time-constant formed by R2/C3 provides a smooth transition from one source to another when S1 is moved to a different position. Each input, of course, has its own gating diode, and a network similar to that shown for the auxiliary input is connected to each switch position. In this way, therefore, the signal is switched electronically, the selector switch merely gating on the appropriate diode.

USE OF I.C.S

Integrated circuits are used not only in the stages of the control section but also, in some designs, in the power amplifiers as well. Basic examples of i.c.s in filter configurations have already been given (Figs. 3.40 and 3.43). Linear i.c.s (i.e. operational amplifiers) reduce the number of discrete components per stage, and an example of a universal input preamplifier, with feedback loop switching for RIAA equalisation, is given in Fig. 3.47.

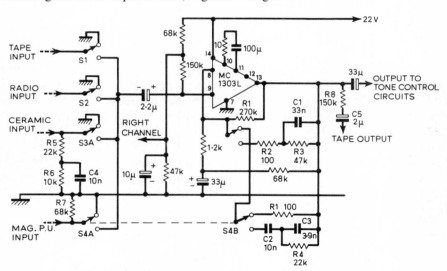

FIG. 3.47. *Universal input preamplifier using an i.c. (Amstrad)*

Switches S1, S2, S3A/B and S4A/B select the sources, and they are arranged so that the sources not active are 'earthed'. With S3A/B and S4A/B 'out' (positions shown) the stage operates in the unequalised mode, the gain then being defined essentially by R1 relative to the tape and radio inputs. With S3A/B 'on', R1 is removed and equalisation network R2/R3/C1 is introduced into the feedback loop relative to the ceramic input. With S4A/B 'on', equalisation network C2/C3/R4 is introduced into the feedback loop relative to the magnetic pickup input.

Further correction for a ceramic pickup is provided by network R5/R6/C4, while R7, in conjunction with the amplifier input impedance, establishes the magnetic pickup load. Signal for tape recording is obtained from the i.c. output through R8/C5.

The circuit shown is for the left channel, the right channel being identical.

This circuit is a part of the Amstrad IC2000 Mk II amplifier which employs a total of three i.c.s in each channel.

Also in this amplifier a tone control for the middle range of frequencies, in addition to the usual bass and treble controls, is employed. This operates in a frequency-selective feedback loop and the RC elements are valued so that only the middle range of frequencies are affected.

Finally, the left and right outputs of the control section are arranged to be of a level and impedance to suit the input circuits of the power amplifiers. In some cases the output is at relatively low impedance from an emitter-follower.

CHAPTER 4

Power Amplifiers and Power Supplies

IT IS THE job of the power amplifiers to accept the signals 'tailored' by the control section and to translate them to a suitable power for driving the loud-speakers. For hi-fi applications the signals delivered by the control section should have a distortion content not much greater than 0.1% over the full dynamic range and accepted frequency spectrum. Thus the power amplifiers must not substantially add to this low distortion yield.

To ensure the least distortion and required power bandwidth use is made of liberal negative feedback, but negative feedback cannot be regarded as the cure for all power amplifier ills. It is a powerful design tool, but applied in excess without due regard to other aspects of the design it can detract from, rather than enhance, the quality of reproduction, even though instrument tests may be taken to indicate otherwise! Over an extended bandwidth, for example, the feedback can change from negative to positive and encourage high-frequency oscillation and 'rings', and if large amounts of feedback are used to extend the power response when relatively low f_T transistors are adopted in the design, transient intermodulation distortion (see pages 43, 102 and 124) can prove troublesome, though may not show up on ordinary tests.

In the open-loop condition, therefore, the power amplifier should have maximum bandwidth and the least possible distortion. The latter calls for accurate design and the former for high f_T power transistors. Since the power transistors are not uncommonly operated in the common-emitter mode, the cutoff frequency is significantly below f_T, particularly when the impedance 'seen' by the power transistors bases is relatively high, it then approximating $f_T/(\beta + 1)$, where beta (β) is the ratio of the d.c. collector current I_c to the d.c. base current I_B.

A greater open-loop bandwidth is achieved by lower base input impedances and current drive, but this tends to increase the static distortion. However, this is reduced to acceptably low levels by the main negative feedback loop and, in some cases, by local feedback in the form of unbypassed emitter resistors, which further increases the bandwidth.

Poor design, resulting in unwarranted stray capacitances, can encourage high-frequency instability and demand the use of 'stabilising' networks, which tend to work against the requirements for an extended high-frequency response.

CLASS A

The stages of the control section are biased so that collector current is maintained at all times throughout a complete signal cycle. This is class A, and is illustrated in Fig. 4.1.

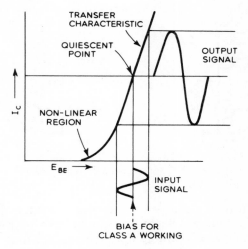

FIG. 4.1. *Class A working illustrated*

Class A is perfectly acceptable—indeed, desirable—for the low power stages, since in small transistors the resulting quiescent current is relatively small. In power amplifiers, however, the very much greater quiescent current demands the employment of large heat sinks to keep the transistor junctions at a stable temperature. Class B operation, as we shall see, avoids such high dissipation and enhances the efficiency.

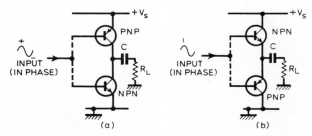

FIG. 4.2. *Two arrangements for complementary push-pull output, where C is the load coupling capacitor and R_L the load*

Nevertheless, there are still (at the time of writing) one or two hi-fi amplifiers being made with class A power amplifier stages. Whatever the class, the output stages of hi-fi amplifiers employ two transistors in push-pull, and with class A the design is such that the current in one increases by the amount that it decreases in the other over a full signal cycle, neither the current through either transistor nor the voltage across it falling to zero.

83

This means, assuming perfect conditions, that the peak current communicated to the load R_L is twice the quiescent current, or $2I_q$. The two transistors are connected in series across the supply V_s, and they can be either the same or complementary polarity. Fig. 4.2 shows two complementary configurations where the drive to the two transistors needs to be of common phase.

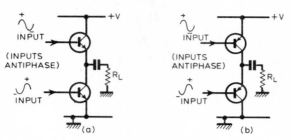

FIG. 4.3. *Two arrangements for non-complementary push-pull output, where C and R_L are as in Fig. 4.2*

Fig. 4.3 shows two common polarity arrangements for npn and pnp pairs respectively. In this case antiphase drive to the two transistors is required. Thus, some form of 'phase-splitting' stage is necessary to drive common-pair output stages.

CLASS A EFFICIENCY

With class A biasing the peak load voltage is $V_s/2$, and since the peak load current is $2I_q$, the optimum load is equal to $V_s/4I_q$ (i.e. $(V_s/2)/2I_q$). The *mean* power in the load, therefore, is the product of the peak voltage and the peak current divided by two, which works out to $V_sI_q/2$. Since V_sI_q is the input power, maximum efficiency can be expressed as

$$\text{Eff.}_{\text{max}}\% = \frac{V_sI_q}{2V_sI_q} \times 100 \qquad (4.1)$$
$$= 50\%$$

CLASS B

By definition, class B assumes a push-pull output stage which is biased to collector current cutoff in the absence of drive signal. When drive is applied, the collector current of one transistor of the pair flows for one half of each complete cycle, while the other of the pair is driven into non-conduction, the conditions reversing during the opposite half of each complete cycle.

However, contemporary practice assumes that a class B amplifier is one in which the bias is deliberately adjusted to provide a small value of I_q in the absence of drive signal. When the biasing is further from theoretical class B and more towards class A, the term class AB is sometimes adopted.

Thus, with the class B used in hi-fi amplifiers, one half-cycle of drive causes the current to rise through one transistor and fall through the other until eventually there is no current in this transistor at some point *after* the start of the signal cycle, the transistors then changing role on the other half cycle.

CROSSOVER DISTORTION

Fig. 4.4 shows the ideal state of affairs for 'pure' class B, based on complementary transistors. Unhappily, this ideal is not attainable (it never is) because the transfer function of each transistor has a bottom region of non-linearity. Moreover, the 'potential barrier' of the base/emitter junction must be outweighed to allow the start of the conducting half-cycle to yield collector

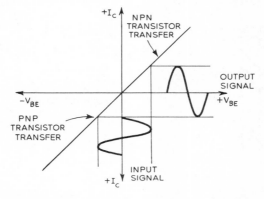

FIG. 4.4. *Ideal push-pull transfer function for a complementary pair (see text)*

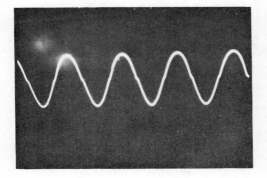

FIG. 4.5. *Oscillogram showing mild crossover distortion*

current. Unless counteracted, therefore, each half-cycle of the signal communicated to the load would not only be distorted, particularly at low power, but the two halves of the signal would fail to re-form to a whole cycle correctly; small steps would occur between the positive and negative half cycles, giving so-called crossover distortion, revealed in mild form by the oscillogram in Fig. 4.5. The net result would be severe high-order harmonic distortion and high intermodulation distortion, having minimal reference to high quality reproduction!

To some extent the problem is solved by biasing each transistor of the pair for a small I_q in the absence of drive signal. The diagrams in Fig. 4.6 (not to scale) attempt to show the conditions with zero I_q and hence high crossover distortion at (*a*) and with a small I_q and far less distortion at (*b*).

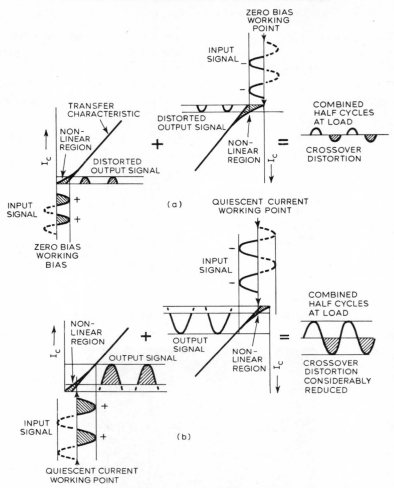

FIG. 4.6. *Theoretical class B operation for zero I_q biasing (a) and practical class B (b). See text for descriptions*

Main advantages of class B over class A are thus low quiescent current, leading to more reasonably sized heat sinks, and higher efficiency. Class B can also ease the power supply problems, since the power drawn from the supply is geared to the power delivered to the load.

The basic stages in Figs. 4.2 and 4.3, with suitable biasing, are also found in class B push-pull amplifiers.

CLASS B EFFICIENCY

Assuming zero I_q, the power drawn by a class B amplifier in the absence of drive is thus zero. Theoretical maximum power is $(V_s/2)^2/2R_L$, which is $V_s^2/8R_L$. The mean current is then $V_s/2\pi R_L$, so the mean supply power is $V_s^2/2\pi R_L$.

Maximum efficiency is thus

$$\text{Eff.}_{\max}\% = \frac{V_s^2}{8R_L} \cdot \frac{2\pi R_L}{V_s^2} \times 100 \qquad (4.2)$$

$$= \frac{\pi}{2} \times 100 = 78.5\%$$

CLASS D

One or two class D amplifiers for audio applications have appeared, but for various reasons have not caught on, one being associated with radiation of the switching operation. Class D differs significantly from class A and class B in that the output transistors are arranged as switches in a single-ended push-pull circuit. The audio information is carried by square waves to the switching transistors such that the width of the square waves (mark/space ratio) varies with the audio signal. The switching transistors convert the width-modulated square waves back to ordinary audio signal, and the switching signal—which is at a high repetition frequency—is removed by low-pass filtering.

The maximum theoretical efficiency of this class of circuit is 100%, and in practice circuits have been engineered with efficiencies exceeding 90%.

CLASS C

Class C amplifiers are not used in audio applications since conduction occurs for only a small part of each cycle. However, they are used extensively in r.f. power amplifiers where the waveform (in this case sinusoidal) is recovered by high-Q tuned circuits.

PI-MODE

Pi-mode describes a scheme evolved some time ago by the Mullard engineers where increasing signal drive causes the power amplifier biasing to change from class A to class AB and then—at full drive—to class B. This reduces the cross-over distortion at medium power levels and eliminates it at low power levels, where in some class B designs, there is a tendency for it to start increasing (for the reasons shown in Fig. 4.6). Class A power amplifiers, of course, exhibit no crossover at all, the normal harmonic distortion falling progressively with reducing power.

The pi-mode has an essentially constant current drain, and because of this complicated power supply circuits, with regulation, are unnecessary. However, the scheme in its original form is not very often found in contemporary amplifiers.

The majority of hi-fi designs are based on quasi-class B (i.e. class B with optimised I_q for the least distortion) and circuits which almost completely eliminate crossover distortion and keep THD and IMD at very low levels. In fact, it is impossible to detect crossover distortion or artefacts on the residual of many well made amplifiers.

87

LOAD COUPLING

The power may be extracted from a capacitance coupled to the load (loud-speaker), as in Figs. 4.2 and 4.3, or direct coupling may be employed, the power supply then being balanced positively and negatively about 'earth' (chassis), as in Fig. 4.8. The d.c. through the coupled loudspeaker is extremely small when the two transistors are correctly balanced, but any imbalance, resulting from a circuit or component fault, could cause a high offset current to flow, and to avoid loudspeaker burnout an electronic cutout, sensing any offset current, or a fuse is fitted to remove the supply or the loudspeaker from circuit in the event of such trouble. A cutout is best since a fuse may be too slow in blowing!

A stereo amplifier integrates the two power amplifiers and a quadraphonic amplifier integrates the four power amplifiers. There might be a switch in some four-channel models allowing the channels to be paired up at virtually double the single-channel power for two-channel stereo operation. As already mentioned, most contemporary amplifiers—whether two-channel or four-channel—integrate also the control section.

PROTECTION

Protection is also given to the output transistors in most designs either by an electronic circuit which removes or reduces the drive in the event of an overload or loudspeaker circuit short or by fuses which remove the power supply should the output stage current rise to an abnormally high value. Loudspeaker fuses might also be incorporated when electronic overload protection is employed.

Since a power amplifier is almost a constant voltage device, it follows that the current will increase as the load resistance is decreased (which is why most amplifiers yield increasing power with reducing load value). A very low value of load, of course, might cause the power transistors to pass a greater current that this parameter of their design permits. If fuses only are used for protection, the power transistors usually have a conservative current rating.

PRACTICAL CIRCUIT

Fig. 4.7 gives the circuit of one channel of a power amplifier, whose push-pull output transistors are arranged as at (a) in Fig. 4.3. This is based on the Armstrong '600' series. Output transistors Tr6 and Tr7 are capable of providing an average continuous wave power of 50 watts into 4 ohms, 40 watts into 8 ohms or 27 watts into 15 ohms. Based on the 83 V supply, it might be concluded from the formulae on page 86 that a greater maximum power should be obtainable. This is not the case because (a) transistors are never 'perfect', (b) the supply voltage falls slightly under sustained continuous wave power and (c) power is lost in the 0.68 ohm resistors in series with the two transistors and in the load-coupling components.

Power is taken via C1, such that during one half-cycle current is drawn from the supply, which charges C1, and during the next half cycle C1 charge is withdrawn.

The parallel L1/R1 in *series* with the load is a stabilising device, which also helps to reduce overshoot into capacitance loads. Another such network consists of a capacitor in series with a resistor connected *across* the output of an amplifier. This, called a Zobel network, presents the loudspeaker to the amplifier as a resistive load.

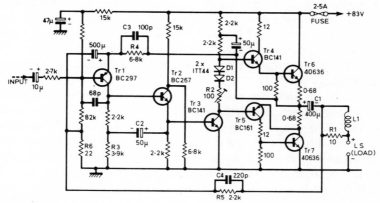

FIG. 4.7. *Quasi-complementary power amplifier (Armstrong). See text for description*

A Zobel network thus serves to neutralise loudspeaker reactance to protect the output transistors from collector breakdown during severe overload or on pulse signal. A loudspeaker contains resistance, capacitance and inductance, and an RC network caters for the inductive component. The Zobel R_z and C_z values can be found from

$$R_z = R_s$$

and
$$C_z = \frac{L_s}{R_s^2}$$
(4.3)

where R_s is the loudspeaker resistance and L_s its inductance. Thus for 4 ohms and $200\,\mu$H R_z would be 4 ohms and C_z $12.5\,\mu$F, but the network can only approximate the requirement. When L and R in parallel are used the values might be chosen empirically for the best compromise.

Drive for the power transistors is obtained from the complementary pair Tr4 and Tr5. Thus, while the base of one output transistor is swinging positively, that of the other output transistor is swinging negatively. Low impedance couplings to Tr6/Tr7 bases are used, which maintain an acceptable power bandwidth. The bases of Tr4 and Tr5 are driven together and in phase from the directly coupled Tr3. Direct coupling, in fact, is used throughout the amplifier, except to the loudspeaker. The quiescent current is set by R2 which is in the series chain across the supply. Diode pair D1/D2 provides temperature compensation, so that the quiescent current remains fairly constant with temperature change of the power transistors.

Tr3 is driven at low impedance from emitter-follower Tr2, which in turn is driven from the collector of the input transistor Tr1. A high impedance coupling between Tr1 and Tr2 is achieved by bootstrapping relative to C2 and R3 (see

Fig. 3.21). Two feedback paths are used, one from the output transistors direct (for d.c. stabilisation) and the other from the load (loudspeaker) side of C1. Both go back to Tr1, the first via R4 and C3 and the second via R5 and C4, the feedback voltage developing across R6. This arrangement provides a zero source impedance at a low frequency (round 25 Hz) and a change towards a positive source impedance at lower frequencies, which can help with loudspeaker damping at low frequencies.

The capacitors across the feedback resistors remove overshoot from pulse and transient waveforms, while also defining the upper cutoff frequency of the amplifier. The 68 pF capacitor across the base and emitter of Tr1 is for phase compensation.

There is no overload protection circuit, but the power transistors are protected from abnormally high current by the input power supply fuse.

This quasi-complementary type of power amplifier circuit is popular with designers of hi-fi equipment, and it is found in a variety of configurations, often with significant differences in design detail reflecting the views of the individual designers. The term *quasi-complementary* stems from the use of a pair of complementary transistors driving into a pair of npn *or* pnp output transistors.

COMPLEMENTARY SYMMETRY POWER AMPLIFIER

Owing to the early dearth of high power transistors of opposite polarity, complementary symmetry power amplifiers were at first limited to a few watts. However, transistors of opposite polarity and matching characteristics, capable of handling quite substantial power, are now readily available, and powerful amplifiers based on the fully complementary configuration are in wide use.

Complementary symmetry or 'fully complementary' signifies that pnp/npn pairs are used for both the driver and power amplifier stages, and several configurations are available to the designer, two of which for the output stage are given in Fig. 4.2. As in the quasi-complementary case, the load is coupled to the mid-point, either directly when split supply operation is adopted or through a capacitor, as in Fig. 4.7, when a single supply rail is used. Complementary symmetry provides both simplicity and stability, and there is no trouble in achieving a low impedance between the emitter and base of both output transistors.

Complementary compound or Darlington configurations are commonly used for each driver and its associated power transistor, leading to two such sections, one for each half cycle. This method avoids class A for the driver, thereby making it possible to run at substantial power without elevated driver stage dissipation.

A circuit (by Bryan Amplifiers Limited) using complementary pairs is given in Fig. 4.8. The compound pairs are Tr8/Tr10 and Tr9/Tr11, and both are driven together from the driver Tr3, which is similar in operation to Tr3 in Fig. 4.7. Input amplifiers are Tr1 and Tr2, the first being an emitter-follower for low impedance drive to Tr2.

It will be seen that Tr2 is arranged with Tr4 as a differential amplifier, which receives a constant-current supply from Tr12, connected to the emitters. Tr12 is itself stabilised by the zener diode at its base. The Tr2 part of the differential stage receives input signal at its base, while the Tr4 part receives negative feed-back signal at its base. R1 and R2 in series form a voltage divider across the output, so the ratio of these two resistors determines the amount of negative feedback applied to Tr4 base. There is also a local a.c. feedback path back to Tr2 base, via the tap on the RC divider, through R3. The low output impedance of Tr1 allows the use of a high degree of feedback.

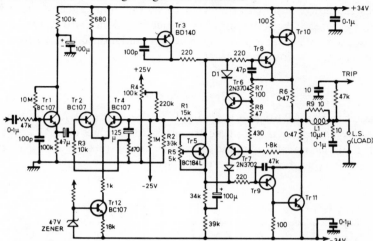

FIG. 4.8. *Complementary symmetry power amplifier (Bryan LE720). This includes short-circuit protection transistors Tr6 and Tr7, differential input Tr2/Tr4 with constant-current supply by Tr12 and direct coupling to the loudspeaker. See text for description*

The preset R4 sets the mid-point voltage for optimum symmetry, while Tr5 controls the quiescent current, adjustable by preset R5. Tr5 acts rather like diodes D1/D2 in Fig. 4.7—as a stabilising device.

HIGH CURRENT PROTECTION

Transistors Tr6 and Tr7 serve to sense an abnormally high current in the power transistors, and then automatically to reduce the drive to keep the current within the rating of the transistors. For example, the voltage developed across R6 depends on the amount of current flowing through the resistor, and hence on the power transistor current. The voltage is divided down to Tr6 base by R7/R8, and the values of the components are chosen so that up to a predetermined current Tr6 is non-conducting, which is 5 A in the circuit given.

Power transistor current in excess of this value, therefore, causes Tr6 to switch on and short-circuit the drive signal through D1, which immediately causes the current to fall. A short-circuit across the loudspeaker terminals in the presence of high drive will thus operate the protection device and prevent the output transistors from exceeding their rating.

Exactly the same function occurs on the other half of the circuit due to a similar action of Tr7, etc.

Protection circuits of a similar nature sometimes trigger on and remain on until a capacitor of a time-constant circuit has had time to discharge. There are

91

others which operate a power supply cutout and need to be reset. There is also a species which operates by sensing abnormally high heat-sink temperature.

Protection circuits of this kind should not be confused with loudspeaker protection which is now being used in amplifiers where there is direct coupling to the loudspeaker. Indeed, the circuit in Fig. 4.8 has direct coupling to the loudspeaker, via network L1/R9, and an electromechanical trip which neatly removes the power supply in the event of serious imbalance of the push-pull stage. It has already been explained that such imbalance will cause d.c. to flow out of the push-pull stage into the loudspeaker, and if the current is high enough it could damage the loudspeaker.

OFFSET PROTECTION

The circuit in Fig. 4.9 is the power supply of the Bryan LE720 amplifier. Split rail supplies are required, and these are provided at values of +34 V and −34 V from the mains transformer and a bridge power rectifier D1 (top right of circuit)—the values being relative to chassis.

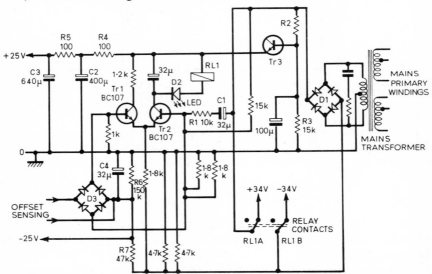

FIG. 4.9. *The split-rail power supply for the Bryan LE720 amplifier (Fig. 4.8). The long-tailed pair Tr1/Tr2 operates the relay RL1 to disconnect the power supply in the event of a fault-condition offset voltage in excess of 5 V appearing at the output. Relative to 'chassis', outputs of +34 V/−34 V and +25 V/−25 V are provided. See text for description*

The +34 V and −34 V supplies are fed to the amplifier through relay contacts RL1A and RL1B, via fuses. Under normal operating conditions, relay winding RL1 is energised by current from Tr2, which is part of a long-tailed pair with Tr1. When RL1 is energised current flows through the light emitting diode D2, which glows indicating that the amplifier is under power, since then contacts RL1A/B are closed.

Bridge rectifier D3 is connected across the output of the amplifier to sense any offset voltage. Under normal conditions, of course, the offset voltage will be extremely small or non-existent. Now, should an offset voltage occur due to power amplifier imbalance, D3 communicates this to Tr1/Tr2 bases, which causes the long-tailed pair to trigger and de-energised RL1, which opens contacts RL1A/B and removes the power supply, while also extinguishing the light emitting diode.

RL1 is re-energised by switching the power supply off, waiting about five seconds and then switching on again. This gives C1 of R1/C1 time-constant time to discharge to restore the normal mode of the long-tailed pair.

The relay operates with either positive or negative offset, and it is insensitive to signal voltages above 20 Hz.

Transistor Tr3 helps with the filtering of the $+25$ V supply fed to the pre-amplifier stages in the control section (not shown), and the voltage is set by the ratio of the base resistors R2/R3. Further filtering of the $+25$ V supply is achieved by R4/R5/C2/C3. This supply is also connected to the $+25$ V input of the power amplifier (Fig. 4.8).

The complementary -25 V input for the power amplifier is obtained from the divider R6/R7 across the -34 V supply line, and is smoothed by C4.

TRANSISTORS FOR 100 W COMPLEMENTARY SYMMETRY AMPLIFIERS

Most power amplifiers are nowadays based on the quasi-complementary or the complementary symmetry circuit, and with power transistors such as MJ802 (npn) and MJ4502 (pnp) along with driver transistors such as MM3007 (npn) and 2N5679 (pnp), by Motorola, audio powers up to 100 W into 8 ohms are now possible from complementary symmetry circuits.

As already noted, the two power amplifier sections of a stereo amplifier are integrated into a common housing (often, nowadays, with the preamplifiers of the dual-channel control section). The same is true with the new generation four-channel amplifiers for quadraphonic reproduction, the four power amplifiers of which can often be switched to form a stereo pair, each of higher total power than when operating in separate single-channel mode (see page 99).

HEAT SINKS

With class A operation the power dissipation of the output transistors is maximum under quiescent conditions; that is, with zero input and output signals. The minimum dissipation and hence the maximum efficiency (see expression 4.1) occurs when the transistors are driven to maximum collector voltage swing and with maximum power being delivered to the load. Power transistors in class A, therefore, dissipate a substantial amount of power under normal operating conditions and thus require careful design with regard to heat sinking.

A class B amplifier with zero I_q receiving sine wave drive has a maximum power dissipation in each transistor at the output voltage where $V_s/2$ is $V_s/3.1416$ (see expression 4.2 and the lead-up formulae). In theory, therefore, a 100 W amplifier could be produced from a pair of power transistors each with a power rating of about 10 W! Now that power amplifiers up to, and sometimes in excess of, 100 W per channel are being demanded by enthusiasts using relatively inefficient loudspeakers and requiring hi-fi-scale loudness over a 60 dB dynamic range in a highly absorbent lounge, one can see the need for class B. Undoubtedly, based on transistors of suitable power rating, class A could yield similar powers, but then massive heat sinks would have to be used, and the amplifier as a whole, particularly if four-channel, would be so large as to be incompatible with the contemporary domestic scene.

Nevertheless, stereo class A amplifiers of 10 or 20 W per channel are popular with some enthusiasts, and at these smaller powers the dimensions are not unduly obtrusive; but with the design advances of class B amplifiers—particularly so far as the suppression of crossover distortion is concerned—there seems little future for class A push-pull power stages, especially now that four-channel amplifiers are becoming the order of the day!

Fig. 4.10. *Heat sink common to both pairs of pair transistors in a stereo amplifier*

There is no universal value for class B quiescent current. The actual value is determined by the design, the nature of the transistors and by the distortion requirements. To eliminate crossover distortion—or, at least, to minimise it—some designs require a greater I_q than others. Since changing the I_q affects the transfer function of the output pair, it follows that there will also be a change in the nature of the distortion. This can be appreciated by adjusting the I_q preset while observing the distortion residual from a distortion factor meter on the screen of an oscilloscope (see Chapter 5, page 127).

From the distortion point of view, therefore, the setting of the I_q preset can be quite critical, which shows how important it is for the design to hold stable the working point of the output transistors with variations in voltage and temperature. With some amplifiers the distortion can be seen to change as the output transistors warm up and when the input voltage is changed. However, as we have seen, most hi-fi amplifiers incorporate some artifice for holding steady the operating point, but some are better able to do this than others!

There may be either separate heat sinks for each power transistor or all the power transistors may share a large, common heat sink. Fig. 4.10 shows a common heat sink accommodating the two pairs of output transistors for two channels, while Fig. 4.11 shows (at the top edge) each output transistor mounted on its own sink.

Heat sinks are chosen with a suitable thermal resistance for the maximum total dissipation of the transistors, so the larger the power of the amplifier, the larger the heat sinks. To improve thermal conductivity silicone grease is applied between each transistor and the surface of the heat sink.

Even though the heat sinks may be quite large on some 40/50 W per-channel stereo class B amplifiers, they may rise only very mildly in temperature when

FIG. 4.11. *In this stereo amplifier each power transistor has its own heat sink*

FIG. 4.12. *Slip-on heat sinks like those illustrated are sometimes used on the driver transistors*

reproducing music; and there may be no significant rise in temperature under quiescent conditions. However, when handling steady-state (i.e. sine wave) signal towards the full power rating of the amplifier (both channels running together), the power dissipation is obviously much greater, and if this condition is sustained the heat sinks will certainly become hot.

On the other hand, quasi-class B amplifiers operating with a fairly high I_q (with the biasing more towards AB) do exhibit hot heat sinks even under quiescent conditions. In fact, the quiescent temperature is a fair indication of the value of I_q adopted by the designer. Some designs need to operate with a fairly high I_q for the least crossover distortion, but this is not always the case. Indeed, some 40/50 W designs may only be running at 10 mA or so of I_q and still exhibit low distortion.

Some of the smaller 'budget' amplifiers use the metal chassis accommodating the printed circuit boards as the heat sink. This is perfectly acceptable when the total transistor dissipation is relatively small, but when it is necessary to run at a fairly high I_q to keep the distortion down, the rise in quiescent temperature can be disturbing, since the whole of the amplifier can then become quite hot.

The nominal dissipation of the driver transistors may also be sufficiently high to demand heat sinking. Small heat sinks, however, are suitable for these, of the kind shown in Fig. 4.12.

SUPPLY REGULATION

With class A the *total* power demanded by the output stage from the power supply is constant, so the regulation of the power supply is less important with this class of amplifier than with class B, where the power drawn increases with power delivered to the load. Nevertheless, owing to the constant power requirement of class A, this class of amplifier must incorporate a supply of sustained high power rating and low ripple content at the constant high current.

Regulation is not always used with class B, however, since a respectably low source impedance can be obtained from the latest type of bridge rectifiers fed from a low resistance secondary winding on the mains transformer (see Fig. 4.9). The output stages of the power amplifiers are usually energised directly from across the reservoir capacitor, so the source impedance is not increased by series resistance. However, separate smoothing and filtering circuits are used for the supplies of the preceding stages and for the preamplifier stages of the control section where, to avoid hum, supplies of very low ripple content are essential.

Some idea of the efficiency of the bridge-type power rectifier can be gleaned from the fact that four Mullard BY126 power rectifiers in bridge formation will yield 24 V d.c. across a 4000 μF reservoir capacitor at a current of 1.6 A from a low resistance mains transformer secondary winding delivering 18 V r.m.s.

Clearly, the regulation of the power supply depends on the source impedance and the effect of the regulation on the minimum-to-maximum range of current drawn. A simple bridge rectifier supply of a 40 W per channel amplifier may be, say, 83 V under quiescent conditions. With one channel driven to full power on sine wave signal into a 4 ohm load the voltage may drop to about 78 V, while a drop towards 70 V may occur with both channels driven to full power together with sine wave signal.

It is for this reason that, without supply regulation (or separate power supplies—see later), the per channel power of a class B amplifier may be a dB or so down when both channels are driven together than when only one channel is driven. It will be recalled that the theoretical maximum power of a class B amplifier is $V_s^2/8R_L$, where V_s is the supply voltage (page 86). Thus, as V_s falls, so will the output power.

96

Since the engineers and technicians whose job it is to review and test-report on hi-fi equipment are keen on evaluating the power capacity of amplifiers with both (or four) channels driven into 8 ohm loads on sine wave signal together (which is a perfectly valid—indeed, desirable—way of testing), the manufacturers of the more costly and powerful type of equipment may adopt supply regulation (thus ensuring very minimal fall in voltage from quiescent up to maximum two-channel drive), so that the per channel power is substantially the same whether just one or both channels together are driven. The *total* output of the amplifier is then greater, of course.

Indeed, to ensure that the rated powerholds when both channels are driven to maximum together, the American Harman-Kardon hi-fi equipment manufacturer employs twin power supplies, a supply for each channel, which also helps with inter-channel isolation.

REGULATED POWER SUPPLY

The (British) Acoustical Manufacturing Company, Limited, maker of the well known *Quad* equipment, is a believer in a well regulated power supply, and the circuit of this for the Quad 303 power amplifier is given in Fig. 4.13. The 303, incidentally, is the power amplifier only, and requires Model 33 control unit to work with it.

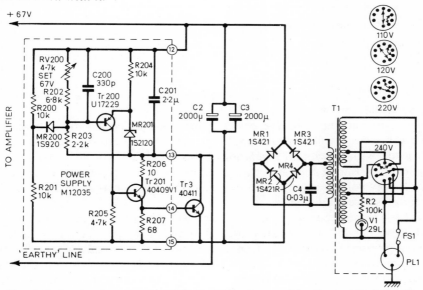

FIG. 4.13. *Regulated power supply of the Quad 303 power amplifier. See text for description*

The mains transformer T1 drives the normal bridge rectifier M1–M4, and the combined $2000 + 2000\,\mu$F electrolytic ($4000\,\mu$F in all) acts as the reservoir. The positive output of the rectifier goes straight to the amplifier, while the negative output passes through regulator transistor Tr3 (from emitter to collector since it is an npn device). Thus, the supply voltage across the amplifier depends on the conductivity of Tr1. This is controlled by emitter-follower Tr201, which itself is driven by Tr200 whose operating conditions are stabilised by zener diode MR201. Since Tr200 base is in communication with the positive supply, any change here will reflect a change into Tr3 base circuit, thereby altering the conduction of this transistor. The circuit is engineered so that a decrease in supply voltage is countered by Tr3 automatically turning on more power, and an increase by Tr3 turning down the power. The supply to the amplifier thus remains constant irrespective of the power drawn by the output stages.

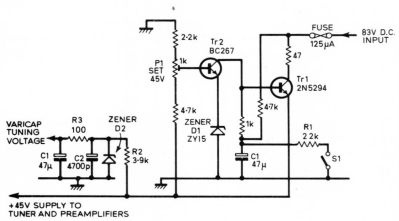

FIG. 4.14. *Preamplifier and tuner regulator of the Armstrong 625/626 receivers, showing also the zener stabilising circuit for the varicap tuning diodes. See text for description*

Preset RV200 adjusts Tr200 base voltage and thus sets the required 67 V supply to the amplifier.

To assist with filtering, the power amplifiers may be fed direct from the supply rectifier, while the preamplifiers may be fed from a simple series transistor, with or without regulation. Tuner-amplifiers in which varicaps are employed for tuning must also feature supply regulation to prevent tuning drift with supply voltage change. The arrangement of the Armstrong 625 and 626 receivers is given in Fig. 4.14.

Tr1 is a series regulator transistor receiving 83 V from the main supply line and delivering 45 V to the tuner and audio preamplifiers. Since the output in this case is positive it emanates from the emitter. Tr1 conductivity is controlled by common-emitter stage Tr2, stabilised by zener D1. Tr2 base samples the voltage on the 45 V line, and any change is counteracted by the resulting conductivity change—the transistor turning on more or less power as required. Preset P1 sets the 45 V output. S1/R1/C1 are associated with a 'muting' arrangement, such that S1 *closes* when the mains is switched off and C1/R1 time-constant then swiftly pulls Tr1 base to chassis potential. This causes a smart collapse of the 45 V supply, which neatly avoids the varicaps tuning over the band 'audibly' as the major electrolytics discharge on switch-off.

The rectifier also includes a thermal delay circuit which prevents switch-on surges and overvoltage at the small-signal transistors, while minimising the switch-on 'thump' effect. The circuit places a 47 ohm resistor in series with the rectifier prior to full warm-up.

Varicap tuning voltage is obtained from zener D2, fed from the 45 V line, via R2. Ripple is reduced by the zener's low impedance, but since even small traces of ripple on the varicaps can precipitate modulation hum, further filtering is provided by C3/R1. C2 in shunt with the zener bypasses noise signals, for which such diodes are renown!

Power amplifier regulation thus makes possible greater per-channel power capacity when both channels are driven simultaneously, and since regulation is tantamount to a very low effective power supply impedance, its employment can reduce low-frequency decoupling problems and interaction between the channels of two- and four-channel amplifiers.

It is noteworthy that the difference between continuous wave average power and the IHF music or dynamic power is to some extent related to supply regulation. Assuming that heat sinks of suitable thermal resistance are used for the power transistors, then there should be very little difference between the IHF music power and the continuous wave average power when the power supply is fully regulated.

POWER BRIDGING

The output of two power amplifiers can be combined to provide a total greater output into a common load. This is called 'power bridging' which was developed by Bell Telephone Laboratories some years ago. Both series and parallel bridging is possible, but for hi-fi applications the latter is preferred since it results in less distortion. With series bridging, where the two outputs are connected in series with the load, the in-phase and out-of-phase distortion components add, giving a net distortion which is the 'average' of both outputs. However, when the two outputs are connected in parallel and applied out-of-phase *across* the load, the in-phase components cancel, so the net result is lower distortion.

With the advent of the four-channel amplifier for quadraphonic reproduction, power bridging has assumed a greater importance than hitherto. In the mono days one rarely contemplated connecting two amplifiers together to secure an output of greater power, and since the introduction of stereo both channels have been fully involved so there has been little need to connect their *outputs* together electrically to obtain a single, higher output for one loudspeaker. It is possible, of course, to run a stereo amplifier from a mono signal into both loudspeakers or to translate a stereo signal to mono (by connecting the left and right signals in parallel somewhere in the control section) so that both loudspeakers are driven together, but neither of these is the same as power bridging.

The advantage of power bridging with four-channel amplifiers is that by suitable switching such an amplifier can be arranged to operate in isolation into four separate loudspeakers for quadraphonic reproduction or into two separate loudspeakers at greater power per loudspeaker for stereo reproduction. The switching provides parallel power bridging of the left front amplifier with the left rear amplifier (for the left stereo loudspeaker) and of the right front amplifier with the right rear amplifier (for the right stereo loudspeaker).

A pioneer of this mode of switching is the American Harman-Kardon incorporation.

With the 'stereo/four channel' switch in the 'four-channel' position all four power amplifiers operate independently, as shown basically in Fig. 4.15. Fig.

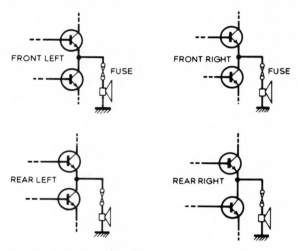

FIG. 4.15. *A four-channel quadraphonic amplifier whose output stages are operating independently*

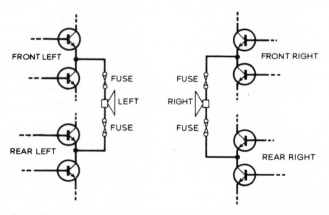

FIG. 4.16. *A four-channel quadraphonic amplifier where switching allows parallel bridging of the two pairs of channels for two-channel stereo operation at greater per combined-channel power. See text for full explanation*

4.16 shows, also in basic form, what happens when the switch is changed to the 'stereo' position. The left loudspeaker is now driven from the paralleled left front and rear amplifiers, while the right loudspeaker is driven from the paralleled right front and rear amplifiers. The Harman-Kardon switching also automatically disconnects the left and right rear loudspeakers in the 'stereo' mode.

The diagrams in Fig. 4.17 show what happens in the paralleled mode. Assuming sine wave signals (*a*) and (*b*) of V_p peak amplitude from the two amplifiers, the combined signal (c) *across* the load is $2V_p$ amplitude; this is because signals (a) and (b) differ in phase by 180 degrees and are of equal amplitude.

The total *peak* power is thus $2^2 V_p^2/R$, where R is the resistance of the load. Since the peak power of one amplifier alone into the same load is V_p^2/R, it can be seen that the combined power of the two is *four* times as great.

Evaluating for total *average* power $W_{tot.}$ we have

$$W_{tot.} = \frac{(V_{amp\,1} + V_{amp\,2})^2}{R} \qquad (4.4)$$

where $V_{amp\,1}$ is the r.m.s. voltage across the load due to amplifier one, $V_{amp\,2}$ the r.m.s. voltage across the load due to amplifier two and R the value of the shared load in ohms.

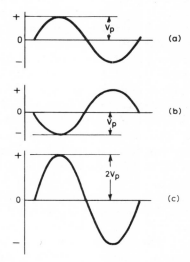

FIG. 4.17. *The signals involved in parallel bridging. (a) and (b) are the signals from the two separate amplifiers and (c) is the signal across a common load shared by the two amplifiers. Since it is assumed that signals (a) and (b) are of equal amplitude, and since they are applied across the load in opposite phase, the amplitude of (c) is equal to the sum of amplitudes (a) and (b). This method of power bridging also cancels in-phase distortion components*

In practice, the maximum available power from parallel bridging is rarely exploited. Four-channel designs are switched so that the parallel-bridged power is about twice or, perhaps, a little more the single channel power. To realise four times the power would demand significant uprating of the heat sinks and power supply(ies).

By comparing the diagrams in Fig. 4.15 with those in Fig. 4.16, it will be appreciated that in order to measure the power in the parallel-bridged mode the r.m.s.-reading voltmeter will need to be connected right across the load, with no 'earthy' reference. Clearly, if one terminal of the voltmeter is 'earthy' one amplifier would have a short across its output, which would blow the fuse.

As discussed in Chapter 2, an hitherto little considered distortion, called transient intermodulation distortion, is now receiving attention. The subject has been investigated in some detail by Matti Otala of the Philips Research Laboratories at Eindhoven, the Netherlands, and a number of papers dealing with various aspects of it have been presented by this engineer*.

When a power amplifier receives from the control section a transient input signal which is faster than the open-loop rise time of the power amplifier, a pulse or overshoot is generated on the input signal due to the delayed feedback signal. Since the overshoot can result in clipping of the input stage or stages of the power amplifier, the gain of the amplifier for other signals appearing simultaneously under this condition is zero, the result then being a burst of 100% intermodulation distortion.

Although not easily measurable (but see Chapter 5, page 124), such distortion is subjectively disturbing, and it is made worse by treble lift at the control section. Its elimination in the main requires the cutoff frequency of the power amplifier in the open-loop condition to be greater than the cutoff frequency of the control section (i.e. preamplifiers). Since it is desirable for the control section response to extend to, at least, 20 kHz, the requirement in essence is for the use of power amplifier transistors of the highest possible f_T.

Moreover, the stability aspects of the power amplifier also warrant particular attention so that the full f_T of the power transistors can be exploited. For example, the open-loop upper cutoff frequency is reduced by the RC networks required to stabilise the amplifier in the presence of feedback, and the greater the feedback, the lower the cutoff frequency provided by the RC components necessary for stabilisation.

Further, the overshoot amplitude also increases with feedback, which makes the transient intermodulation distortion approximately proportional to the amount of feedback.

A good case exists, therefore, for the use of the least negative feedback consistent with the harmonic and regular intermodulation distortion requirements, and in some designs this will constitute a compromise between acceptable transient intermodulation distortion and harmonic and the usual intermodulation distortion, such that adjusting the feedback *either* up or down will result in subjective impairment of the quality of reproduction.

In addition to the use of high f_T power transistors and a 20 kHz or so control section upper frequency response, other suggested methods for reducing transient intermodulation distortion include the use of unbypassed emitter resistors and low base and/or collector resistors both to increase the upper cutoff frequency of the power amplifier, the use of lead compensation networks for stability and the use of relatively large collector currents and collector/emitter voltages for the input transistors to enhance the overload margins.

---

* See, for example, 'Circuit Design Modifications for Minimising Transient Intermodulation Distortion in Audio Amplifiers', *Journal of the Audio Engineering Society*, June 1972, Vol. 20, No. 5, and 'Transient Distortion in Transistorised Power Amplifiers'. *IEEE Transactions on Audio and Electroacoustics*, Vol. AU-18, September 1970, and Transient Intermodulation Distortion in Commercial Audio Amplifiers, *JAES*, May 1974, Vol. 22, No. 4.

It has further been suggested that the open-loop frequency response of the power amplifier should establish the required preamplifier frequency response, such that the 'usable' frequency response is not enhanced by the negative feedback. In other words, if 20 kHz is accepted as the frequency response required for hi-fi reproduction, then this should be available from the power amplifier *without* feedback. Also, that the upper frequency cutoff *with* feedback to be at least *20 kHz times* the feedback loop gain (i.e. 630 kHz for 30 dB feedback, 2 MHz for 40 dB, etc.).

F.E.T POWER AMPLIFICATION

Likely to constitute a significant breakthrough in hi-fi power amplifier technology is the recently (1974) announced *power* field effect transistor (f.e.t.). This, based on an invention by a Professor Jun'inchi Nishizawa of the Electronic

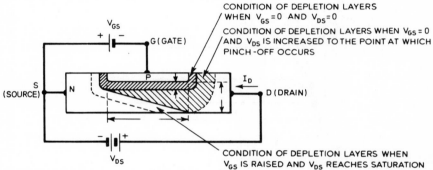

FIG. 4.18. *Elementary impression of conventional f.e.t., showing the condition of its depletion layers when under voltage*

Communications Research Laboratory at Tohoku University, where he is one of the leading instructors and for which—along with other intensive work on semiconductors—he received the Gakushi'insho science award, has been developed by the Yamaha Nippon Gakki Company Limited of Japan under commission from the Technological Development Foundation of Japan, and acknowledgements are given to the Yamaha Company for the appropriate information of the development which follows.

The power f.e.t. differs from the conventional type of 'pentode' small-signal f.e.t. in that its IV characteristic and input impedance are more like those of a thermionic triode valve and that it has a power dissipation of 300 W.

Fig. 4.18 gives a cross-sectional impression of conventional f.e.t. construction and shows how the conduction channel alters with different supply conditions, while Fig. 4.19 gives the output characteristics. The current channel of a f.e.t. is formed between two depletion layers in the semiconductor, and the device operates by the voltage between the gate (which is high impedance since in a junction f.e.t. it is essentially a reverse-biased diode) and source electrodes (V_{GS}) altering the cross-sectional area of the current channel by virtue of the depletion layers closing in or moving out, so that the drain current (I_D) is controlled. As V_{GS} is increased (negatively with respect to the source for an n-channel f.e.t., as shown in Fig. 4.19) the two depletion layers close in and eventually meet

103

along the entire length of the channel. The channel resistance thus increases so that I_D falls. When the two depletion layers meet no I_D can flow and the device is then said to be pinched-off. The V_{GS} required for this condition is called the pinch-off voltage (V_P).

Further, when the voltage between the drain and source electrodes (V_{DS}) is increased from zero *at a constant* V_{GS}), I_D initially increases linearly with V_{DS}

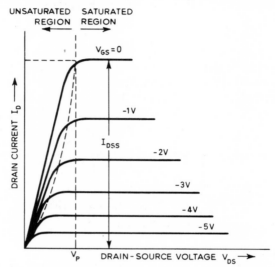

FIG. 4.19. *Characteristics of conventional f.e.t., showing pinch off voltage (V_P) and V_{DSS}.*

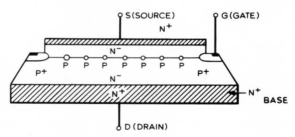

FIG. 4.20. *Elementary impression of power f.e.t., where the current flow is vertical through the device (see text)*

(i.e. linear ohmic range), but as I_D rises the current channel narrows and its resistance rises so that the rate of change of I_D diminishes. Eventually, the depletion layers almost meet, but this time at the drain end of the channel only, which again gives the pinched-off condition. (For more information see the Mullard book on Field Effect Transistors.)

Only the $I_D - V_{DS}$ or output characteristics are given in Fig. 4.19. Another characteristic is $I_D - V_{GS}$ whose curve for a normal f.e.t. is of parabolic form, thereby signifying the essentially square-law of the f.e.t. such that $I_D \propto V_{GS}^2$.

However, the newly developed power f.e.t. differs from the small-signal f.e.t. in that the design is such that the current flows vertically through the device and that a 'grid' is interposed between the source and the drain (Fig. 4.20). It retains still the essentially square-law characteristic and possesses a frequency range in excess of that of an ordinary bipolar power transistor, the treble roll-off, in fact, depending chiefly on the distribution of the input capacitance, as shown in Fig. 4.21. The voltage gain and frequency characteristics of the device are detailed in Fig. 4.22.

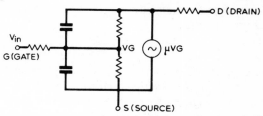

FIG. 4.21. *The h.f. roll-off of a power f.e.t. is governed by the distributed capacitance at the input, as shown*

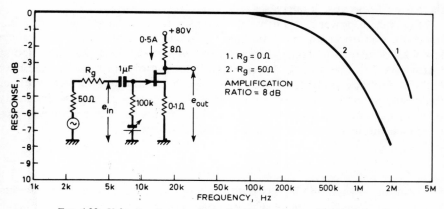

FIG. 4.22. *Voltage gain versus frequency characteristics of power f.e.t.*

Parameters of the power f.e.t. and those of the associated driver f.e.t. (the latter in parenthesis) are given in Table 4.1 below.

Table 4.1

V_{DS} ....200–300 V (300–500 V)
P_D ....300 W (10 W)
I_{DSS} ....10 A (0.1 A)
μ ....5 typical (50)
D_R ....5 ohms (1 k)
g_m ....1 k mmhos (50 mmhos)
where P_D is the power dissipation, I_{DSS} the drain-to-source shortcircuit current at $V_{GS} = 0$, μ the voltage amplification ratio, D_R the drain internal resistance and g_m the transconductance.

Advantages of the power f.e.t. over the ordinary bipolar power transistor are in general improved upper-frequency response, elimination of 'notch' distortion due to the storage of minority charge carriers because such effects are absent with majority charge carriers operative in f.e.t.s, better temperature stability, high impedance drive and less tendency for secondary breakdown. Moreover, the essentially square-law of the f.e.t. means that third- and odd-order harmonics are minimised, while even-harmonic distortion can be virtually eliminated by carefully balanced push-pull amplifier design.

Distortion stems from the non-linearity of the transfer characteristic as has already been noted, such that

$$I_D = I_{DSS}(1 - V_{GS}/V_P)^n \qquad (4.5)$$

When $n = 2$, the expression would signify only the presence of first and second order terms, but since n is not exactly equal to 2, f.e.t.s are not completely free from some third- and higher-order terms. However, there is an important distortion distinction between f.e.t.s and bipolar transistors and that is the third harmonic distortion contribution of a f.e.t. is much lower than that of a bipolar transistor, which is why a f.e.t. has more favourable intermodulation and cross-modulation figures than a bipolar transistor. The distortion tends to fall with increasing I_D because it decreases as $|1 - V_{GS}/V_P|$ increases.

Thus, with a power f.e.t. push-pull amplifier most of the second- and even-harmonic distortion can be eliminated by careful balancing, while for a given low level of distortion less negative feedback is required for f.e.t.s than bipolar transistors. In other words, the intrinsic distortion of a f.e.t. power amplifier without feedback can be lower than that of a bipolar transistor power amplifier under similar conditions. Less negative feedback can result in improved stability over an extended bandwidth, which in turn results in better transient performance and less transient intermodulation distortion.

F.E.T. POWER AMPLIFIER DESIGN

A prototype power amplifier based on a pair of the power f.e.t.s and f.e.t. drivers has been developed by Yamaha. Circuit design is fairly conventional, there being two-stage differential amplification and symmetrical drive from a direct-coupled source-follower, with direct coupling to the loudspeakers. Bias to the driver and power f.e.t.s is from specially compensated circuits (patents pending), which is said to provide good d.c. stability without the need for power supply regulation. Preset adjustment allows for the compensation of differences between the f.e.t. characteristics, and to ensure that the available transient performance is not impaired bootstrapping circuits and electrolytic capacitors have been avoided wherever possible, as also have large-value stabilising time-constant circuits.

The output f.e.t.s are biased for class AB operation, virtually eliminating cross-over discontinuity, and the relatively high quiescent current is adequately handled by the robust heat-sinked f.e.t.s.

Since f.e.t.s are less temperature sensitive than bipolar transistors, temperature compensation is not necessary, neither can thermal runaway occur, for I_D tends to fall with increasing temperature.

Independent power supplies are adopted for the left and right channels, and this means that the per-channel power yield remains the same with only one channel fully driven or with both channels fully driven simultaneously. A triple, non-stabilised power supply with outputs of $+85\,V$, $-85\,V$ and $-200\,V$ is used.

The loudspeakers are protected in the event of a rise in offset voltage (due to the direct coupling) by an electronically controlled relay circuit which activates to remove the loudspeakers from the output stages should the offset rise above $\pm 2\,V$.

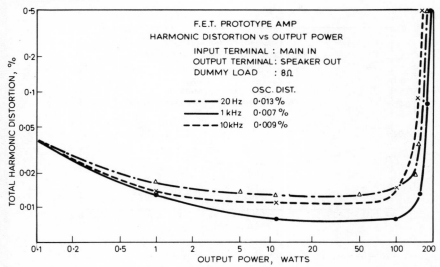

FIG. 4.23. *Harmonic distortion versus output power of prototype f.e.t. power amplifier. Distortion essentially even harmonic*

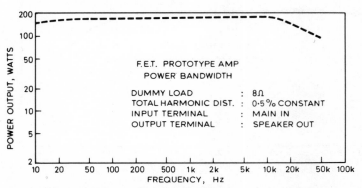

FIG. 4.24. *Power bandwidth of prototype f.e.t. power amplifier*

The power push-pull stages use f.e.t.s of 300 W permissible drain dissipation (at $T_C = 25\,°C$) while the driver stages also use lower power vertical junction type f.e.t.s but of higher voltage and gain (see Table 4.1).

The primary parameters of the prototype amplifier are: continuous power output both channels driven into 4- or 8-ohm loads over 20 Hz–20 kHz: 150 + 150 W (180 W at 1 kHz one channel driven). THD at rated power: 0.1%; at 1 W 0.04%. IMD: as THD. Frequency response: 5 Hz–100 kHz ($-1\,dB$) at 1 W.

Power bandwidth: 5 Hz–50 kHz (IHF, distortion constant 0.5%). Hum and noise: 110 dB (A weighting). Damping factor at 1 kHz: 100 ref. 8 ohms. Input: 0.775 V (50 k). Output load: 4–16 ohms.

The curves in Figs. 4.23, 4.24, 4.25 and 4.26 show respectively harmonic distortion versus output power, power bandwidth, harmonic distortion versus frequency and damping factor versus frequency of the Yamaha prototype.

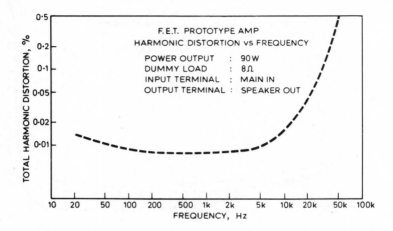

FIG. 4.25. *Harmonic distortion versus frequency of prototype f.e.t. power amplifier*

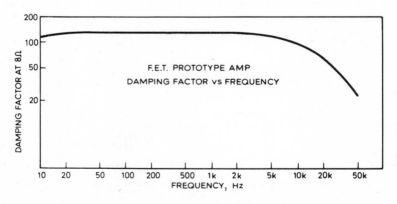

FIG. 4.26. *Damping factor versus frequency of prototype f.e.t. power amplifier*

It is probable that by the time this book is published f.e.t. power amplifiers will be available in the UK from Yamaha and, possibly other manufacturers,* and this must surely signify third-generation high fidelity reproduction—from thermionic triodes through tetrodes to bipolar transistors and to f.e.t.s, which are almost like the triode valve but much more powerful and efficient and not requiring an output transformer.

*Including JVC, Pioneer and Toshiba.

CHAPTER 5

Adjustments and Measurements in Amplifiers

THE GENERAL BASIC setup required for testing amplifiers is given in Fig. 5.1. The load should be resistive and suit both the power and value requirements of the amplifier, the generator should deliver very low distortion sine wave signal (in the general case) at about 600 ohms and include a meter (internal or external) indicating the r.m.s. level of the signal delivered, the attenuator should switch

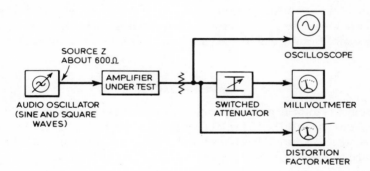

FIG. 5.1. *Instrument setup for basic evaluation of audio amplifiers (see text for full description)*

over tens and units of decibels (tenths can also be useful) and should be capable of withstanding the full r.m.s. voltage across the load, the millivoltmeter should be scaled in r.m.s. voltage and have a sensitivity of at least 1 mV full-scale deflection, the oscilloscope should have a Y bandwidth of at least 1 MHz and the distortion factor meter should read down to at least 0.1% full-scale.

POWER OUTPUT

With the amplifier adjusted for 'flat' and volume control maximum the input signal should be increased at the generator either until peak clipping just occurs on the oscilloscope or until the distortion factor meter indicates a required level of distortion (1% distortion factor occurs in most cases just at the sine wave peak clipping point). The r.m.s. voltage across the load is then measured and the average power calculated using expression 2.10 (Chapter 2).

ADJUSTMENTS AND MEASUREMENTS IN AMPLIFIERS
DISTORTION FACTOR

Using the millivoltmeter and the load value to calibrate the power delivered, the distortion factor can be measured at any power or frequency within the range of the instrument. However, to reduce the effect of noise, it is desirable to reduce the power from maximum by turning down the amplifier's volume control. By switching the audio generator off and measuring the noise only, expression 2.2 (Chapter 2) can be used to evaluate the true total harmonic distortion.

With a two- or four-channel amplifier it is desirable to measure both the power capacity and the distortion factor per channel with all channels operating at the same power together. The required power amplifier inputs can often be achieved merely by switching the control section to mono; but in some instances it may be necessary to arrange for separate input feeds to the control section from the common audio oscillator.

MAINS INPUT

Since the power capacity and hence the distortion at full power are affected by the voltage of the power supply (page 96, Chapter 4), it is essential that the mains input voltage be monitored and, if necessary, adjusted to suit the amplifier while power and distortion measurements are being made. A variable voltage mains transformer and accurate a.c. voltmeter are required for this.

DAMPING FACTOR

The damping factor is generally measured at one-quarter the power rating of the amplifier and at 40 or 50 Hz. The voltage across the load at the appropriate power is noted on the millivoltmeter and the load is then removed. The change in voltage is a function of the damping factor, which can be evaluated from expression 2.7 (Chapter 2). Since the change in voltage is very small when the source impedance is very small, a digital type of audio voltmeter is required for accurate measurement.

POWER BANDWIDTH

There are two ways of measuring power bandwidth, one by setting up the amplifier so as to measure the rated power at 1 kHz, and then adjusting the audio oscillator, with the signal input to the amplifier remaining constant, from very low to very high frequency, noting the l.f. and h.f. points where the power is 3 dB below the 1 kHz power. This is known as the half power bandwidth and is shown diagramatically in Fig. 2.9, Chapter 2. It is possible, however, that the distortion may be high at the −3 dB frequencies.

The other method takes account of distortion, the power bandwidth then being measured, as just explained, but this time using the distortion factor meter to measure a specified value of distortion at the l.f. and h.f. terminal frequencies, as shown in Fig. 2.10, Chapter 2.

ADJUSTMENTS AND MEASUREMENTS IN AMPLIFIERS

INPUT SENSITIVITY

With the amplifier operating in the 'flat' condition and the volume control at maximum, the 1 kHz input voltage required at the selected input for the related output power corresponds to the sensitivity of that particular input. The sensitivity might be different from the specification if the test is made with a stereo amplifier switched to the mono mode. Thus, each channel of a two- or four-channel amplifier should be measured for sensitivity independently.

HUM AND NOISE

The millivoltmeter and attenuator are adjusted to establish a 0 dB reference when a 1 kHz signal is applied to the input being tested and the amplifier is delivering its rated output. The oscillator signal is then removed and the amplifier input (see under DIN 45-500, page 44), or shorted. With the volume control at maximum and the amplifier in the 'flat' condition, the sensitivity of the readout is increased to determine by how many decibels the hum and noise is below the rated output.

WEIGHTED HUM AND NOISE

A weighting filter is required for this test in the readout circuit, and the weighting values should be as in Table 5.1 below.

Table 5.1

10 Hz	−70.5 dB	200 Hz	−10.8 dB	4.0 kHz	+1.0
12.5	−63.4	250	−8.6	5.0	+0.5
16	−56.7	315	−6.5	6.0	−0.1
20	−50.4	400	−4.8	8.0	−1.1
25	−44.6	500	−3.2	10.0	−2.4
31.5	−39.2	630	−1.9	12.5	−4.2
40	−34.5	800	−0.8	16.0	−6.5
50	−30.2	1 kHz	0	20.0	−9.2
63	−26.1	1.25	+0.6		
80	−22.3	1.6	+1.0		
100	−19.1	2.0	+1.2		
125	−16.1	2.5	+1.2		
160	−13.2	3.15	+1.2		

This weighting takes account of the annoyance value of the hum and noise and obviously gives a more favourable ratio than the unweighted measurement.

The circuit of a filter which has a response approximating the weighting values is given in Fig. 5.2.

INPUT OVERLOAD

With the amplifier in the 'flat' condition and the volume control adjusted for an output 12 dB below the rated power, as determined by the level of the input signal, the input from the oscillator at 1 kHz is increased until the output waveform just shows peak clipping. If this is caused by preamplifier overload the clipping will hold steady as the volume control is adjusted. It is important to establish this. The overload threshold of the input corresponds to the r.m.s. voltage applied to the amplifier from the oscillator for this condition. The overload can also be referred to a specified value of distortion factor instead of to the threshold of peak clipping.

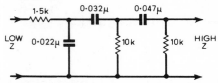

FIG. 5.2. *Circuit of weighting filter providing approximately the weighting values given in Table 5.1*

A stereo amplifier switched to the mono mode may have an overload value which differs from that in the stereo mode.

STEREO SEPARATION

The separation of one channel from another can be determined by loading both channels and by arranging one to be driven to the rated power. The readout is then connected across the load of the non-speaking channel and the sensitivity increased to measure by how many decibels the output from this channel is below the rated output. For a true evaluation it is necessary for the input of the non-speaking channel also to be loaded either with a shorting plug or with a load corresponding to the source for which the input under test is designed (i.e. magnetic pickup cartridge). Channel separation can be measured at any frequency, though the frequencies of most interest are 100 Hz, 1 kHz and 10 kHz. Four-channel quadraphonic amplifiers can be measured similarly.

FREQUENCY RESPONSE PLOTS

Curves can be constructed of the overall frequency response of the amplifier, of the responses of the tone controls, of the RIAA equalisation and of the filters by using the setup in Fig. 5.1. A reference is established for 0 dB at 1 kHz and, with the amplifier delivering about 20 dB below its rated power, the frequency of the input signal is changed over small intervals, starting at 20 Hz and continuing to 20 kHz, and the dB difference from the reference at each frequency is plotted to form a response curve. If a 0 dB reference is established on the millivoltmeter, the switched attenuator can be used to measure any dB change— up or down—at each test frequency. This is more accurate than relying on the dB divisions of a millivoltmeter.

HARMONIC DISTORTION

For this test an audio wave analyser is required. The setup as in Fig. 5.1 can be employed, but a wave analyser is connected across the load in place of the distortion factor meter. Each harmonic is then tuned in and recorded separately. Total harmonic distortion can be evaluated from expression 2.3, Chapter 2.

ADJUSTMENTS AND MEASUREMENTS IN AMPLIFIERS

INTERMODULATION DISTORTION

The wave analyser can also be used for tuning in intermodulation components when two signals are applied simultaneously to the input of the amplifier, as explained in Chapter 2. The total intermodulation distortion can then be evaluated from expression 2.4, Chapter 2.

It is generally more convenient, from the calculation point of view, anyway, to employ an intermodulation test set which automatically sums the intermodulation components of interest, giving a readout of total IMD.

DISTORTION RESIDUAL OSCILLOSCOPE DISPLAY

For certain adjustments, as well as for evaluating the subjective sensation of certain types of distortion, notably crossover distortion, an oscilloscope display of the distortion factor residual can be very useful (Fig. 2.3, for example). This also facilitates evaluation of the approximate ratio of noise to total harmonic distortion.

Most distortion factor meters are equipped with an output for connecting to the Y input of an oscilloscope, and if the oscilloscope is a double- or split-beam model both the output signal and the distortion factor residual can be displayed simultaneously, as shown by the distortion factor residual oscillograms in this book.

PHASE RESPONSE

The angle by which the signal at the output of an amplifier differs from the signal at the input indicates the amount of phase shift occurring in the amplifier. The phase response is thus the angle of variation over the passband of the amplifier. The amplifier stages themselves will, of course, produce specific phase shifts, and it is possible that the output signal will be 180 degrees out of phase with the input signal, depending on the nature of the stages and the number in cascade.

Negative feedback, of course, relies on the output signal fed back to the input being 180 degrees out of phase with the input signal. This condition is substantially met at 1 kHz. At increasing or decreasing frequency either side of 1 kHz, however, the phase tends progressively to shift positively or negatively. Within the amplifier's passband the phase shift is (or should be!) insufficient to change the feedback from positive to negative.

Hi-fi quality power amplifiers are designed for an adequate phase margin, which is defined as the angle by which the phase differs from 180 degrees at the upper and lower frequencies where the loop gain falls to unity. If the loop gain is greater than unity at the frequency or frequencies where the phase shift reaches a full 180 degrees, then the amplifier changes into an oscillator! To avoid spurious oscillation at high frequencies, well outside the amplifier's passband, lag compensation networks are commonly employed, but as these roll-off the open-loop response they can encourage transient intermodulation distortion, as explained in Chapter 4 (page 102).

Low-frequency phase shift, and hence low-frequency instability, can arise due to inadequate decoupling or common impedance supply circuits.

113

Phase shift in amplifiers, therefore, can be of prime importance from the stability aspect. Moreover, greater attention of recent times is being paid to it from the reproduction point of view, for after all a change in phase at a particular frequency is tantamount to a change in transit time of a signal component of corresponding frequency through the amplifier. Phase, of course, is important so far as stereo and quadraphony are concerned.

Fig. 5.3 shows how an oscilloscope can be used to measure phase shift. The amplifier is arranged to receive suitably attenuated output from the audio oscillator, and the signal across the output load, at any required level and

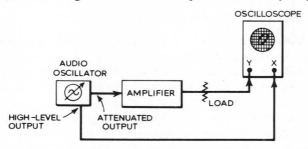

FIG. 5.3. *Instrument setup for measuring phase shift*

frequency, is applied to the Y input of the oscilloscope. The oscilloscope's time-base is switched off and the horizontal sweep provided by high-level signal from the audio oscillator. The amplitudes of the Y and X traces are balanced by removing the Y signal and adjusting the X gain control for a suitable horizontal datum amplitude, reconnecting the Y signal, removing the X signal and adjusting the Y attentuator for a corresponding vertical amplitude.

When the two signals are applied simultaneously the trace will give an indication of the phase difference between them, as shown by oscillograms (*a*)

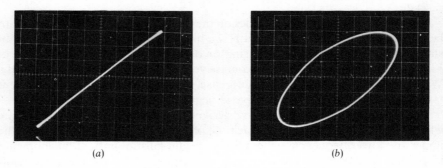

(*a*)   (*b*)

FIG. 5.4. *Phase shift oscillograms, (a) zero degrees and (b) about 42 degrees, but see text. The slight kinks on these displays indicate mild distortion*

and (*b*) in Fig. 5.4. The instruments used for obtaining these were the Radford Low Distortion Oscillator and the Telequipment D53 Oscilloscope. The Radford oscillator is convenient in this respect since it has two outputs, one via the switched and continuously variable attenuators and the other at maximum.

114

Fig. 5.5 shows that the ratio of dimensions A and B give the sin of the phase difference. In Fig. 5.4(b) A/B is approximately 2/3 (= 0.66), which makes the angle about 42 degrees or, complementary, 318 degrees. In Fig. 5.4(a), of course, the ratio is 0/3 (= 0), so the angle is zero degrees or, complementary, 360 degrees. In other words, the phase shift of (b) with respect to (a) is about 42 degrees.

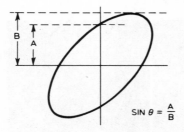

$$\text{SIN } \theta = \frac{A}{B}$$

FIG. 5.5. *Method of measuring phase shift from an oscilloscope display*

A perfect circle implies a ratio of 1/1 (= 1) and an angle of 90 degrees or, complementary, 270 degrees. When the trace is inclined into the other two quadrants the angle ranges from 180 degrees straight line, though ellipses to the circle at 90 degrees.

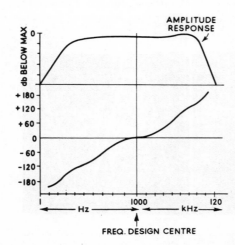

FIG. 5.6. *Amplifier amplitude and phase characteristics*

When the phase shift in a complete amplifier (i.e. control section plus power amplifier section) is measured it will be found that the tone controls and filters affect the phase. At 1 kHz and with the tone controls centre (i.e. 'flat' response) and filters switched out the relative phase shift should be zero (Fig. 5.4(a)).

A diagram showing the phase response relative to the frequency response of an amplifier is given in Fig. 5.6.

CLIPPING

Another steady-state test is that for peak clipping. The instrument setup in Fig. 5.1 is suitable. In this case (as distinct from preamplifier overload tests) the amplifier's volume control is set at maximum, tone controls 'flat' and filters out and the oscillator signal advanced until peak clipping is displayed on the oscilloscope, as shown in Fig. 5.7.

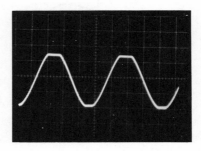

FIG. 5.7. *Peak clipping of a sine wave signal*

This shows reasonably symmetrical clipping, and the power at which the clipping just occurs can be measured. Asymmetrical clipping is shown on the sine wave in Fig. 5.8. If one peak clips significantly before the other in a power amplifier the centre-point balance of the two output transistors is generally in error.

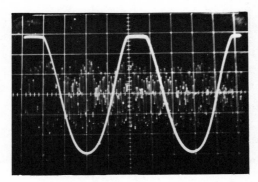

FIG. 5.8. *Asymmetrical clipping of a sine wave signal on one trace and music signal on the other trace. Since both amplifiers for the sine wave and music signal were of similar characteristics, the oscillogram shows that the amplifier carrying the music signal is working well within its dynamic range*

The other trace in Fig. 5.8 shows music signal whose peaks fail to reach the clipping point, indicating that this amplifier, which has the same characteristics as that in which the sine wave clipping is occurring, is working within its dynamic range.

It is absolutely necessary to avoid peak clipping, and as transient peaks of music can rise to remarkably large amplitudes, an amplifier should never be

116

operated at a level such that the overload margin is diminished (see Chapter 1). The oscillogram in Fig. 5.9 gives an impression of the high amplitude to which

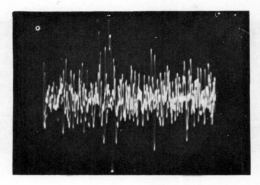

FIG. 5.9. *This oscillogram shows clipping of music signal transients. The distortion arising from this can be fatiguing*

music transients can rise; in fact, slight clipping of the maximum amplitude transient can be seen in this oscillogram (also see Figs. 3.18 and 3.19). This sort of effect can occur when an amplifier of insufficient power yield for the size of the room and sensitivity of the speakers is operated well towards maximum in an endeavour to achieve a more realistic sound intensity.

TRANSIENT TESTS

In the main, the tests and measurements detailed in the foregoing relate to steady-state signal. Other equally as important tests measure, or give an evaluation of, the transient performance of an amplifier. These include stability, rise time, slewing rate (see expression 2.14, Chapter 2) and transient inter-modulation distortion.

RISE TIME

A useful signal for transient appraisal is the square wave provided its rise time is significantly smaller than that of the amplifier (see Chapter 2). Figure 5.10 gives some examples of rise time using a square wave. The oscillogram at (*a*) shows the rise time of the Radford Low Distortion Oscillator (which also has a square wave output). The time scale here is 0.5 μs/cm (horizontal division), so the rise time is less than 0.1 μs, as specified for this instrument.

The oscillogram at (*b*) shows the same signal after passing through an amplifier, the time scale now being 5 μs/cm, thereby indicating an amplifier rise time close to 10 μs. Oscillogram (*c*) shows the same signal and the same amplifier, but this time with the treble filter switched on. The time scale is 5 μs/cm, as at (*b*), so the rise time, due to the filter, has increased to about 30 μs.

117

Expression 2.8, Chapter 2, gives the relationship between rise time and high-frequency response, and based on this the amplifier responsible for Fig. 5.10(b)

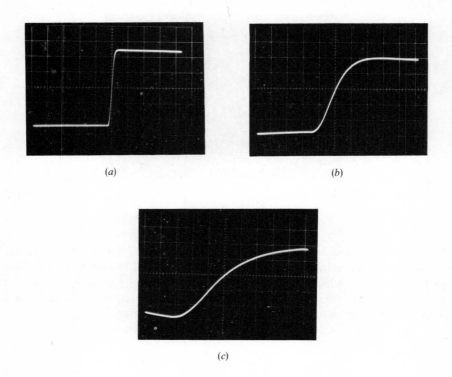

(a)   (b)

(c)

FIG. 5.10. *Rise times. (a) less than 0.1 μs. (b) 10 μs. (c) 30 μs. See text*

would have its upper −3 dB point at 35 kHz. With the filter active (Fig. 5.10(c)), the −3 dB point occurs at about 11.6 kHz. Slewing rate is dealt with in Chapter 2.

SQUARE WAVE TESTS

Examples of square wave tests have already been given (see Chapter 2, for example). The test rig in Fig. 5.1 (but without the distortion factor meter) is suitable for square wave displays, and the power produced is best calculated from the peak-to-peak amplitude of the displayed waveform with reference to the graticule on a calibrated oscilloscope. Most audio voltmeters are mean-reading type, since the a.c.-to-d.c. conversion is done immediately before the meter movement. The meter is then scaled in r.m.s. values of a sine wave. With signals other than true sine wave, therefore, errors in indication can occur. For example, a sine wave of 20 V pk-pk amplitude (as measured on a calibrated oscilloscope) will indicate 7 V r.m.s. on such a meter (i.e. $20/2 \times 0.707$), but a square wave of 20 V p-p amplitude will give an indication of 1.11 times the r.m.s.,

118

average or peak value, since a square wave is unique in that all these values are the same.

A peak responding meter, on the other hand (i.e. where the signal is rectified at the input and used to charge a capacitor to the peak value of the input waveform), will give virtually the same indication from a sine wave *or* square wave signal of a given amplitude.

There is merit in making square wave tests at the nominal half power level of the amplifier, and this is easily arranged by adjusting the signal level so that

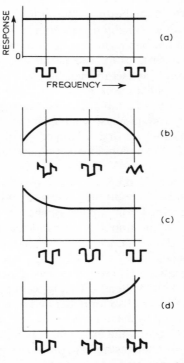

FIG. 5.11. *Square wave evaluation of frequency response characteristics. (a) perfectly flat response.*
(b) bass and treble roll-off. (c) bass lift. (d) treble lift

the pk-pk amplitude of the square wave is equal to the pk-pk amplitude of a sine wave whose r.m.s. value corresponds to an audio power in the load which is 6 dB below the amplifier's rated power.

It will be understood, of course, that the rise time of the oscilloscope's Y channel should be several times smaller than the rise time of the amplifier under test or, in other words, the Y channel frequency response should be several times greater than the frequency response of the amplifier.

Evaluation of the frequency response characteristic of an amplifier (or, indeed, any active or passive network) is possible by examination of the nature of the waveform after it has passed through the amplifier (or network).

The diagrams in Fig. 5.11 give an impression of the output waveforms at three frequencies (low, medium and high) after passing through amplifiers of the responses indicated. It is assumed that the input waveform is a true square wave of very small rise time. In practice, slight variations in waveform shape will be observed, depending on the actual test frequency and precise nature of the response characteristics.

With a hi-fi amplifier adjusted for a 'flat' response, filters switched off, the waveforms should not be as at (b) since there would (or should be) greater extension of the bass and treble responses. A good hi-fi amplifier will exhibit an almost perfect square wave at 1 kHz, slight corner rounding at 10 kHz and tilt at 40 Hz, as shown by the series of oscillograms in Fig. 5.12. The input waveform is also shown on the bottom trace at (b).

It is possible to obtain a virtually perfect square wave at 1 kHz by adjusting the tone controls about the 'flat' positions, but if there is early bass roll-off such adjustment merely compensates for the deficiency, so it is not a conclusive indication that the controls are set to their 'neutral' positions. A phase test all the way through the amplifier (see Fig. 5.4), in conjunction with square wave tests, is a more accurate way of establishing the electrical centres of the controls. A subsequent frequency response test will clinch the matter.

Poor stability is indicated by rings (damped oscillation) at the start of the square wave horizontals, but no amplifier should be so prone when driving into a resistive load.

One effect of square wave testing is that the period of the wave might effect the amplifier's d.c. operating conditions, and to avoid this very narrow pulses are sometimes used, obtained from a pulse generator, as distinct from a square wave generator. These test the amplifier more in keeping with music signal, but square waves subject the amplifier to more rigorous conditions and are favoured by the author.

Pulsed sine wave signals are also sometimes used for amplifier tests, but these have been found to be better suited for testing pickups and loudspeakers.

The low frequency stability of an amplifier and also any shortcomings in the power supply are indicated by a square wave at low repetition frequency. The oscillograms in Fig. 5.13 give some examples. The kinks or pulses at the start of the 'horizontals' reveal small instability tendencies, while the waveform at (c) shows very poor low-frequency response as well. This series is at 40 Hz. The tilt is due to differentiation of the true squarewave by the amplifier.

A sine wave at 40 Hz has a time period of 1/40, or 25 ms, which means that each positive and negative horizontal of a 40 Hz square wave has a time period of 25/2 ms.

The stability of an amplifier is generally at its best when the output load is resistive. Loudspeaker loads, however, are not like this, since they contain components of both inductance and capacitance, as well as resistance. Electrostatic loudspeakers are essentially capacitive (the Quad, for example, is approximately simulated by 15 ohms in parallel with $2\,\mu F$ and $20\,\mu H$ in series with the RC parallel combination). The analogue of dynamic loudspeaker systems depends on the impedance of the driver units employed and on the nature of the frequency divider networks. As would be expected, therefore, the electrical analogue of these can differ significantly between makes and models, and the manufacturers rarely give detailed information on this—which seems such a pity.

120

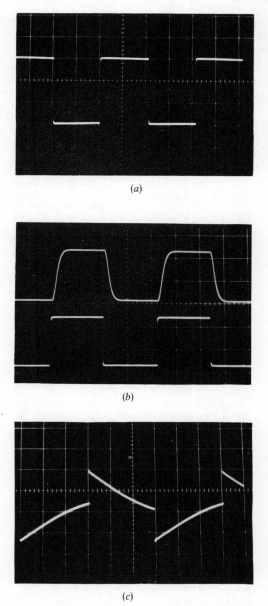

(a)

(b)

(c)

FIG. 5.12. *Square wave tests into a resistive load. (a) 1 kHz. (b) 10 kHz, also showing input waveform at bottom trace. (c) 40 Hz*

A resistor shunted by a capacitor is the worse condition from the amplifier's stability point of view, and the value of the capacitor which precipitates instability is sometimes taken as a measure of the amplifier's stability.

Thus, square wave tests with the amplifier driving into capacitively reactive loads are revealing. Quite a few reviewers make this test with 8 ohms in

121

parallel with $2\,\mu\text{F}$ and not many amplifiers get away without some trace of ringing or overshoot when loaded in this way.

A couple of examples are given in Fig. 5.14, (a) at 1 kHz and (b) and 10 kHz. Since the ring is very quickly damped, giving virtually an overshoot effect, this sort of performance is perfectly acceptable. Far less acceptable, however, would be a lightly damped prolonged ring.

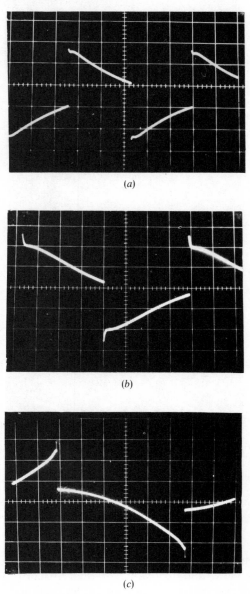

(a)

(b)

(c)

FIG. 5.13. *Waveforms showing signs of instability at 40 Hz into a resistive load*

122

To establish more conclusively the amplifier's stability, the $2\,\mu F$ capacitor should be removed from the resistive element and a capacitor box connected in place to see whether instability is encouraged at any intermediate value of. capacitance.

In general, amplifiers have better stability with a particular inductive load, such as a dynamic loudspeaker system.

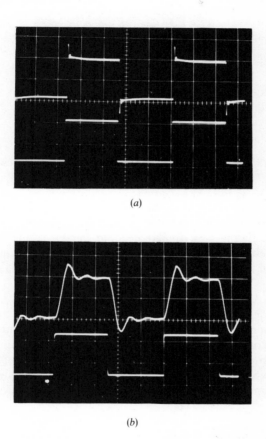

(a)

(b)

FIG. 5.14. *Square wave tests into a load of 8 ohms in parallel with $2\,\mu F$. (a) 1 kHz. (b) 10 kHz*

Stability depends on the overall design, including the amount of negative feedback adopted and on lag and lead compensating networks. However, deliberate overcompensation of the open-loop response as a means of minimising overshoot into a capacitive load is a singularly masking technique which can lead to impaired open-loop high frequency response and hence to transient intermodulation distortion (see Chapters 2, 4 and 5).

More sanitary is the use of a resistor and inductor parallel combination in series with the output, as shown in the Armstrong circuit in Fig. 4.7 and in the Bryan circuit in Fig. 4.8.

Transient intermodulation distortion is difficult to evaluate accurately, but some idea of how an amplifier behaves in this respect can be gleaned by using a test waveform of combined sine and square waves, as shown in Fig. 5.15.

The test setup in Fig. 5.1 can be used, but the distortion factor meter will not be required, and the waveforms need to be combined as shown in Fig. 5.16.

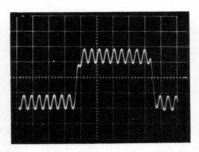

FIG. 5.15. *Combined sine wave and square wave transient intermodulation distortion test (see text). Here the amplitude refers to the graticule divisions of 1 cm in terms of 10 V/cm and the sweep in terms of 100 μs/cm*

The three resistors form a star network, and since the two signal sources will have approximately the same impedance and since it is this impedance which is used to couple the combined source to the input of the amplifier under test, each resistor will have the same value, and this can be calculated from

$$R = Z\frac{n-1}{n+1} \tag{5.1}$$

where Z is the common impedance and n the number of inputs.

Since we are concerned only with two inputs and since Z in most cases will be 600 ohms, R becomes 200 ohms. Note, however, that the network is correctly 'matched' only when the output arm is terminated into 600 ohms (see Fig. 5.16). Each signal component at the output will then be 6 dB below the output from each generator.

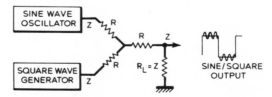

FIG. 5.16. *Method of connecting sine wave oscillator and square wave generator for composite square sine waveform (see text)*

The waveform in Fig. 5.15 was obtained from across the resistive output load of an amplifier, the square wave component being 1 kHz and the sine wave component 20 kHz. This display signifies that the amplifier is free from serious transient intermodulation distortion at least, for in severe cases the amplitude of the sine wave component at the commencement of each positive and negative half cycle of square wave is visibly suppressed or cut off altogether, owing to the 'blocking' effect already explained.

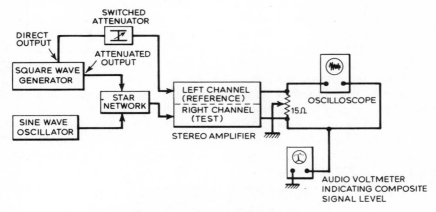

FIG. 5.17. *Test rig for transient intermodulation distortion appraisal*

As mentioned earlier. accurate evaluation of this distortion is difficult, particularly in absolute terms, and at the time of writing research is in hand in an endeavour to derive a more meaningful test and absolute expressions of distortion percentage.

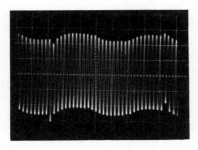

FIG. 5.18. *Transient intermodulation distortion oscillogram obtained by cancellation of the square wave component at the output of the amplifier under test. Y is 2 V/cm and X 200 μs/cm*

One scheme which enhances the evaluation is based on the cancellation of the square wave component of the composite output waveform just prior to oscilloscope display. One such method has been described by J. R. Stuart (*Wireless World*, September, 1973).

The author has experimented along similar lines, and the display shown in Fig. 5.18 was obtained from the test rig given in Fig. 5.17. Here it is the right channel of a stereo amplifier which is being evaluated, and to the input of this is applied the composite square/sine signal. The left channel is used purely as a reference and through this is passed only the square wave signal, via a separate attenuator.

The two channels are correctly loaded at the output (the illustration shows a potentiometer of 16 ohms total value, but two 8-ohm loads could be used with the tap connected to chassis, of course). Since the oscilloscope is connected across the two 'live' outputs of the amplifier and since the square wave of the composite signal is in phase with the square wave alone, the square wave component is removed from the composite signal from the display point of view. Thus, when the level of the square wave signal is adjusted accurately to correspond to that of the square wave component of the composite signal, only the sine wave component is displayed on the oscilloscope.

Any change of amplitude of the sine wave signal, or mutilation of this signal, at the transition points is then more easily observed.

Fig. 5.18 shows mild amplitude changes at the transition points. The test signal was the same as that used for obtaining the display in Fig. 5.15 (i.e. 1 kHz square wave and 20 kHz sine wave), and the oscilloscope was adjusted for 2 V/cm amplitude and 200 μs/cm sweep.

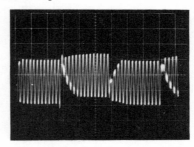

FIG. 5.19. *Display of more severe transient intermodulation distortion (see text)*

A more severe display of transient intermodulation distortion is shown by the oscillogram in Fig. 5.19. Here the test amplifier was operating at 1 dB or so below peak clipping and was subjected to a very small degree of treble lift. This shows clearly how the amplitude of a sine wave type signal can be severely mutilated when accompanying a transient-type signal. Notice that the sine waves gradually return to normal, unclipped amplitude as the feedback assumes control.

Tests so far appear to indicate that transient intermodulation distortion could have most adverse subjective impact when the amplifier is operated towards peak power capacity on signal peaks and on programme material which contains both fast-rise transients and high-amplitude, high-frequency signal components—and that goes for most wide dynamic range music. The effect is also aggravated by treble boost when the signal peaks rise towards the amplifier's power capacity, as the theory of the phenomenon predicts.

ADJUSTMENTS

There are two primary internal adjustments of hi-fi amplifiers, one which sets the mid point voltage between the output transistors and the other which adjusts the quiescent current (I_q).

The first mentioned, which not all designs include, is merely adjusted to establish symmetrical clipping of sine wave peaks when the amplifier is driven a shade beyond its power capacity. When included, it is usually located in the base circuit of the preamplifier stage to whose emitter is connected the d.c. feedback resistor (see Fig. 5.20). Since the stages of the power amplifier are

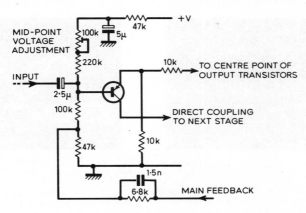

FIG. 5.20. *Showing the position of the mid-point voltage preset of a class B amplifier* (*see Fig. 4.8*)

directly coupled, the preset regulates the d.c. conditions for balance relative to the two output transistors. In the circuit in Fig. 4.8 (Chapter 4), R4 is also such a preset.

QUIESCENT CURRENT ADJUSTMENT

The most critical adjustment is that for I_q. This one regulates the standing bias applied to the two output transistors, and its location is shown by R2 in Fig. 4.7 and R5 in Fig. 4.8.

The I_q is the current taken by the output transistors in the absence of drive signal. Some presets are arranged so that the I_q is adjustable from zero (pure class B—and inevitable crossover distortion) to 100 mA or, perhaps, more, yielding virtually class A biasing (see Chapter 4).

However, few class B designs are capable of handling the large I_q required for class A operation, and if the I_q is turned up too much the power transistors dissipate more heat than the sinks can dispose of, so that the transistors ultimately burn up.

On the other hand, too little I_q will encourage crossover distortion, but this is rarely indicated in full force by testing for distortion factor or harmonic distortion, though a test of IMD will often show higher-order components under this condition.

The service manual or notes of the amplifier will (or should!) give the recommended I_q, and this may range from as low as 10 mA to 40 or even 50 mA, depending on the design and power of the amplifier. The I_q can be measured either by breaking the d.c. circuit of the output transistor pair and inserting a milliammeter (making sure that the meter is adjusted initially to a suitably high current range) or by measuring the voltage across an emitter resistor and working out the current from Ohm's law. For example, 10 mV measured across 0.5 ohm works out to 20 mA. This method calls for a d.c. voltmeter of high sensitivity (i.e. full-scale deflection around 100 mV).

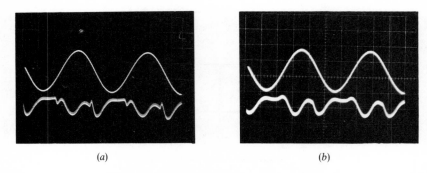

(a)   (b)

FIG. 5.21. *Distortion residual oscillograms.* (a) *showing crossover artefacts and* (b) *how these have been reduced by adjustment to* I_q. *The* I_q *must not be increased to a value significantly in advance of that recommended. Abnormally hot sinks would indicate an excessive* I_q *(see text)*

As shown in the circuits of Figs. 4.7 and 4.8, thermal stabilisation of the operating point is achieved either by a transistor or diode arrangement which samples the temperature, thereby compensating for the current change through the transistors as their temperature changes. It is desirable, therefore, to let the amplifier warm up on half-power drive before making final adjustments of I_q.

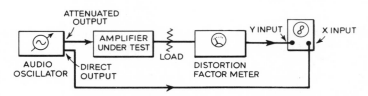

FIG. 5.22. *Instrument setup for Lissajous figure display of distortion factor residual*

It is also highly desirable to monitor the distortion factor residual on an oscilloscope (using test setup Fig. 5.1) while the I_q is being adjusted, for even though the I_q might be set exactly as specified in the service manual there may be quite high amplitude crossover, and it may only require a small increase from the recommended I_q value to eliminate the distortion (or, at least, reduce it to an insignificant level).

The distortion should first be monitored at 1 kHz and, if necessary, the distortion at this frequency cleared or reduced, after which an examination should be made at 10 kHz. If crossover is now present, it may need only a minor I_q advancement to reduce it. It would then be prudent to recheck at 1 kHz to ensure that crossover has not been introduced at this frequency.

Fig. 5.21 shows two distortion factor oscillograms. (*a*) signifies crossover artefacts and (*b*) shows dramatically how these were reduced by a small I_q adjustment. These oscillograms refer to 10 kHz and 10 W into 8 ohms.

The distortion factor residual can be displayed as a Lissajous figure* by switching off the oscilloscope's timebase and obtaining the horizontal sweep from the input sine wave test waveform, as shown in Fig. 5.22. Such a display of distortion residual is given in Fig. 5.23, and from this it is possible to deduce the primary harmonic—second in this example.

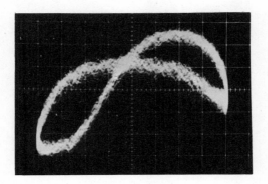

FIG. 5.23. *Lissajous figure display of distortion factor residual, signifying that the distortion is essentially second harmonic*

Crossover distortion can be responsible for subjectively depressing reproduction, particularly at very low levels. It is instructive to listen to the change in quality as the I_q preset is adjusted over its range, taking in severe crossover artefacts at one extreme and essentially low-order harmonics at the other extreme. This subjective test has most impact at very low levels, and to emphasise

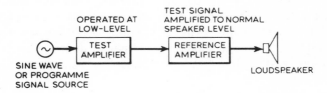

FIG. 5.24. *Setup for evaluating crossover distortion subjectively (see text)*

the difference in quality as the preset is adjusted the test amplifier can be connected to the input of a reference amplifier. This, of course, makes it possible to listen to very low signals from the test amplifier at full loudspeaker power, via the reference amplifier (see Fig. 5.24).

The test can also be made with sine wave input signals, while the distortion factor residual is being monitored. A series of tests of this kind have been made

* See, for example, the author's book by the same publisher entitled *Radio, Television and Audio Test Instruments.*

by the author using several sets of observers, and the results indicate that cross-over distortion is one of the most disturbing kinds of distortion—with transient intermodulation distortion possibly a short distance behind, but detailed subjective tests of this distortion still need to be conducted and fully evaluated.

Finally, Fig. 5.25 illustrates some of the instruments referred to in this chapter and which are employed in the laboratory of the author's company. The

FIG. 5.25. *Some of the instruments used by the author's company, showing author at work.* (*See text for more information*)

important ones, reading from left to right, are Marconi wave analysing equipment, including TF2330 and TF2334, Eagle multirange K1400, Taylor a.m. signal generator 68A/M, Taylor valve voltmeter 172A, Tech. Instruments decade attenuator TE-111, instruments by J. E. Sugden, including Si451 millivoltmeter, distortion measuring unit Si452 and low distortion sine/square oscillator Si453, Grundig MV20 audio millivoltmeter, Marconi f.m. generator TF995B/2, Taylor f.m./a.m. generator 61A, Radford Low Distortion Oscillator and Distortion Measuring Set and Telequipment D53 oscilloscope with interchangeable Y amplifiers. There is also equipment for monitoring the mains supply voltage and for adjusting the voltage applied to equipment under test. On the bench can be seen the TEAC AG-6500 tuner-amplifier.

CHAPTER 6

Loudspeakers and Headphones

THE ELECTRICAL ANALOGUE of the sound pressure waves at source is translated back to sound pressure waves by the loudspeaker or headphone set, which is thus a transducer having a function complementary to that of the microphone.

MOVING COIL LOUDSPEAKER

The moving coil unit is in majority application at the time of writing, and in principle is no different today from the first one ever made, many years ago. A coil of wire, called the speech coil, secured to the centre of a cone (or diaphragm) is free to move as a 'piston' in a radial magnetic field, the coil and hence the cone thus deflecting when current is passed through the coil. This is

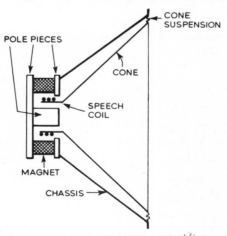

FIG. 6.1. *Basic components of a moving coil loudspeaker unit*

the well-known motor principle. When signal current is passed through the coil the cone is caused to vibrate to the pattern of the audio information carried by the signal and, excluding distortion, the sound pressure waves so produced have correspondence to those produced in the first place to form the signal. The main components of a moving coil loudspeaker unit are shown in Fig. 6.1.

The force acting on the cone due to the current-carrying speech coil can be expressed

$$F = BIk \tag{6.1}$$

where F is the force in dynes, B the radial flux density in gauss, I the current in amperes/10, l the conductor length in cm and k a factor (less than unity) which takes account of the deviation from 90 degrees between the angle of the magnetic flux and current.

The force is made as large as possible by the use of a strong magnet and by winding the conductor into the form of a coil. The current depends on the power of the driving amplifier, and when large power is to be handled the diameter of the conductor is made sufficiently large to avoid overheating. Special attention is also paid to the construction of the speech coil and the method of securing it to the cone.

IMPEDANCE

The speech coil is composed of inductance, distributed capacitance and resistance, the elementary analogue being given in Fig. 6.2. Thus from the signal

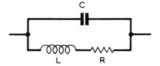

Fig. 6.2. *Electrical analogue of loudspeaker unit, describing impedance*

(a.c.) point of view the speech coil represents an impedance, which is measured at 400 Hz or 1 kHz (Fig. 6.3). The preferred DIN value is 4 ohms, other values

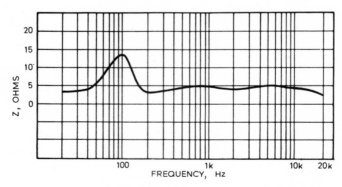

Fig. 6.3. *Loudspeaker system impedance characteristic*

being 8 and 16 ohms. Loudspeakers made on the Continent of Europe are commonly 4 ohms, though 8 ohms is preferred in the UK and often in the American areas.

132

POWER CAPACITY

Since contemporary amplifiers are essentially constant voltage devices owing to the high negative feedback yielding a very low source impedance, it follows that the lower the impedance of the loudspeaker, the greater will be the audio power abstracted by it. However, some amplifiers are designed so that the power optimises at a specific impedance, often around 4 or 8 ohms. Very few, if any, modern amplifiers give the highest power at 15 or 16 ohms.

It would be possible to use a matching transformer between, say, a 15-ohm loudspeaker and a transistor amplifier, so that the amplifier is looking into 4 ohms, where the highest power is produced, but this technique is not very desirable because the transformer coupling and shunt losses can rise to quite high values at infrabass frequencies, where the load can then appear as a short-circuit to the amplifier! Although the programme signal itself may not carry information much below 30 Hz, significant infrabass power can be produced by very low rumble and disc ripple effects, particularly when a good pickup is used with an amplifier whose response extends down to sub-bass frequencies.

Because a loudspeaker constitutes an impedance, rather than a 'pure' resistance, the power abstracted by it is

$$W = EI \cos \theta \tag{6.2}$$

where W is the electrical power in watts, E the signal voltage across the loudspeaker, I the signal current through it and $\cos \theta$ the cosine of the phase angle between E and I.

This becomes important when measuring the efficiency of a loudspeaker (expression 1.23, Chapter 1). It is possible, of course, to apply a signal at a frequency where the impedance is essentially resistive, the power then being EI, but since this places the efficiency calculation at one frequency only, pink or white noise is sometimes used to appraise the 'average' efficiency.

As an example, for an 'average' sound pressure of 96 dB (12μb) at 1 metre under hemispherical free-space conditions (à la DIN 45-500), pink noise can be applied via an amplifier, the product of the noise voltage and the noise current at the loudspeaker then giving the 'average' input power. Since average reading audio meters are generally used to measure the noise E and I, a correction should be made by subtracting 1.05 dB from the result.

As we have seen (Chapter 1), 96 dB at 1 metre under hemispherical free-space conditions corresponds to an acoustical power emission of about 25 mW, so a loudspeaker requiring, say, 9 W for this would have an 'average' efficiency of 0.277%, which is not a particularly untypical value when measured this way.

PHASE ANGLE

A phase angle versus frequency characteristic is given in Fig. 6.4. This is not particularly typical and does not refer to the loudspeaker whose impedance characteristic is given in Fig. 6.3. This shows that the loudspeaker is resistive at two frequencies only—60 Hz and about 200 Hz.

The phase angle characteristic is influenced by the overall loudspeaker system design, as also is the impedance characteristic (see later). While the impedance

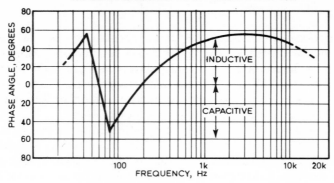

FIG. 6.4. *Loudspeaker phase angle characteristic (see text)*

characteristic is sometimes given, the phase angle characteristic is rarely given or stated by the manufacturer, which seems a pity.

RESONANCE FREQUENCY

This commonly refers to the low-frequency resonance, which is the natural frequency of the cone assembly where heavy vibration occurs, governed by the associated values of mass and compliance (see expression 1.27, Chapter 1). At frequencies below resonance the pressure output falls off at the rate of 12 dB/octave. The resonance frequency is influenced by the acoustical loading of the unit, and is recognisable as the peak in the impedance characteristic and the dip in the phase angle characteristic (Figs. 6.3 and 6.4).

LOUDSPEAKER BAFFLE

Because sound is emitted from both sides of the cone, that from the rear tends to cancel that from the front as the frequency is reduced and the sound wavelength approaches the size of the cone. This arises because a compression wave is developed by one side of the cone while a rarefaction wave is developed by the other side, a so-called 'acoustical short-circuit' then occurring.

The effect is significantly reduced when the unit is mounted on a baffle board which increases the distance between the rear and front sound sources. Even so, when the sound wavelength becomes approximately equal to the baffle size destructive interferences and loss of low-frequency emission result.

For reasonable low-frequency reproduction (down to about 50 Hz), the baffle needs to be about 3 metres, and to avoid a cancellation dip a little above the bass roll-off frequency the unit needs to be mounted substantially asymmetrically on the baffle.

A similar surface area can be retained in a more convenient form by arranging for the baffle to take the form of an open-backed box; but this sort of acoustical loading, which is adopted in radio and television receivers, etc., is not very desirable since it encourages various types of air resonances.

The large, flat baffle is thus rarely encountered in hi-fi sound reproduction nowadays. Some enthusiasts, though, approach a near infinite baffle effect by mounting the unit on a wall dividing two rooms. To avoid irregularity of middle and treble response, however, the unit needs to be mounted to avoid the aperture acting as a cavity resonator.

When a unit is mounted on a flat baffle the sound pressure output falls off at the rate of 6 dB/octave below the baffle cutoff frequency.

When a loudspeaker unit is mounted over an aperture in a totally closed box the rear wave is completely suppressed, a method of acoustical loading which at one time was referred to as 'infinite baffle'. At low frequencies the air trapped within the box adds to the stiffness of the normal cone-restoring stiffness, such that the total compliance is decreased and the loaded resonance frequency increased.

In the early days of this type of loading quite large boxes were required for a reasonable low-frequency performance. Of more recent times, however, bass units have been developed specifically for this type of loading, which exhibit a very low bass resonance resulting from a cone assembly of relatively high mass and high compliance. In fact, a large proportion of the total cone restoring compliance results from the air trapped in the box. This type of loading, attributed to American Edgar Villchur, is now more accurately referred to as acoustical suspension.

Owing to the low bass resonance of the driver, the loaded low-frequency response still provides a useful bass output, even when quite small boxes are used. An example axial pressure response of an acoustical suspension loudspeaker system is given in Fig. 6.5.

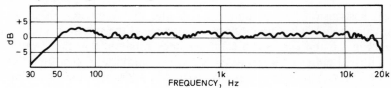

FIG. 6.5. *Pressure response characteristic of well designed acoustical-suspension loudspeaker system*

To maintain a useful bass output when the driver unit is equipped with only a small diameter cone, substantial linear cone movement is essential, the cone then acting as an air piston. Moreover, since the system is essentially pneumatic, the cone, its surrounding suspension and the joints of the box must all be sensibly air-tight, since significant air leakage into the box would be likely to create high distortion and lower the system's power handling capacity.

Acoustical suspension drive units are designed to have large cone movements without the speech coil leaving the magnetic gap, along with air-tight cones and suspensions. In the small system, the effective compliance is almost wholly established by the trapped air, which means that the bass resonance frequency cannot be decreased by increasing the normal cone-restoring compliance. Instead, the mass is increased which, as would be expected, decreases the efficiency of the system.

135

DAMPING

The loudspeaker system needs to be suitably damped to avoid ringing and overhang effects, and this is achieved by electromagnetic damping, due to the amplifier's low source impedance and hence resulting high damping factor, and by the introduction of a material into the box which possesses a high value of acoustical absorbitivity; some commonly used materials being rockwool, long-haired wool, bonded acetate fibre and polyurethane foam.

The damping is a function of the system's Q value (sometimes called 'magnification factor')

$$Q = \frac{2\pi f M}{R} \tag{6.3}$$

where f is the design centre for the low-frequency resonance, M the total mass and R the total loss resistance. Fig. 6.6 gives the electrical analogue of an

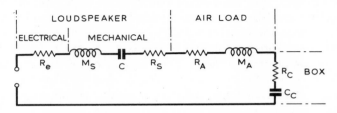

FIG. 6.6. *Electrical analogue of acoustical-suspension loudspeaker system, where R_e is the electrical damping, M_s the mass of the cone assembly, C_s the compliance of the suspension, R_s the acoustical resistance of the suspension, R_a the resistive component at front of cone, M_a reactive component at front of cone, R_c resistive component at rear of cone and C_c the reactive component at rear of cone*

acoustical suspension system and Fig. 6.7 the low-frequency response for different values of Q. Assuming that the resonance of the system is established, then from Fig. 6.6 and expression 6.3 it becomes apparent that the Q value can be best adjusted either by altering the electrical damping R_e (i.e. by adjusting the B and l factors of expression 6.1, assuming a given value of amplifier's

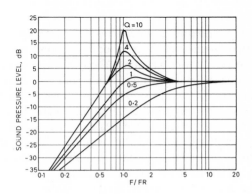

FIG. 6.7. *Low-frequency response of acoustical-suspension loudspeakers system for different values of Q (see text)*

source impedance) or the resistive component R_c of the box loading on the rear side of the cone, which includes the damping material.

The loudspeaker's motor system (expression 6.1) is normally engineered to suit the effective source impedance of the 'average' amplifier, so the R_c component is usually adjusted for a Q between about 0.8 and 1.5. Most people prefer a low Q and the application of mild bass boost at the amplifier, than an underdamped system which can precipitate 'boomy' bass, especially when the electromagnetic damping is below optimum.

ISOTHERMAL EFFECT

A byproduct of the acoustical damping R_c is an apparent increase in the volume of the box—that is, an increase in air compliance. The pressure changes inside the box are rapidly occurring and consequently approximately adiabatic (i.e. no heat exchange with surroundings). For this condition the compliance can be expressed as

$$C = \frac{V}{\gamma p a^2} \qquad (6.4)$$

where C is the compliance, V the volume, γ the ratio of specific heats, p the pressure and a the area.

The presence of the damping material in the box produces an isothermal effect owing to heat storage, and when the filled box behaves totally isothermally the compliance is

$$C = \frac{V}{p a^2} \qquad (6.5)$$

where the symbols are as in expression 6.4.

Since the value of γ for air is 1.41, it follows that the damping will increase the compliance and hence the effective volume of the box by a factor of 1.41 under optimum conditions, thereby reducing the bass resonance by about 17%. Cellular damping material, such as polyurethane foam, has good heat storage properties, but the density required for optimum heat storage may differ from that required for a Q value between 0.8 and 1.5. However, there are damping techniques which provide both the optimum damping and maximum heat storage—i.e. the optimum isothermal effect.

At frequencies above $f = c/2l$, where c is sound velocity (344 m/s) and l the largest internal side of the box in feet, standing waves occur in the box, as in a room, and these are also damped by the internal packing, this being necessary to avoid irregularity of the pressure response characteristic.

The box must be rigid and free from panel resonances, and the high-frequency absorbitivity of the damping material must be high enough to inhibit rear panel reflection of the waves which, if the cone is acoustically transparent, would result in significant high-frequency colouration due to the reflected waves passing through the cone. From this aspect, the greater the depth of the box, the better, but the cones of driver units intended for acoustical suspension loading are often designed for optimum acoustical opacity.

MIDDLE AND HIGH FREQUENCIES

The loading so far considered refers to the bass end. The treble emission is generally handled by a separate high-frequency unit, and in many designs there is also a third unit for the middle range of frequencies. Since the high-frequency unit (often called a tweeter) is acoustically closed at the rear, it is not affected by the low-frequency pressure changes in the box, and so can be mounted normally on to the front panel, along with the bass unit.

When a mid-range unit is employed, however, this is commonly of the open-backed type, so needs to be isolated from the internal box pressure changes by a small, internal enclosure.

Both the high-frequency and middle-frequency units are commonly based on the moving coil principle, but the diameter of the cones or diaphragms indicate the range of frequencies over which they are effective. The diameter of a mid-range unit is between 4 and 8 in and handles frequencies over about 750 Hz to 5 kHz. The treble unit is much smaller, often with a Melinex diaphragm of about 1 in diameter, shaped in the form of a dome to broaden the high-frequency radiation pattern.

Horn loading is sometimes adopted for the middle and treble frequencies, and the high-frequency driver may use a ribbon 'diaphragm' instead of the conventional cone or domed diaphragm. The ribbon forms the conductor, and for low mass it is thin, though often corrugated. It is suspended in a very powerful magnetic field. Horn loading then provides an efficient coupling between the unit and the air.

The size of a horn is determined by the wavelength and hence the frequency of the sound over the operational bandwidth. For high frequencies the dimensions are not inconveniently large, and there are commercially designed loudspeaker systems incorporating treble and mid-frequency horns, but for correct unit loading at bass frequencies a large horn is required. Nevertheless, bass horns are adopted by some enthusiasts, these being built either below the floor or on to or into a wall, sometimes incorporating the corner of a room.

The small horn system uses a form of folded horn, allowing the length dimension to be accommodated in a more practical volume. The corner of a room might also be used to extend the mouth of the horn, thereby making it responsive to lower frequencies (see later).

FREQUENCY-DIVIDING NETWORKS

When more than one loudspeaker unit is used in a loudspeaker system a frequency-divider network is required so that the units receive signals only over the frequency range for which they are designed. For example, the bass unit may handle frequencies up to 500 or 750 Hz, the mid-range unit frequencies from about 500 Hz to 5 kHz and the high-frequency unit frequencies from 5 kHz upwards. The high-frequency unit thus establishes the upper-frequency limit of the system while the bass unit and the box or enclosure establish the lower-frequency limit.

There are two types of frequency divider, one the approximately constant impedance type and the other the constant impedance type. The 'order' of the filter determines the roll-off rate, and for two-unit systems Figs. 6.8, 6.9 and 6.10 give configurations for 6, 12 and 18 dB respectively (sometimes called quarter-, half- and full-section), series at (*a*) and parallel at (*b*). The circuits in Figs. 6.8 and 6.9 are constant impedance and in Fig. 6.10 approximately constant impedance. The captions give the formulae required for working out the component values.

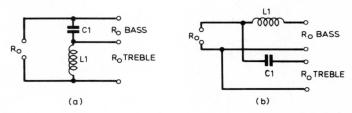

(a) (b)

FIG. 6.8. *6 dB (quarter-section) frequency dividers, (a) series and (b) parallel. $L_1 = R_o/(2\pi f_o)$ and $C_1 = 1/(2\pi f_o R_o)$, where f_o is the crossover frequency at which the attenuation is -3 dB and the power to the bass and treble units equal. C is in farads and L in henrys*

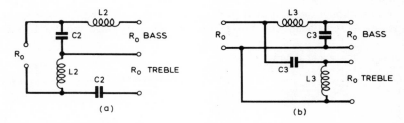

(a) (b)

FIG. 6.9. *12 dB (half-section) frequency dividers, (a) series and (b) parallel. $L_2 = R_o/(2\sqrt{2}\pi f_o)$, $C_2 = 1/(\sqrt{2}\pi f_o R_o)$, $L_3 = R_o/(\sqrt{2}\pi f_o)$ and $C_3 = 1/(2\sqrt{2}\pi f_o R_o)$, where f_o is the crossover frequency at which the attenuation is -3 dB and the power to the bass and treble units equal. C farads and L henrys*

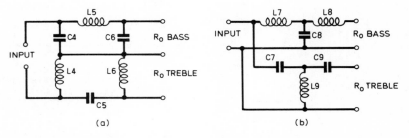

(a) (b)

FIG. 6.10. *18 dB (full-section) frequency dividers, (a) series and (b) parallel. $L_4 = R_o/(1+m)(2\pi f_o)$, $L_5 = 2R_o/(2\pi f_o)$, $L_6 = R_o/(2\pi f_o)$, $C_4 = (1+m)/(2\pi f_o R_o)$, $C_5 = 1/(4\pi f_o R_o)$, $C_6 = 1/(2\pi f_o R_o)$, $L_7 = (1+m)R_o/(2\pi f_o)$, $L_8 = R_o/(2\pi f_o)$, $L_9 = R_o/(4\pi f_o)$, $C_7 = 1/(1+m)(2\pi f_o R_o)$, $C_8 = 1/(\pi f_o R_o)$ and $C_9 = 1/(2\pi f_o R_o)$, where f_o is the crossover frequency at which the attenuation is -3 dB and the power to the bass and treble units equal and m about 0.6 to provide the most nearly constant image impedance value in the passband. C farads and L henrys*

The half-section or 12 dB type are commonly adopted. The rate of attenuation of the 6 dB type is rarely rapid enough for all but simple type of loudspeaker systems. Study of the parallel configurations shows that the filter to the bass unit is low-pass and that to the treble unit high-pass, in the simple 6 dB case there being merely an inductor in series with the bass unit and a capacitor in series with the treble unit. Fig. 6.11(*a*) shows a simple quarter-section divider which provides a crossover at about 5 kHz when the component values shown

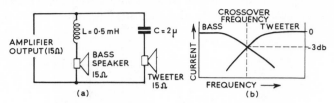

FIG. 6.11. *Simple 6 dB divider (a) and response (b)*

are used with 15-ohm units. The approximate response characteristics are shown at (*b*).

To obtain an even response over the spectrum, particularly when three units are employed, fixed or variable resistors might be used to adjust the power to the units.

The composition of a three-unit divider used in the Heathkit AS-9530 loudspeaker system is given in Fig. 6.12, along with the individual and overall

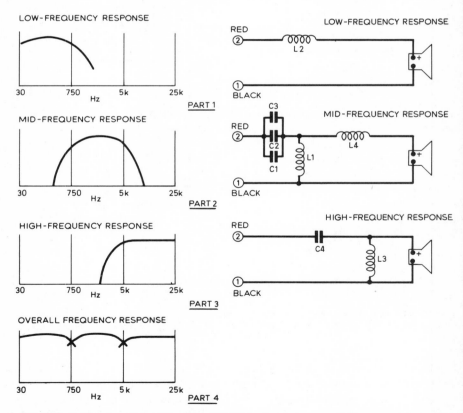

FIG. 6.12. *Sectional analysis of Heathkit AS-9530 loudspeaker system divider network (see text)*

frequency responses. Part 1 shows a quarter-section (solitary inductor) for the bass unit and Part 3 a half-section for the high-frequency unit. Part 2 is a half-section bandpass filter for the mid-frequency unit, and Part 4 shows the complete response characteristic. This system uses three KEF units, type B139 for bass, type B110 for middle and type T27 for treble.

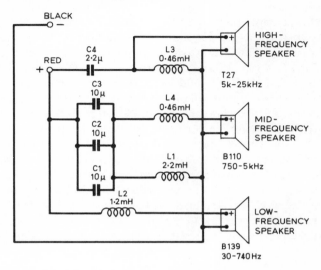

FIG. 6.13. *Complete divider circuit of Heathkit AS-9530 loudspeaker system (see text)*

The complete divider circuit, with component values for 8 ohms, is given in Fig. 6.13, which also reveals the frequency ranges and the correct phasing of the three units.

DIVIDER COMPONENTS

The capacitors can be either paper or electrolytic. However, with the latter the polarity is important, and since the capacitors are concerned with a.c. (signal current) they should be of the bipolar type. Alternatively, two ordinary electrolytics wired positive-to-positive or negative-to-negative (see Fig. 6.14) can be used for each capacitor. However, it must be remembered that when two capacitors are connected in series the total value is reduced since $1/C_{tot.} = 1/C_1 + 1/C_2$. Thus, the connection of two $2\,\mu F$ capacitors in series will give a total value ($C_{tot.}$) of $1\,\mu F$.

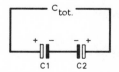

FIG. 6.14. *A bipolar electrolytic can be constructed by connecting two electrolytics in series back-to-back, as shown. $1/C_{tot}$ then equals $1/C_1 + 1/C_2$*

141

The inductors must not be of the metal core type, as such cores can result in bad distortion. Some of the recent ferrite cores, however, are being used successfully, though there is the possibility that ringing (due to inadequate damping) or magnetostriction effects might precipitate certain types of distortion.

Many enthusiasts prefer air-cored coils, the formers of which can be made of wood, plastics or any other type of insulating material (not metal). Lacquer-insulated copper wire of 1.2 mm diameter is suitable for most divider applications, and on a core of 70 mm overall diameter, 25 mm inner diameter and 25 mm width 175, 210, 245 and 270 turns of such wire will yield inductance values of about 0.78, 1.12, 1.57 and 1.95 mH respectively.

A core of similar diameters but of 40 mm width will provide respective values of 2.78, 3.15 and 3.9 mH from 300, 340 and 375 turns.

7.8 mH requires about 515 turns on a former of 100 mm overall diameter, 25 mm inner diameter and 40 mm width.

It will be appreciated, of course, that the inductors possess distributed capacitance as well as resistance, so some power will be lost, but this should be small when the wire is of a reasonable diameter. Clearly, the divider network will modify the electrical analogue of the loudspeaker system 'seen' by the amplifier, and the damping due to the low source resistance of the amplifier will be less at each unit owing to the resistive and reactive components of the divider.

DOUBLE-CONE UNITS

As a means of obtaining a wide response from a single unit, a double-cone assembly might be adopted. The main low- and middle-frequency cone is designed so that above a certain frequency, called the mechanical crossover frequency, the speech coil becomes decoupled and little or no energy is radiated by the main cone. However, tightly coupled to the speech coil is a second cone of very small mass, which 'couples in' at the mechanical crossover frequency, thereby maintaining the response into the high-frequency part of the spectrum.

This kind of unit avoids the need for divider networks, of course, but the system designer has less control over the frequency response, greater flexibility being provided by two or more separate units.

Sometimes the double-cone unit is designed to respond to the low-middle, middle and high-frequency parts of the spectrum, a second unit, coupled by way of a divider, then being used for the bass frequencies.

Another scheme (Tannoy) takes the form of a horn-loaded high-frequency unit concentrically located in the main cone. The main cone handles the bass and middle frequencies. The two units are coupled through a frequency dividing network, with rear-of-cabinet controls for regulating the treble roll-off and energy delivered by the high-frequency unit.

BASS-REFLEX LOADING

Although the acoustical-suspension type of bass loading accounts for the majority of the smaller loudspeaker systems currently in use, there are still quite a few systems being designed and in use employing the so-called bass-reflex loading. Because an aperture is an important part of the enclosure, the terms 'vented-box', 'ported' and 'tunnelled' are sometimes used to describe the system.

Like the other systems so far described, the bass-reflex loudspeaker is a direct-radiator system. The box has two main apertures, one to accommodate the driver unit and the other, called the vent or port, which allows air to move in and out of the enclosure in sympathy with the air pressure changes inside.

The vent is often a simple aperture, though sometimes (particularly when the dimensions limit the volume of the enclosure) it extends into the enclosure

FIG. 6.15. *Inside of Rectavox Omni MkII loudspeaker system, showing the bass and treble units, the tube extension from the vent and the frequency divider network at the bottom*

from the aperture as a tunnel or duct (see Fig. 6.15, for example). The air in the vent behaves as an internal mass since it is reactive, and the vented enclosure exhibits the characteristics of a Helmholtz resonator (see Chapter 1).

When the enclosure is tuned by its volume and vent dimensions to the un-loaded resonance f_o of the bass unit, the air in the vent at f_o moves in phase with the cone. Under this condition there is maximum air compression in the enclosure, which neatly damps the driver's bass resonance.

Below f_o the cone is tightly coupled to the mass of air in the vent, which yields a lower resonance. Above f_o the enclosure stiffness is coupled to the cone owing to the high mass reactance of the air in the vent, which yields an upper, essentially undamped resonance. The lower and upper resonances are shown in Fig. 6.16, which is an impedance characteristic.

Clearly, when the air in the vent moves in phase with the front of the cone the low-frequency emission is augmented. However, below f_o the vent emission tends to cancel the cone emission, as the former then swings towards phase coincidence with the *rear* of the cone.

Attributes of a bass reflex enclosure are good low-frequency power handling owing to the relatively heavy acoustical damping on the cone at f_o, small low-frequency distortion owing to the smaller excursions of the cone around f_o, extended bass response for a given enclosure size and driver unit, small electrical peak impedance and good acoustical damping at low-frequency. However, the vent area and enclosure volume need to be carefully 'matched' to the bass driver for these attributes to be fully realised.

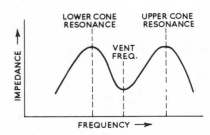

FIG. 6.16. *Impedance characteristic of a bass-reflex enclosing, showing the two peaks referred to in the text. Damping of the peaks is possible by an acoustical resistance unit at the vent (see text)*

When the area of the vent approximates to that of the cone of the driver unit, the vent radiation characteristic would appear to optimise. However, some small-volume systems are optimised by extending the vent into the enclosure, as shown in Fig. 6.15. This has the same effect as making the vent smaller (to suit the volume of the enclosure) while maintaining an air movement equivalent to that of a larger area vent.

A more recent technique, based on the bass-reflex principle, utilises an 'auxiliary bass radiator' mounted alongside the ordinary driver unit. The diaphragm of the auxiliary bass radiator is designed for a critical compliance and mass and hence loading to the enclosure, and it takes the place of the vent of the regular bass-reflex enclosure. It is thus activated by the air compressions at low frequencies inside the enclosure, thereby augmenting the bass radiation from the driver. In effect, the radiation from the rear of the driver's cone is brought out, in phase, to the front of the enclosure, which enhances the bass efficiency. The nature of the loading and the characteristics of the auxiliary bass radiator ensure that the phasing at low frequencies remains coincident with the bass driver. At higher frequencies the enclosure behaves as a correctly damped closed box.

The vent of a bass-reflex enclosure is sometimes damped deliberately by an acoustical resistance unit (ARU, Goodmans). This not only reduces the radiation from the vent, but it also provides even damping of both bass peaks in the response and allows the use of significantly less air volume in the enclosure than required for correct operation without vent damping.

It is noteworthy that the concept of the bass reflex enclosure was introduced in 1930 by A. L. Thuras, under U.S. patent No. 1 869 178, yet the system is still in use today.

OTHER TUNED OR RESONANT SYSTEMS

Another resonant enclosure takes the form of a tuned column of air with the unit positioned at one end (or at some calculated distance from the end) and the other end either open or closed, depending on the precise design. When the pipe is open at the far end, the dimensions are such that low-frequency sound is radiated in phase with the cone of the driver, the bass then being augmented, as by the bass reflex enclosure.

When the far end of the pipe is closed, the dimensions of the pipe and hence the column of air are such that the air resonance assists the cone motion at low frequencies owing to the low value of air-load impedance at resonance.

There have been several variations in the design of column enclosures over the years, and the technique in one or two guises is with us still today. Owing to the nature of unit loading, the term transmission line is sometimes used to describe this sort of enclosure. The term has been borrowed from transmission line theory owing to the analogy between an electrical transmission line and a column of air under conditions of resonance.

When one end of a pipe is excited by sound and the pipe is a quarter the wavelength of the sound, the wave reflected back is in phase at the source when the far end of the pipe is open. The reflected wave when the pipe is a half wavelength is out of phase at the source. The opposite conditions occur when the pipe is closed. These properties are exploited by the column enclosure, and the basic approach is an open pipe, with the driver mounted at one end, of a length providing an anti-resonance coinciding with the driver's bass resonance. Length l of an open pipe for anti-resonance at frequency f is given by

$$l = \frac{c}{2f} - 1.7\sqrt{\frac{A}{\pi}} \qquad (6.6)$$

where c is the velocity of sound in air and A the cross-sectional area of the pipe.

To partly combat the disadvantage of anti-resonances at every quarter wavelength, the driver may be mounted one-third of the pipe length from the closed end, which cancels the first resonance (i.e. the third harmonic) above the fundamental.

An enclosure which has some of the properties of the column enclosure is the acoustical labyrinth, the 'pipe' of which is formed by a wooden maze built within the enclosure (Fig. 6.17). The rear of the cone thus drives a long folded pipe, lined with sound absorbing material, the mouth of which opens either at the front or rear of the enclosure to 'exhaust' the very low-frequency sound waves.

Some designs are for virtually complete absorption of the rear radiations from the cone, so that the load applied to the cone is pretty well resistive. The heavy damping results in a smooth fall in bass output since the cone is then operating under conditions approaching constant velocity.

The effectiveness of a labyrinth is limited at low frequencies by its length, and for a nearly linear response down to about 70 Hz the pipe length, measured on a centre line, should be in the region of 2.13 m when the loaded bass resonance of the driver is about 40 Hz. That is, the 'pipe' length should be about a quarter of the wavelength of the sound at the loaded bass resonance of the driver. For example, if the loaded bass resonance of the driver is, say, 30 Hz (11.4 m wavelength), then the 'pipe' length should be a quarter of this, which is about 2.85 m for the most linear bass response.

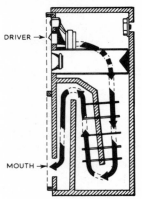

FIG. 6.17. *Acoustical labyrinth loudspeaker system (see text for full description)*

This sort of acoustical loading reduces the bass resonance frequency of the driver, so if the unloaded resonance is, say, 50 Hz, then the loaded resonance may fall to around 40 Hz—which is opposite to the effect provided by the acoustical suspension type of loading.

An advantage of the acoustical labyrinth is that it has almost complete freedom from resonances. It also appears to be regaining popularity in various modes.

ELECTROSTATIC PRINCIPLE

The electrostatic principle is adopted both by loudspeakers and headphones. High-frequency electrostatic units have been available for many years, but of more recent times complete systems have been developed using the principle —notably the Quad Acoustical full-range electrostatic loudspeaker.

As shown by the elementary diagram in Fig. 6.18, two plates are employed

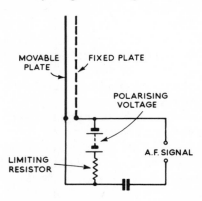

FIG. 6.18. *Showing basic electrostatic loudspeaker principle*

146

as in a capacitor. One is fixed and the other very thin and movable, mounted so that it can vibrate without touching the fixed plate. Audio signal voltage is applied across the plates, and as this produces electrostatic forces between the plates varying at the audio frequency, the thin plate vibrates in sympathy with the audio information. This is the normal electrostatic action.

However, in this simple case the movable plate will be attracted towards the fixed plate on every half-cycle of signal, so that two vibrations will occur on each full-cycle. This is avoided by the application of a polarising voltage in series with the signal, as shown in Fig. 6.18. The polarising voltage results in an initial attraction of the movable plate, and provided the peak signal voltage does not exceed the polarising voltage, the plate will vibrate in correct correspondence to the audio information. The limiting resistor is to prevent the polarising source from bypassing the signal circuit.

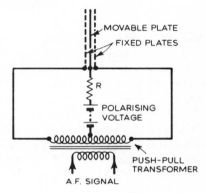

FIG. 6.19. *The basic scheme of the push-pull electrostatic loudspeaker*

For top-quality applications, however, a push-pull arrangement is used (Fig. 6.19). This substantially removes not only second and even-numbered harmonics, but it also keeps odd-numbered harmonics at a low level. Total harmonic distortion, in fact, can be kept below 1%, which is a low order for loudspeakers.

With the push-pull arrangement the movable plate is sandwiched by two perforated fixed plates which, relative to the movable plate, are energised by equal and opposite-phase signal voltages from a transformer with a centre-tapped secondary winding. A balanced mode of operation is thus achieved.

HORN LOADING

As already noted, horn loading is not uncommon at middle and high frequencies; but for bass reproduction (unless folded or extended by the boundaries of the room) they are often far too large (particularly in pairs) for the average domestic scene. Bass horns, nevertheless, have been built below floor level or into room walls, with the mouth 'exhausting' into the room.

A horn-loaded loudspeaker is noted for its high electrical/acoustical efficiency, and within its useful bandwidth the movement of the cone or diaphragm of the driver is much less for a given acoustical output than for baffle loading. The horn can be regarded as an acoustical transformer which transforms the high pressure and low velocity sound energy at the driver to low pressure and high velocity sound energy required for coupling to the outside air. Such efficient loading and coupling lead to good damping, low distortion and relatively flat frequency response within the useful bandwidth.

Although horns can be exponential, parabolic, conical and hypex, the exponential law is that most commonly adopted, with either circular or square cross section. With folded horns, an approach towards the exponential is achieved by the integration of several conical sections.

In general, horns are designed* to cover only a part of the audio spectrum, and single horns are often used as woofers or as tweeters, but not for full frequency range reproduction. Compromises resulting from attempts to widen the horn bandwidth significantly impair the reproduction by the creation of resonances, etc.

The cross-sectional area of an exponential horn doubles each time the distance along the axis is increased by a factor known as the 'flaring constant', which influences the cut-off frequency. A horn reproducing down to 30 Hz may be up to 4 m long with a 1.5 m mouth diameter operating from a driver of about 300 mm cone diameter.

The mouth diameter for the least low-frequency resonances should not be less than one-third of the lower limit cutoff wavelength. Clearly, then, a correctly engineered horn loading down to about 30 Hz is a massive device, hence the attempts which are made to reduce the size by folding and by extending the mouth by the room boundaries for domestic application.

The resistive component of the throat impedance tends to fall swiftly below about 1.2 times the flare cutoff frequency, and although some output is obtained at lower frequencies the harmonic distortion rises. The fundamental resonance of the driver should not be less than the flare cutoff frequency, preferably not less than 1.2 times the cutoff frequency to ensure that the driver loads adequately at its fundamental resonance.

Resistive loading at frequencies below the flare cutoff frequency is sometimes achieved by the use of an air chamber between the driver and the horn proper. This is designed to introduce a capacitive reactance of a value which corresponds to the inductive reactance of the horn at the flare cutoff frequency. This technique is sometimes used with folded horns of limited size designed for the domestic scene.

The greatest efficiency in the smallest space is achieved when the cross-sectional area (A_x) at any distance (x) from the throat is given by

$$A_x = A_o \varepsilon^{mx} \tag{6.7}$$

where A_o is the throat area, m the flaring constant and ε the base of natural logarithms (2.718 28).

The cutoff frequency (f_c) is given by

$$f_c = mc/4\pi \tag{6.8}$$

where m is the flaring constant and c the velocity of sound in air.

*J. Dinsdale, Horn Loudspeaker Design, *Wireless World*, March, May and June 1974.

LOUDSPEAKER CONTROL

Apart from that provided by the acoustical properties of the enclosure loading, loudspeaker control is achieved by negative feedback which, as has already been shown (Chapter 2), applies a very low effective source impedance across the loudspeaker, thereby damping its free motion electromagnetically. The effectiveness of this method of control is limited by the value of resistance which appears in series with the driver and source due to the connecting cable and components of the frequency divider. The amplifier's source resistance, for example, may be only about 0.1 ohm, while the series resistance may be ten times or more this value.

Various schemes have been tried over the years to improve loudspeaker control, and one relies on the amplifier/loudspeaker being integral, so that a short cable of low resistance can couple direct from the amplifier to the driver. In this case it is the amplifier which drives the bass unit, the frequency dividing to the middle- and high-frequency units occurring before the output of the amplifier. Sometimes there is an amplifier for each driver! At the time of writing loudspeaker systems integrating a bass amplifier are being made; in fact, there appears to be a revival of the scheme for enhancing and/or extending the bass response of large and even small loudspeaker systems.

There have also been other methods of applying overall negative feedback round the amplifier/loudspeaker circuit, using both electrical and acoustical loops, with the aim of achieving a speech coil velocity proportional to input amplitude (i.e. constant velocity motion) and completely independent of frequency. Some of the early ideas derived a suitable feedback voltage from an auxiliary speech coil attached to the cone, from a microphone placed close to the cone and from a special bridge circuit connected across the amplifier output, whose one arm constituted a value-scaled replica of the impedance of the loudspeaker connected as the second arm, the bridge then being completed by two fixed resistors of suitable value for balance. None of these ideas really caught on.

PHILIPS MOTIONAL FEEDBACK

However, of very recent times Philips have developed the acoustical feedback-path type of control to an acceptable and viable commercial state, and have named it motional feedback. A block diagram of the scheme is given in Fig. 6.20.

All the items shown in the diagram, including the drivers, form an integrated system within an enclosure volume of a mere 12 litres and external dimensions of 38 × 28.5 × 22 cm. Motional feedback is applied to the bass unit (woofer), which is a standard 8 in Philips unit with a built-in transducer. A small printed circuit board positioned just above the speech coil fixing point accommodates the transducer in rubber clamps such that it is able to react resiliently to cone accelerations.

The transducer, being ceramic, is matched into the feedback circuit by a field effect transistor, and the resulting error signal is applied to the comparator along with the input signal. The source or input signal is applied via an active filter which passes signals up to 500 Hz to the low-frequency channel. Another filter at the input of the low-frequency channel attenuates signals below about 35 Hz, corresponding to the resonance frequency of the bass driver, so that the input signal at the comparator, which is an adding network, lies in the range of about 35–500 Hz. These frequencies are handled by the 40 W amplifier and drive the bass unit.

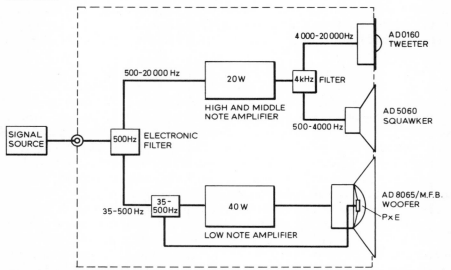

FIG. 6.20. *Block diagram of the Philips motional feedback loudspeaker system with integrated amplifiers, etc.*

The feedback tends to maintain constant velocity motion of the cone. The transducer effectively 'measures' the acceleration of the cone, and provided the cone acts as a piston its acceleration is proportional to input amplitude; any deviation from this condition comes under the corrective influence of the feedback.

The system thus reduces low-frequency harmonics and overhang effects; it also lowers the resonance frequency, thereby making it possible for a relatively small volume enclosure to provide a very useful low bass output.

The middle/high frequency channel is filtered over the range 500 Hz–20 kHz approximately, and a separate 20 W amplifier is used for this range of frequencies, the output of which drives the middle-frequency unit (squawker) and the high-frequency unit (tweeter) via a 4 kHz frequency divider.

Each system is mains powered with its own on/off switch; but in addition to this there is automatic electronic switching which puts a system in the 'stand by' condition after a period of about two minutes following the cessation of a signal input; the system then automatically switching on when input signal is re-applied.

There are two signal sockets, one which accepts the programme signal from a preamplifier and the other which allows the feeding of a second system—and that a third system, and so on—with the same signal. It is thus possible to develop a multi-output system of very high total power.

How well the bass is maintained for such a small enclosure volume is revealed by the response curve in Fig. 6.21, applicable to loudspeaker system Type RH532.

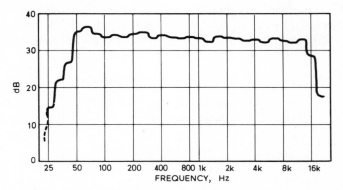

FIG. 6.21. *Frequency response of the Philips motional feedback loudspeaker system, Type RH532*

Philips have also developed a four-channel preamplifier programme source for feeding the motional feedback loudspeaker systems, which includes f.m. stereo and a.m. radio tuners and 'electronic' record player.

HEADPHONES

Most headphones used for high quality applications are either moving coil or electrostatic. The principles already expounded for loudspeakers are applicable basically also to headphones. However, with headphones the acoustical loading is achieved by the intimacy of the ear units to the ears, so that even the very small units are capable of providing very good bass performance.

One problem with headphones is resonances at high frequencies resulting from cavity effects and cone or diaphragm break-up. Electrostatic headphones are somewhat less vulnerable to these, and are, indeed, noted for their very transparent sound delivery, devoid of enclosure and room coloration effects.

A recent development by Wharfedale is the Isodynamic headphone set which, while working on the dynamic principle, has an action similar to that of electrostatic counterparts. This results from a thin diaphragm which carries printed circuit coils operating in a transverse magnetic field. Thus the drive is evenly distributed—as with the electrostatic principle—over the whole area of the diaphragm, which alleviates the break-up at certain frequencies, sometimes characteristic of the less sophisticated type of moving coil headphone set.

The Wharfedale headphones are significantly less sensitive than the more conventional magnetic variety, and they can, in fact, be connected direct to the loudspeaker terminals of an amplifier. Most other moving coil type, however, need to be connected to the output of an amplifier via an attenuator. Typical sensitivity is 100 dB sound pressure at the ears for an input of about 1 mW at 1 kHz, though some models may require a greater input than this for a similar pressure.

151

Impedances range from 4 to 8 ohms up to 1000 or so ohms. However, most amplifiers equipped with a headphone jack socket will accommodate a wide range of impedances with little apparent change in performance.

The simplest attenuator is shown in Fig. 6.22, which consists merely of a resistor in series with each ear unit to the appropriate amplifier channel output. The resistor value ranges from about 100 to 200 ohms, depending on the requirement.

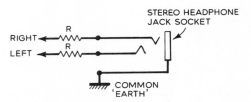

FIG. 6.22. *Simple resistive attenuation used in many amplifiers for feeding a stereo headphone set. R may range from 100 to 220 ohms (about ½–1 watt). This diagram also shows that by convention the tip of the jack plug is connected to the left ear unit and the ring to the right unit, the sleeve being the common 'earth' for both units*

Better attenuation is provided by a network shown in Fig. 6.23 (for one channel only), with the resistor values arranged so that the unit is loaded across a low value resistance for the best damping, though the relative importance of damping with headphones is somewhat debatable. Nevertheless, some manufacturers feel that the importance is sufficiently great to warrant including the ear units in the amplifier feedback paths, so that the low source impedance becomes fully affective, which it does not, of course, when the basic method of attenuation is adopted.

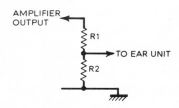

FIG. 6.23. *With this sort of attenuator the ear unit is loaded by the relatively low value of R_2. R_2 should have the lowest value consistent with the required output and with $R_1 + R_2$ not being smaller than the load requirement of the amplifier. The wattage rating of the resistors should be suitable for the music power of the amplifier*

Electrostatic headphones, on the other hand, need to be energised in most cases from a control unit (sometimes mains powered) located between the headphones and the amplifier. This unit contains a signal voltage step-up transformer and some method for producing a polarising voltage.

While valve amplifiers need a dummy load across the output when normal headphones are used without the loudspeaker, transistor amplifiers are troubled less in this way (they are more vulnerable to a low resistance load—i.e. short-circuit). Nevertheless, there is often merit in maintaining a reasonably low value load, even if this is above that provided by the loudspeaker. Some transistor amplifiers are distressed when operated under full-signal drive without an output load.

CHAPTER 7

Disc Recording

DESPITE RECENT developments in the field of magnetic tape recording, including high energy tapes, noise reducing artifices and cassette and cartridge systems, the gramophone record still remains very much in the forefront of the domestic sound scene.

Although there are still a few mono releases, the basic record is cut for two-channel stereo, which is mono compatible. More recent records, however, are cut for four-channel stereo (quadraphonic) replay, and these have different degrees of stereo and mono compatibility. The four channels are achieved from the single groove either by a matrixing process or by an ultrasonic carrier and frequency-phase modulation. The four channels are reclaimed either by a complementary matrix or a special demodulator at the reproducing amplifier.

Most gramophone records start as very high quality tape recordings, the edited material then being recorded in disc form on to a lacquer blank, from which the stamper is ultimately derived, and it is this which is used to press the discs for mass distribution.

The lacquer blank carries all the features of the final record, and the tool used to cut the groove and impart the modulation in mono, stereo or four-channel form is the complement of the replay stylus. This is activated by the cutter head, which is the complement of the replay cartridge. A lathe-like arrangement causes the cutter head to traverse the blank radially at a rate for the required groove pitch, and a variable groove spacing unit is incorporated to accommodate high modulation amplitude levels.

Single-channel mono information is imparted to the groove by lateral vibrations of the cutting-tool, so that 'wriggles' corresponding to the audio signal are cut into the groove. On replay these cause sympathetic vibrations of the pickup stylus, which in turn create a signal e.m.f. of characteristics similar to those of the original signal.

AMPLITUDE AND VELOCITY

Two factors associated with the vibrating cutting-tool or stylus are amplitude and velocity. For a constant velocity, the amplitude is small at high frequencies and large at low frequencies, and for a constant amplitude the velocity is large at high frequencies and small at low frequencies. Mathematically, therefore, we have

$$V = 2\pi f A \tag{7.1}$$

and

$$A = \frac{V}{2\pi f} \tag{7.2}$$

where V is the peak velocity in cm/s (or m/s), A the peak amplitude in cm (or m) and f the frequency in Hz.

Fig. 7.1 gives the graphical illustration of this, where at (a) wave B has twice the frequency and half the amplitude of wave A for constant velocity ($S_1 = S_2$)

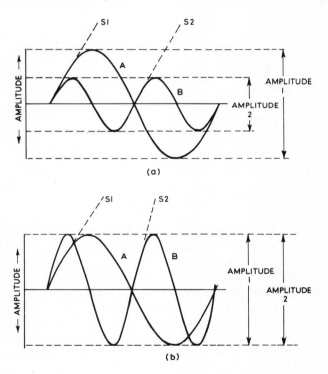

FIG. 7.1. *Showing constant velocity (a) and constant amplitude (b). See text for full details*

and at (b) wave B has twice the frequency and twice the velocity of wave A for constant amplitude ($A_1 = A_2$).

To help avoid groove collapse at low frequencies and high modulation level, signals of frequency below 1 kHz are recorded at a progressively reducing level, while to improve the replay signal/noise ratio signals of frequency above 1 kHz are recorded at a progressively increasing level. The net result approximates to constant amplitude recording, which necessitate complementary equalisation on replay, as explained in Chapter 3 (see Fig. 3.3).

DISC RECORDING

The disc recording characteristic currently adopted is that sponsored by the Record Industry Association of America, and is thus often referred to as the RIAA characteristic; it is also embodied in British Standard 1928:1955, and is sometimes referred to by this number. The recording characteristic in Table 7.1 is the complement of the replay equalisation characteristic given in Fig. 3.3.

Table 7.1

Frequency, Hz	dB	Frequency, Hz	dB
20	− 18.6	3 000	+ 4.7
30	− 17.8	4 000	+ 6.6
50	− 17.0	5 000	+ 8.2
60	− 16.1	6 000	+ 9.6
70	− 15.3	7 000	+ 10.7
80	− 14.5	8 000	+ 11.9
100	− 13.1	10 000	+ 13.7
150	− 10.2	12 000	+ 15.3
200	− 8.3	14 000	+ 16.6
400	− 3.8	16 000	+ 17.7
500	− 2.6	18 000	+ 18.7
700	− 1.2	20 000	+ 19.6
1 000	0		
1 500	+ 1.4		
2 000	+ 2.6		

The complementary curve for replay is defined by time-constants of 3180, 318 and 75 μs.

DISC PARAMETERS

The cutting-tool yields a vee-shaped groove which has a nominal width at the top of 0.0025 in (62 μm). The width can vary from its nominal value with changing amplitude of low-frequency recording signal. The space between adjacent grooves is called 'land', the nominal dimension of which is 0.0015 in (37.5 μm). The angle between the groove walls is 90 degrees, and the groove has a depth of about 0.00125 in (31 μm) and a bottom radius of about 0.00015 in (3.75 μm). These parameters apply to all 45 and 33⅓ records, though with the new four-channel techniques there will undoubtedly be some (minor) changes.

It will be understood that a record is cut such that the cutting tool moves on a true radius across the disc. On replay this condition is not always met, since many pickup arms are of the pivoted type. The lack of correlation produces distortion, but pickup arms are designed and set up to minimise it (see Chapter 8).

Modern records are also being cut so that the vertical cutting angle is 15 degrees,* and the latest cartridges are designed to play at a corresponding angle when correctly set up, thereby ensuring the least distortion from lack of correlation in this respect (see Chapter 8).

On replay various types of distortion occur, one of which is tracing distortion, and attempts have been made deliberately to introduce a complementary form of distortion during recording so that there is cancellation on replay.

* New IEC and DIN standards put the angle at 20 degrees.

DISC RECORDING

RECORDING LEVEL

Recording level may be given in terms of amplitude or velocity. Amplitudes up to 0.005 cm are present on the latest records, the limit being imposed by playing time requirement (assuming variable groove spacing) and the cutter's acceptability of large amplitude l.f., especially as a difference signal. The maximum peak velocity is limited by geometric and mechanical factors of the cutter/groove interface; but fairly recent work carried out by Shure implies that peak velocities approaching 50 cm/s or higher are present at high frequencies on the modern disc of wide dynamic range (see Chapter 3 and Fig. 3.17). Standard reference recording level is often given as 3.54 cm/s.

A function of frequency and velocity (or amplitude, of course) is acceleration, and the modern record can have accelerations exceeding those which would be produced by 1000 times the pull of gravity! The modulus of acceleration due to a steady-state signal can be expressed as

$$\alpha = 2\pi f V$$

or
$$(2\pi f)^2 A \qquad (7.3)$$

where α is the modulus of acceleration, f the frequency in Hz, V the velocity in cm/s, and A the amplitude in cm. At a frequency of 10 kHz and a velocity of 10 cm/s, the modulus of acceleration works out to 628×10^3, and referred to the dyne, which is unit force corresponding to the pull of gravity on 1/980 gram at latitude 45° at sea level, the effective acceleration is in the order of 640 g ($628 \times 10^3/980$), which is 640 times the pull of gravity! Such large accelerations assume importance at the pickup, where the effective mass of the stylus tip needs to be accelerated similarly; a very small effective tip mass thus being required to keep the resulting force to a practical value.

STEREO RECORDING

On a stereo disc the left channel is recorded on the inner wall and the right channel, separately, on the outer wall. Fig. 7.2 gives the basic elements of an

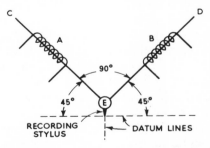

FIG. 7.2. *Elementary impression of stereo cutting head*

electromagnetic stereo recording head, with coil A corresponding to the left channel and coil B to the right channel. Moving up and down these coils are armature links C and D, which are coupled to cutter mounting E. Since the armature links are at an angle of 90 degrees from each other and 45 degrees from the surface of the disc, it follows that vibration of C will operate the cutter to record only on one wall of the groove and vibration of D will operate the cutter to record only on the other wall. The left and right channel signals are thus conveyed to coils A and B. Fig. 7.2 shows the cutter at rest in relation to the dotted datum lines.

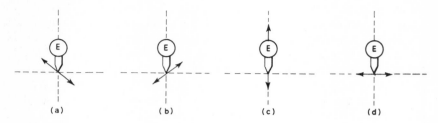

FIG. 7.3. *Vibration modes of cutter for different signal conditions; (a) left channel only, (b) right channel only, (c) left plus right channel antiphase and (d) left plus right channel inphase*

The diagrams in Fig. 7.3 shows how the cutter moves or vibrates under various signal conditions, at (*a*) when coil A only is energised (left channel), at (*b*) when coil B only is energised (right channel), at (*c*) when both coils are energised with anti-phase signals and at (*d*) when both coils are energised with in-phase signals. These vibrations give rise to groove modulation cuts as shown respectively at (*a*), (*b*), (*c*) and (*d*) in Fig. 7.4.

FIG. 7.4. *Groove cuts resulting from the cutter vibration modes given in Fig. 7.3. (a) left channel only, (b) right channel only, (c) left plus right antiphase and (d) left plus right inphase (mono cut)*

It will be appreciated, of course, that the relative movements of the armatures depend on the phase of the signals in the windings. The windings are conventionally phased so that when the left and right channel signals themselves are in-phase the cutter vibrates laterally, giving a 'mono' cut. This condition exists, for example, when the cutter signals are originally derived from a stereo microphone located at the centre of the 'sound stage', assuming, of course, that the phasing of the signals all the way through the system, from microphone to cutting head, is correctly retained.

It is this phasing which is partly responsible for the mono compatibility of a stereo record, for from the foregoing it will be realised that a mono cartridge will yield an output from the lateral components of the cut without significant loss of information. A mono cartridge, in effect, sums the left and right signals, the net result of which is a correctly balanced mono signal.

For a mono cartridge to operate correctly on a stereo record, however, it must possess a reasonable value of vertical compliance to cater for the vertical components of the cut, even though these produce no output.

A stereo cartridge with the two channels connected together in-phase will provide the same results; but if the two channels are connected anti-phase there will be cancellation of all in-phase information.

FOUR-CHANNEL DISCRETE

Regular stereo is enhanced by the use of more than two information channels between the source and the listening room (see Chapter 12), and the art from the domestic point of view at the time of writing is veering from two-channel stereo towards four-channel stereo, now commonly referred to as 'quadraphony', a term which is semantically offensive in some circles owing to the amalgam of Latin and Greek derivatives alternative terms 'quadrasonic' and 'tetraphonic' have been suggested.

The most obvious way of conveying the four lots of information is through four separate channels in isolation (as with the two *isolated* channels used for regular stereo). At the source four separate microphone systems are employed to collect the information, so the problem lies in maintaining isolation of these four microphone channels right up to the four loudspeakers in the listening room.

With magnetic tape as the storage medium this is not difficult since each channel can have its own tape track, but with gramophone records there is only the one groove and the two walls which already accommodate the two-channel stereo information. Nevertheless, techniques have been evolved which make possible the accommodation of additional information (for the two rear channels) in the one groove. One is by a 'multiplexing' technique, using an ultrasonic carrier and frequency modulation, and the other, which has various forms, is by a matrixing arrangement.

The multiplexing arrangement is referred to as 'discrete' since, as with tape, it permits the conveyance of the four lots of information in virtual isolation (i.e. minimal crosstalk between any of the four channels). Such a system has been developed by the Victor Company of Japan (JVC) with RCA, and is called CD-4 after its characteristics of stereo compatibility, 'discreteness' and four-channel. CD-4 records (sometimes called 'Quadradiscs') are made by RCA, Warner Bros., Electra and Atlantic.

CD-4 RECORD

CD-4 records have two signals recorded on to each wall of the groove. One wall contains the sum of *right* front and *right* rear information, recorded in audio frequency (30 Hz–15 kHz at time of writing) as a regular disc, along with the difference signal of these two channels recorded as frequency or phase modulation on an ultrasonic carrier, and the other wall contains the sum of the *left* front and *left* rear information, again recorded in audio frequency, along with the difference signal of these two channels, also recorded as frequency or phase modulation on an ultrasonic carrier.

A large modulation index and hence desirable frequency characteristics of the difference signals are achieved by the carriers ranging from about 20 to 45 kHz.

Fig. 7.5 shows the frequency disposition on both walls of the groove. The carriers centre around 30 kHz (i.e. modulation from −10 kHz to +15 kHz), and the difference signals are frequency modulated up to 800 Hz, after which the modulation changes to phase, and after 6 kHz back to frequency again. In the interests of pickup tracking stability and other factors, the difference signal channels are recorded at a level 19 dB below that of the sum channels.

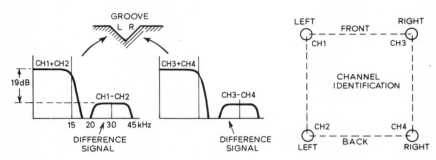

FIG. 7.5. *Frequency disposition on the two walls of a CD-4 record, and channel identification*

Fig. 7.6(a) gives a block diagram of the CD-4 recording system. The input matrix converts the four input signals from the tape machine into sum and difference signals which, after equalisation to the RIAA standard, drive the cutter head in the usual way, via the recording amplifier. However, the level of

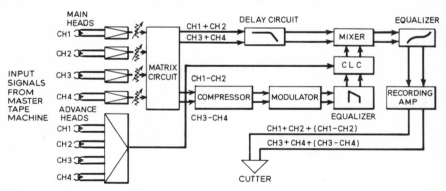

FIG. 7.6(a). *Block diagram of the recording system for a CD-4 record (see text)*

the difference signals is initially compressed for noise reduction (see Chapter 12). The converted signals next pass through the modulator, and after level compensation by the equaliser in this channel they then drive the automatic carrier level controller (CLC), which automatically increases the carrier level with increasing level of direct signal for signal/noise ratio enhancement of the difference signals. It will be seen that the CLC is in receipt of direct, but advanced, input signals for this monitoring function. The difference signals are finally mixed with the sum signals and pass with the latter through the RIAA equaliser and hence to the cutter head, via the recording amplifier.

DISC RECORDING

Owing to the high recording frequencies involved (i.e. up to 45 kHz in the present state of the art), CD-4 records need to be cut at half normal speed and hence at half the final frequency, a value which is compatible with contemporary cutter heads.

To maintain the high frequencies on replay a wide response cartridge is required along with a special stylus, but more about this in Chapter 8.

Clearly, since the two walls carry the left and right information, just like a stereo record, the CD-4 record is stereo compatible, but it is not compatible with the matrix type of four-channel records.

RIAA STANDARD

The RIAA standard for four-signal discrete records is given in Bulletin No. E7 (the RIAA standards for matrix discs are given later in this chapter). The four recorded signals are identified as

$$L_s = \text{left sum}$$
$$L_d = \text{left difference}$$
$$R_s = \text{right sum}$$
$$R_d = \text{right difference}$$

and the four input signals are identified as

$$L_F = \text{left front}$$
$$L_B = \text{left back}$$
$$R_F = \text{right front}$$
$$R_B = \text{right back}$$

The four input signals are combined and specified thus

$$L_s = L_F + L_B$$
$$L_d = L_F - L_B$$
$$R_s = R_F + R_B$$
$$R_d = R_F - R_B$$

The L_s signal is recorded on the inner wall of the groove and the R_s signal on the outer wall of a standard stereo groove. The L_d and R_d signals frequency modulate two 30 kHz carriers and the resultant sideband frequencies are confined to the range 20 kHz–45 kHz. The modulated carriers are superimposed on the L_s and R_s signals respectively, which themselves are recorded to the RIAA characteristic (Table 7.1). Above 20 kHz constant velocity recording is used.

The reference level of the L_s or R_s signal is equivalent to the amplitude of a 1 kHz signal which produces a peak velocity of 3.9 cm/s in the plane of the modulation. Each unmodulated 30 kHz carrier is recorded to 3.54 cm/s level in the plane of the modulation. When the L_d or R_d signal is equal to a 1 kHz reference level, the peak deviation of the 30 kHz carrier is 2.2 kHz.

The 30 kHz carriers are frequency modulated by the L_d or R_d signal which

161

is modified by a pre-emphasis network with a characteristic which is constant voltage below 800 Hz and above 6 kHz and with a 6 dB/octave slope rising with frequency between 800 Hz and 6 kHz, as shown in Fig. 7.6(b).

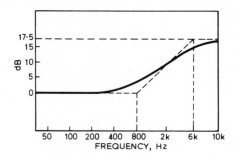

FIG. 7.6(b). *Four-channel discrete disc modulation characteristics—pre-emphasis, where*

$$\lambda \,(dB) = 20 \log_{10} \sqrt{\left[\frac{1+(2ft_1)^2}{1+(2ft_2)^2} \right]},$$

$$t_1 = 199\,\mu s \text{ and } t_2 = 26.5\,\mu s$$

When the L_s or R_s signal is positive, the corresponding groove wall is modulated away from the centre of the record, and when the L_d or R_d signal is positive, the corresponding carrier is deviated higher in frequency.

The L_s signal and the R_s signal are delayed by 40 μs with respect to the corresponding L_d and R_d signals.

The L_d and R_d signals are compressed in two frequency bands of 200 Hz to 2 kHz and above 2 kHz prior to the application of the pre-emphasis. At 630 Hz the rise-time is 5 ms when the level is increased instantaneously from -30 dB to -10 dB, and the restoring time is 100 ms for a corresponding reduction in level. Above 2 kHz the rise-time is 0.5 ms for an instantaneous level shift from -40 dB to -10 dB, and the restoring time is 10 ms. The difference signals L_d and R_d are correspondingly expanded during reproduction. This corresponds to the JVC Automatic Noise Reduction System (ANRS—see Chapter 10). The filter characteristics for the four-channel disc are given in Fig. 7.6(c) and the compressor characteristics in Fig. 7.6(d).

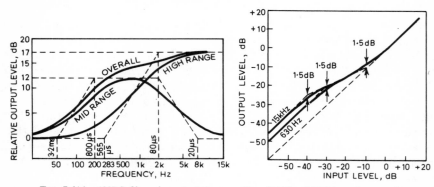

FIG. 7.6(c). *ANRS filter characteristics*   FIG. 7.6(d). *ANRS input/output characteristics*

The CD-4 system has undergone various improvements since its inception, one being the adoption of a new waveform compensator, called Neutrex, which modifies the recorded waveform such that the tracing distortion during replay is significantly reduced.

MATRIX RECORDS

With matrix records the signals corresponding to the four input channels are 'combined' or coded electrically into two channels and then recorded on the two walls of the groove in the same way as a stereo record (Fig. 7.7). This sort of coding makes it possible to derive four-channel information at the reproducing

FIG. 7.7. *A four-channel matrix accepts the four input channels, left front (L_f), right front (R_f), left back (L_b) and right back (R_b) and puts them onto the two outputs left total (L_t) and right total (R_t) for recording as stereo on to a single groove. The matrix at the reproducing end (decoder) is the complement of that at the recording end (coder)*

end by passing the complex two-channel information into a complementary decoding matrix which has four outputs.

Isolation between the four channels is far less well retained than with the discrete systems, however, and various degrees of crosstalk occur between channels, depending on the characteristics and complexity of the particular matrix system adopted.

Image location is achieved by the relative phases (see Chapter 12) and intensities of the sound from the four loudspeakers. Subjectively desirable quadraphony is less dependent on the same amount of channel separation as required for good stereo. Crosstalk between the two stereo channels significantly narrows the sound stage, ultimately reaching the mono state when the separation goes to zero. With quadraphony the situation is not quite the same as this, since the effect with decreasing separation is a reduction in the *area* of the sound stage, with image localisation tending to hold within the diminishing area (Chapter 12).

Several psycho-acoustical principles govern the subjective assimilation of quadraphony, including things like quadrature image shift, front source dominance, rear image contraction, etc., and recently developed matrix systems take these principles into account.

In the simple case, a matrix is a network of symmetrically disposed resistors as shown in Fig. 7.8, where the four inputs, corresponding to left front (L_f), right front (R_f), left back (L_b) and right back (R_b), are combined to two outputs, corresponding to left total (L_t) and right total (R_t).

Relative outputs depend not only on the levels of the input signals, but also on their phase, the nature of the matrix and the attenuation (or gain) and phase shift of the elements used in its makeup. If it is assumed, in the simple case, that the coefficients of coding and decoding are equal (the requirement for the least crosstalk between wanted and unwanted outputs) and that the power

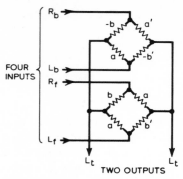

FIG. 7.8. *Basic coding matrix (see text)*

delivered in the two-channel mode is 'normalised' from any input, tantamount to resistors marked a' in Fig. 7.8 being equal to those marked a and those marked b' being equal to those marked b, then the equations for matrixing can be written

$$L_t = aL_f + bR_f + aL_b - bR_b$$
$$R_t = bL_f + aR_f - bL_b + aR_b$$

(7.4)

Solving for complementary decoding the equations become

$$L_{f'} = aL_t + bR_t$$
$$R_{f'} = bL_t + aR_t$$
$$L_{b'} = aL_t + bR_t$$
$$R_{b'} = -bL_t + aR_t$$

(7.5)

where $L_{f'}$, $R_{f'}$, $L_{b'}$ and $R_{b'}$ are the derived signals destined for the left front, right front, left back and right back loudspeakers.

By substituting the factors at the right-hand side of equations 7.4 for factors L_t and R_t at the right-hand side of equations 7.5, and assuming balanced unwanted signals for a central front image and $a^2 + b^2 = 1$ (for 'normalised' power), it can be found that the relative values for resistors (elements) $a' = a$ and $b' = b$ are 0.924 and 0.382 respectively (i.e., $0.924^2 + 0.382^2 = 1$). That is, a is about 2.4 times larger than b (with phase reversal on arms b and b' for back feeds).

Final decoding equations work out to

$$L_{f'} = L_f + 0.707R_f + 0.707L_b$$
$$R_{f'} = R_f + 0.707L_f + 0.707R_b$$
$$L_{b'} = L_b - 0.707R_b + 0.707L_f$$
$$R_{b'} = R_b - 0.707L_b + 0.707R_f$$

(7.6)

These equations show clearly that the crosstalk in the four-channel mode is appreciable between the wanted channel and the two adjacent channels, working out to 1/0.707, which is 1.414:1 or 3 dB. However, between the wanted channel and its diagonally opposite number the separation is theoretically ultimate (due to phase cancellation) since there are only three terms in each equation; for example, for $R_{b'}$ there is no L_f term.

The main systems which have been adopted at the time of writing are the SQ CBS system and the Sansui QS system and variants of these; there are others, including Electro-Voice, and additions will almost certainly appear as time goes on.

The RIAA (Recording Industry Association of America Inc.) have issued standards (approved and issued September 12, 1973, Bulletin No E7) for 'quadraphonic' disc records covering two types of matrix encoding and discrete four-signal discs. Type 1 matrixing is a process by which two separate type 1 matrix encoded signals are recorded in a single groove in a manner that is compatible with standard two-signal stereo and mono playback. The signals are identified as

Two recorded signals	*Four input signals*
L_T = left total	L_F = left front
R_T = right total	L_B = left back
	R_F = right front
	R_B = right back

SQ CBS TECHNIQUE

The preliminary processing (i.e. encoding) corresponds to the SQ technique whose records are made by CBS (Columbia), Capitol (USA) and EMI, the encoding equations being

$$L_T = L_F - j0.707L_B + 0.707R_B$$
$$R_T = R_F + j0.707R_B - 0.707L_B \qquad (7.7)$$

where j signifies a nominal 90 degree leading phase angle, leading positive and lagging negative. In all cases j signifies 90 degree front/back differential held ± 10 degrees over at least 100 Hz–10 kHz by two chains of second-order filters. Four such stages are used in simple decoders.

The inner wall of a standard stereo record groove is modulated by the L_T signal and the outer wall by the R_T signal, the recording conforming to the RIAA standard (Table 7.1).

The signal phasing is such that when the L_T and R_T signals are in phase the corresponding groove is modulated laterally.

The decoding equations are thus

$$L_{F'} = L_T$$
$$R_{F'} = R_T$$
$$L_{B'} = -0.707(-jL_T + R_T) \qquad (7.8)$$
$$R_{B'} = 0.707(L_T - jR_T)$$

Variations of the technique are in use, including 'blending', where deliberate crosstalk is introduced between the left and right channels (one blend is 10% front and 40% back), and so-called 'gain riding' logic circuits. As revealed by the first two equations in 7.8, front separation is infinite in the basic case, and it is the purpose of the (optional) extras to enhance the front-to-back separation. For example, 'auto logic' adjusts the levels to suit the nature of the signals such that the effective instantaneous front-to-back centre separation is increased. Since the logic circuits tend to respond to transients, the 'gain riding' is introduced by those signals which the ear/brain recognise as the sound source, and following the initial image localisation the sound field resumes to normal continuity.

The 'blending' circuits, which may be automatic or 'passive', help to correlate the reproduced image with that of the original sound so, for example, that an image derived, say, from a centre-front source will be reproduced at a similar angular position with the least rear interaction (see also Chapter 12).

Type 2 RIAA matrix recording (QS technique, see below) corresponds to the stereo standard (as type 1) for the L_T and R_T signals. When the two signals are phase coincident and of equal level the recording is such that their reproduction occurs due to the movement of the stylus tip in directions parallel to the record surface and lateral to the sound groove.

The nature of the encoding is such that a signal produced by a sound source located in the front half of the original sound field is distributed in phase to the L_T and R_T signals and that a signal produced by the sound field at the rear half is distributed to the L_T signal with a phase lead of 90 degrees from the front signal, and to the R_T signal with a phase lag of 90 degrees from the front signal.

When a signal is located in the left half of the sound field it is distributed in greater proportion to the L_T signal than the R_T signal and, conversely, when a signal is located in the right half it is distributed in greater proportion to the R_T signal than the L_T signal.

When a signal produced by a sound source lies in the centre of the original sound field it is distributed in equal proportions to the L_T and R_T signals, so that its content in the L_T signal has a phase lead of 90 degrees from its content in the R_T signal.

The RIAA Bulletin expresses both the ideal type 2 and a modified type 2 (where a full 360 degrees circumference cannot be satisfied) mathematically.

QS SANSUI TECHNIQUE

This is a Japanese technique whose records are produced under the Pye label in the UK, and the RIAA type 2 matrix recording standard is based on this. One set of encoding equations for the QS technique is

$$L_T = L_F + 0.414R_F + jL_B + j0.414R_B$$
$$R_T = 0.414L_F + R_F - j0.414L_B - jR_B$$

$$(7.9)$$

and the corresponding decoding equations

$$L_{F'} = L_T + 0.414R_T$$
$$R_{F'} = 0.414L_T + R_T$$
$$L_{B'} = -j(L_T - 0.414R_T)$$
$$R_{B'} = j(-0.414L_T + R_T)$$

$$(7.10)$$

166

where j signifies a nominal 90 degree phase shift, leading positive and lagging negative.

These equations reveal that the front separation is 0.414% or about 7.6 dB. However, because the basic QS matrix is symmetrical, unwanted sounds occurring either side of the position corresponding to the original sound help subjectively to localise a sound image to the position originally intended.

The QS decoder might also be equipped with enhancement circuitry. One such piece of circuitry is arranged to vary the phasing at a fast rate above and below the nominal phase to create a random phase condition at the back of the listening room, which is said to give presence enhancement.* Another QS scheme is called 'Variomatrix' which tends to improve the separation.

ELECTRO-VOICE TECHNIQUE

This is another American technique whose encoding equations in one form are

$$L_T = L_F + 0.3R_F + L_B - 0.5R_B$$
$$R_T = 0.3L_F + R_F - 0.5L_B + R_B \tag{7.11}$$

The corresponding set of decoding equations are

$$L_{F'} = L_T + 0.2R_T$$
$$R_{F'} = 0.2L_F + R_T$$
$$L_{B'} = 0.76(L_T - 0.8R_T)$$
$$R_{B'} = 0.76(0.8L_T + R_T) \tag{7.12}$$

and for Type EVX-44

$$L_{F'} = L_T + 0.2R_T$$
$$R_{F'} = 0.2L_T + R_T$$
$$L_{B'} = 0.63(0.4L_T + jL_T)$$
$$R_{B'} = 0.63(L_T + j0.4L_T) - 0.63(0.4R_T + jR_T) \tag{7.13}$$

where in Type EVX-44, j signifies a nominal 90 degree phase shift, leading positive and lagging negative.

It would appear that the EVX-44 decoder (the first set of equations correspond to Type EVX-4) has greater compatibility with QS records than SQ decoders and with SQ records than QS decoders.

FOUR-CHANNEL COMPATIBILITY

Clearly, the CD-4 demodulator is incompatible with matrix discs in the four-channel mode. Image error results when a basic QS decoder is used to play an SQ record, while rear and one side error is apparent when an SQ decoder is used to play a QS record. The QS Variomatrix decoder is more accommodating to SQ software.

*Discontinued. Variomatrix encoding now used almost exclusively for QS replay.

DISC RECORDING

STEREO/MONO COMPATIBILITY

All 'quadraphonic' records will play through a stereo system with varying degrees of accuracy. Owing to the processing of a CD-4 record, this will yield good stereo, particularly when played with a Shibata, Pramanik (B & O) or Ichikawa stylus, which should be used for four-channel replay anyway (see Chapter 8).

SQ records also yield good stereo owing to the inherently high value of front separation, but QS records are less objectively accommodating in this respect.

CD-4 records play as ordinary stereo records through a mono system, but some matrix records in mono playback mode tend to suffer from attenuation of centre back information, which can be detected by switching a matrix replay system to mono while a matrix disc is playing or by playing a matrix disc on a stereo system switched to mono. This is applicable to SQ and QS software, the left back and the right back sounds of the latter being 7.7 dB down on the front sounds.

The foregoing encoding equations reveal aspects of compatibility. Consider the coefficients of the equations in terms of A, B, a and b where, in the equations which follow, these have been substituted for the numerical coefficient values.

$$L_T = AL_F + BR_F + aL_B - bR_B$$
$$R_T = BL_F + AR_F - bL_B + aR_B$$

The degree of stereo separation between the front channels can be determined by comparing the value of A with the value of B and between the back channels by comparing the value of a with the value of b.

The decoding equations, on the other hand, can be used to determine the differences between the front-to-back levels. If these are also considered in terms of coefficients C, D, c and d, such that

$$L_{F'} = CL_T + DR_T$$
$$R_{F'} = DL_T + CR_T$$
$$L_{B'} = cL_T - dR_T$$
$$R_{B'} = dL_T + cR_T$$

then comparing $C + D$ with $c + d$, taking account of phase shifts where appropriate, will give an assessment of the relative output of the centre front to the centre back.

For the interested reader, a detailed analysis of compatibility is given in the paper 'Playback Effects from Matrix Recordings' by Howard M. Durbin, *J. Audio Eng. Soc.*, November 1972, Volume 20, No. 9.

Other useful references are:

Geoffrey Shorter, 'Four-Channel Stereo', *Wireless World*, January and February, 1972.

Peter Scheiber, 'Four Channels and Compatibility', *J. Audio Eng. Soc.*, April 1971, Volume 19, No. 4.

Duane H. Cooper and Takeo Shiga, 'Discrete Matrix Multichannel Stereo', *Audio Eng. Soc.*, June 1972, Volume 20, No. 5.

R. Itch, 'Proposed Universal Encoding Standards for Compatible Four-Channel Matrixing', *J. Audio Eng. Soc.*, April 1972, Volume 20, No. 3.

Benjamin B. Bauer, Daniel W. Gravereaux and Arthur J. Gust, 'A Compatible Stereo-Quadraphonic (SQ) Record System', *J. Audio Eng. Soc.*, September 1971, Volume 19, No. 8.

T. Inoue, N. Shibate and K. Goh, 'Technical Requirements and Analysis of Phono Cartridges for Proper Playback of Four-Channel Records', *J. Audio Eng. Soc.*, April 1973, Volume 21, No. 3.

T. Inoue, N. Takahashi and I. Owaki, 'A Discrete Four-Channel Disc and its Reproducing System (CD-4 System)', *J. Audio Eng. Soc.*, July/August 1971, Volume 19, No. 7.

More information is also given on 'quadraphony' from the record playing aspects in Chapter 8 and from the reproducing aspects in Chapter 12.

Disc Reproduction

THE MODERN PICKUP consists of an arm and a cartridge. The cartridge is the electrical part (transducer) which converts to electrical signal the information recorded on the walls of the groove, and the arm is the device which accommodates the cartridge and allows it to traverse the record in a manner which introduces the least distortion on the signal and which allows the minimum of force to be used between the stylus and the groove for the conversion.

Many arms are designed so that the cartridge end can be detached. The detachable part is called the headshell, and it is into or on to this that the cartridge is fitted. Few arms are designed with the headshell permanently fixed to the arm as a means of minimising the effective mass (the latest SME arm, for example), and there are even fewer on which the transducer is permanently integrated.

The record player consists of the pickup and a turntable unit, the latter designed to turn the record with the minimum of long- or short-term speed variation and with the minimum of mechanical or electromechanical noise.

PICKUP CARTRIDGES

The cartridge derives its electrical output from the vibrations imparted to the stylus from the passing modulation 'wriggles' recorded on the walls of the groove. Signal generation can be achieved by a variety of well known electrical principles, including piezo-electric, electromagnetic, resistive (i.e. strain-gauge principle), photoelectric and capacitive (i.e. electrostatic). All these have been used, but by far the most popular at the time of writing is the cartridge based on the electromagnetic principle, of which there are various types.

MAGNETIC CARTRIDGES

Cartridges which use electromagnetism are commonly referred to simply as magnetic cartridges. One mode is the moving coil cartridge whose basic features are given in Fig. 8.1. This is the complement of the moving coil loudspeaker, whereby a freely supported coil of wire in a magnetic field is caused to vibrate,

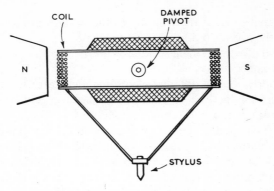

FIG. 8.1. *Basics of moving-coil cartridge*

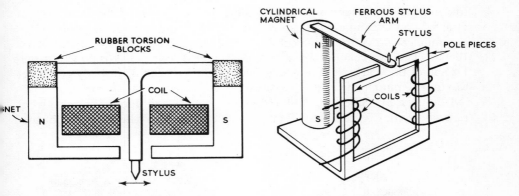

FIG. 8.2. *Basics of moving-armature pickup*   FIG. 8.3. *Basics of variable reluctance cartridge*

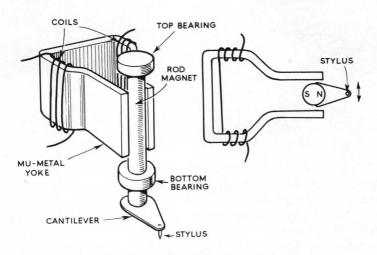

FIG. 8.4. *Basics of moving-magnet cartridge*

171

this yielding a signal e.m.f. in the winding to the pattern of the vibrations and hence to that of the groove modulation.

Instead of a coil of wire a single conductor in the form of a 'ribbon' may be used, the result being a ribbon cartridge.

Elementary impressions of different electromagnetic arrangements are given in Figs. 8.2, 8.3 and 8.4. In all these the signal voltage is produced by a changing magnetic flux through the coil. Only one channel is shown in these simple examples; the two channels required for stereo and for four-channel matrixing (Chapter 7) are obtained by the use of two identical electromagnetic systems each angled by 45 degrees relative to the surface of the record and 90 degrees to each other with a common stylus coupling, as shown in Fig. 7.2 (Chapter 7).

Modern two-channel cartridges exhibit some remarkable electromechanical engineering in miniature. The stylus assembly and its mounting is commonly built upon a plastics moulding which can be pushed on to or slipped into the main housing. The stylus assembly also carries either a low mass magnet (moving magnet system) or ferrous metal armature (variable reluctance system) coupled to the cantilever which, when slipped on to or into the main body, communicates electromagnetically with the signal coils and their pole pieces therein. The two-channel signals are delivered to four pins positioned at the far end of the body, and the fixing holes or slots on the main body correlate to $\frac{1}{2}$ in (12.7 mm) fixing centres on the headshell, which is the standard.

Examples by Goldring, Audio-Technica, Shure and Pickering are given respectively in Figs. 8.5, 8.6, 8.7 and 8.8. The extracted stylus assembly of the

FIG. 8.5. *Goldring magnetic cartridge in which the flux is introduced to the armature by an internal magnet (induced magnet principle). This works rather like a variable reluctance cartridge*

FIG. 8.6. *Audio-Technical magnetic cartridge. This is based on the moving magnet principle, but uses two low-mass magnetics mounted in vee-formation*

Pickering, which carries a small groove-cleaning brush, is shown in Fig. 8.9. The tube protruding from this carries the armature which is attached to the stylus cantilever and which pushes into the main part of the body in which are the coils and pole pieces.

Some early pickups used the metal stylus (then called 'needle') as the armature, the system being after the style of that in Fig. 8.2. Decca have followed

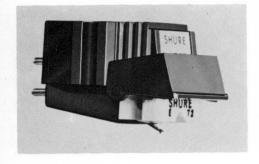

FIG. 8.7. *Another magnetic cartridge, by Shure*

FIG. 8.8. *This Pickering magnetic cartridge includes a small brush on the stylus assembly which trails on the record and removes dust*

this principle all the way through to the present state of the art, exemplified in the Mark IV and the more recent Mark V (London) cartridges. Decca call this 'positive scanning', and one version of the Mark IV cartridge is shown in Fig. 8.10.

The electrical part of this works on the so-called 'sum-and-difference' principle, whereby a lateral sensing coil and two vertical sensing coils are adopted, as shown in Fig. 8.11. The system operates in the manner explained below.

Assuming that only the left channel of a stereo record carries modulation, then the e.m.f.s produced by coils C, D and E will be equal. However, the phasing

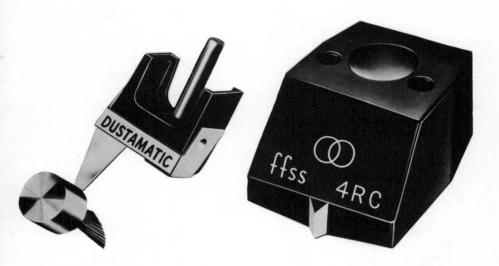

FIG. 8.9. *The stylus assembly of the Pickering cartridge. This slips into the main body*

FIG. 8.10. *Decca sum-and-difference 'positive scanning' cartridge, which is one of the Mark IV models. There is now a Mark V, called the London*

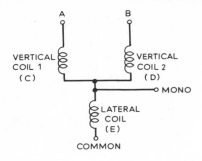

FIG. 8.11. *The sensing coils of the Decca sum-and-difference magnetic cartridge (see text for explanation)*

FIG. 8.12. *Moving-coil cartridge by Ortofon. This needs an external matching transformer (see text)*

of the coils is such that the e.m.f. of coil E adds to the e.m.f. of coil C, so that an output occurs at left terminal A with respect to the common terminal. Since coils C and D yield anti-phase signals the e.m.f. of coil D is subtracted from the e.m.f. of coil E, which results in cancellation and hence no output at right terminal B with respect to the common terminal.

With only the right channel recorded the converse effect occurs; that is the e.m.f. of coil D will add to the e.m.f. of coil E and produce an output at terminal B relative to the common terminal, while the e.m.f.s of coils C and E will cancel so that no output occurs at terminal A.

For mono operation (also see Chapter 7) of this cartridge it is necessary only to use the e.m.f. yielded by the lateral sensing coil, for which a terminal is provided.

An example moving-coil cartridge is shown in Fig. 8.12, which is by Ortofon. Owing to the relatively small signal voltage yield of moving-coil and ribbon cartridges a step-up transformer (or specially-matching, low-noise transistor preamplifier) is required for coupling it to the 'standard' magnetic input sensitivity of contemporary amplifiers. To keep down the weight of the cartridge, this is usually arranged nowadays as a separate add-on unit.

All magnetic cartridges produce signal voltages in proportion to the velocity of the modulation (see Chapter 7), and since records are recorded on a rising (with frequency) velocity characteristic (i.e. essentially constant amplitude) equalisation is required in the reproducing amplifier to produce a 'flat' (with frequency) output, see Chapters 3 and 7 in particular.

PIEZO-ELECTRIC CARTRIDGES

Early piezo pickups used a natural crystal element, such as Rochelle salt, as the signal generator, and these were called 'crystal' pickups. More recent species, particularly those used for better quality reproduction, use specially 'polarised' ceramic, and are thus called ceramic pickups or cartridges. Crystal pickups and cartridges are still being made but are mostly confined to those areas where quality of reproduction and record wear are not regarded as of major importance. They are thus found mostly in the inexpensive record player. The crystal pickup produces, in general, a greater signal (see under Cartridge Output, page 179) voltage for a given level of modulation than a better quality ceramic.

In both cases* the signal voltage stems from piezo-electricity which is produced when crystal elements of the type mentioned are mechanically deflected or stressed. The output can be regarded as a 'charge' across the plates of a capacitor (those either side of the crystal element) which varies in sympathy with the groove modulation.

Two-channel stereo piezo-electric cartridges employ two elements in the general 45/45 degree configuration coupled to the common stylus. The pair is sometimes cemented together to form a 'bimorph' and the elements are cut or processed so that the output from one occurs as the result of torque and from the other as the result of flexure, for which reasons they are termed 'twister' and 'bender' respectively. Lateral components activate the twister and vertical components the bender. Another arrangement consists of a 90 degree vee-shaped configuration, making it possible to employ two twisters, which require less stylus energy for a given output than benders.

A selection of stereo cartridge arrangements is given in Fig. 8.13. A well-known ceramic cartridge is the Deram by Decca, which is illustrated in Fig. 8.14. This is being made still (at the time of writing) and has evolved through a number of stages, the latest version employing an elliptical stylus.

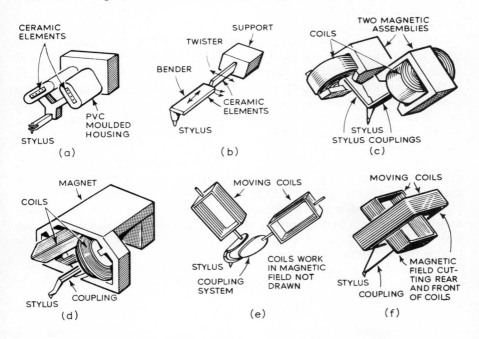

FIG. 8.13. A selection of cartridges; (a) and (b) piezo-electric (the Decca Deram uses type a); (c) and (d) basically variable reluctance types; (e) and (f) moving-coil types

*Strictly, it is the crystal cartridge which works on the piezo-electric principle. The ceramic cartridge works on the different but related principle of electrostriction (ref. Electrostriction, McGraw-Hill Encyclopaedia of Science and Technology, Vol. 4, p. 613).

FIG. 8.14. *The well-known Decca Deram cartridge in recent format*

STYLI

Latest stylus tips are sapphire and diamond, the former being confined to the less exotic crystal and ceramic cartridges. Replacement generally involves changing the complete stylus assembly (Fig. 8.9) in the case of magnetics or the cantilever in the case of crystal and ceramics. Some cartridges, in which the stylus is an integral part of the design, like moving coil and the Decca sum-and-difference London and B & O types, need to be returned to the manufacturer/dealer for attention, though the general scheme is that a new replacement cartridge is supplied on a part-exchange basis.

Early microgroove records required a stylus of 25 μm (0.001 in) radius; but the latest mono, stereo and matrixed (excluding CD-4) discs call for the smaller radius of 12.5 μm (0.0005 in). Clearly, the smaller the tip radius, the better will be the tracing of high-frequency modulation, particularly towards the end of the groove where the groove/stylus velocity is falling and hence the waves of the modulation closing up. However, if the radius is much smaller than 12.5 μm (0.0005 in) the stylus tends to 'bottom' in the groove and generate more noise than necessary.

This is overcome by the biradial or elliptical stylus which has a major axis of around 17.5 μm (0.0007 in) across the groove to prevent 'bottoming' and a minor axis of about 7.5 μm (0.0003 in) for modulation tracing. There are variations in the major and minor radial dimensions; but in all cases the aim is to achieve optimum high-frequency and short wavelength modulation tracing with the least noise due to 'bottoming' effects. The improved high-frequency tracing that the elliptical stylus provides is illustrated in Fig. 8.15.

STYLI FOR CD-4 RECORDS

As told in Chapter 7, CD-4 four-channel records contain modulation frequencies up to at least 45 kHz, and since these records operate at the standard $33\frac{1}{3}$ r.p.m. it follows that the high-frequency waves will be extremely compressed, particularly at the inner diameters of the record. For maximum definition of the waves, therefore, which is essential for proper demodulation of the 'multiplex' information, the stylus tracing radius must be as small as possible.

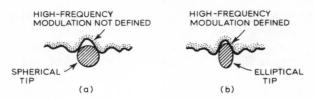

FIG. 8.15. *Showing how an elliptical tip defines high-frequency modulation better than a spherical tip whose radius must be sufficiently large to avoid groove 'bottoming'*

This has led to the creation of a new 'multiradius' stylus of facets shown at (*a*) in Fig. 8.16. For comparison the features of the elliptical stylus are shown at (*b*). The CD-4 stylus has sides which are cut sharply away behind the groove contact area so that the actual defining radius is even smaller than that of the elliptical stylus. Moreover, as viewed from the front, (*c*) and (*d*) in Fig. 8.16, the

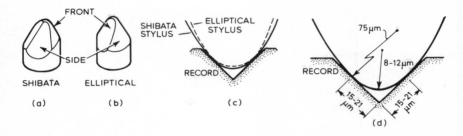

FIG. 8.16. *The CD-4 Shibata stylus compared with the elliptical stylus, and in profile (see text)*

sides are less rounded than the elliptical stylus, which allows maximum vertical contact with the groove walls. This offsets the smaller fore-aft contact surface area and thus distributes the tracking weight over a greater area.

The stylus is cut from nude diamond which demands sophisticated cutting techniques and machinery with measuring accuracy in terms of microns. Because the stylus makes contact with the groove over a larger than normal area, the actual pressure in the groove is comparable to that produced by a conventional stylus tracking at a lower force. It is thus possible to operate a cartridge with a CD-4 stylus at a greater tracking weight than a cartridge with a conventional stylus for a given rate of wear; but, of course, the cartridge must be designed to accommodate this extra weight in terms of its compliance.

The type of stylus described is called 'Shibata', after its maker. Another also designed for CD-4 disc replay is the 'Ichikawa'.*

While on the subject of CD-4 record replay it is noteworthy that to avoid high distortion and to ensure that the modulated carrier wave holds to a usable level towards the end of the groove, the groove is concluded before the inner diameter of a conventional stereo record is reached. This, of course, reduces the playing time, which is far better than either running out of carrier or into high distortion (or both!). Recent techniques are combating this shortfall.

*That used in the recent B & O MMC 6000 four-channel cartridge is called a Pramanik stylus.

177

The author has played a CD-4 record with a light-tracking cartridge responsive to 45 kHz equipped with a good elliptical stylus; but the results were not as good as obtained with a cartridge specifically designed for a 45 kHz response carrying a Shibata or Ichikawa stylus. Perfect replay in the stereo mode, however, is possible from a CD-4 record with a light-tracking stereo cartridge and elliptical stylus; though there is less wear with a Shibata or Ichikawa stylus.

In the four-channel mode, of course, the capacitance of the pickup connecting leads (to the demodulator) must be very small to prevent attenuation of the modulated carrier wave.

There are two main ways by which the high-frequency performance of a cartridge may be upgraded, one is to lower the mechanical impedance of the vibratory system by mass reduction, and the other is to raise the upper-treble resonance frequency either by hardening the record material or by increasing the contact area between the tip of the stylus and the record.

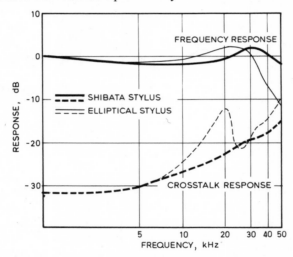

FIG. 8.16(e). *Frequency response and separation performance of CD-4 cartridge using Shibata and elliptical styli, showing improvement obtained with the Shibata stylus*

Cartridges for CD-4 application must, of course, be good high-frequency trackers, which implies very low effective tip mass; but also, owing to the greater area of contact with the record of the CD-4 type styli, the upper-treble resonance frequency is automatically increased. The Shibata stylus, for instance, has a four time larger contact area and, with a given CD-4 cartridge, the curves in Fig. 8.16(e) show the improvement in both high-frequency response and upper-treble separation provided by the Shibata stylus over an elliptical stylus.

PLAYING MATRIX RECORDS

Any good quality stereo cartridge is suitable for playing matrix records since all the information is recorded as audio signal and accommodated in the normal way on the left and right walls of the groove.

DISC REPRODUCTION

Back now to mono and stereo play, a compromise stylus dimension is 17.5 μm (0.0007 in) spherical. This is sometimes found in the less advanced type of magnetic cartridge and is suitable for playing both the earlier microgroove records and the latest mono and stereo releases; it is also suitable for matrix discs, though the better definition afforded by the elliptical stylus is generally preferred.

The elliptical stylus is also suitable for playing the earlier microgroove records since its major radius prevents groove 'bottoming'.

STYLI FOR 78 RECORDS

None of the styli mentioned is suitable for playing the very early 78 r.p.m. records. Radii from 62.5 μm (0.0025 in) to 100 μm (0.004 in) are required for these records. Some of the recent magnetic cartridges with detachable stylus assemblies can be equipped with an assembly carrying a stylus of radius suitable for 78 r.p.m. records. Quite a few of the cartridge manufacturers themselves are able to supply such assemblies. Alternatively, a service of considerable value to collectors of early 78s is provided by Expert Pickups Limited. This firm specialises in fitting 78-type styli to customers' own stylus assemblies or cantilevers. Radii up to 100 μm (0.004 in) are available.

Incidentally, we talk of 'spherical' tips, while what is actually meant of course is a cone with a hemispherical end!

CARTRIDGE OUTPUT

The output from a cartridge is referred to recorded velocity, and a nominal value from many of the recent magnetics is 1 mV r.m.s. per cm/s r.m.s. velocity at 1 kHz, sometimes given as 5 mV referred to a recording level of 5 cm/s.

Few cartridges of the moving-magnet and variable reluctance species yield an output as high as 2.5 or even 3 mV per cm/s. On the other hand, moving-coil and ribbon cartridges have a much lower direct output, not uncommonly around 50 or 100 μV per cm/s. However, after the step-up transformer or transistor 'booster' the output approximates that from a high-output variable reluctance cartridge, often being as high as 3 or 4 mV per cm/s.

A high output magnetic cartridge can, of course, encourage preamplifier overload when the overload margin of the preamplifier is poor or mediocre (see Chapter 3).

OUTPUT FROM PIEZO CARTRIDGES

While the output from a magnetic cartridge is proportional to the recording velocity, the output from a piezo cartridge is proportional to the *amplitude* of stylus deflection. Nevertheless, the output is often referred to a given velocity at 1 kHz, usually at the 'standard' recording level. Crystals can have an output of 1 V or more, but those destined for better quality service generally have a lower output than this, and this applies particularly to the better class ceramics, whose nominal output may be between 50 and 200 mV.

179

CARTRIDGE LOADING

Cartridge output is influenced by the load connected across it, and with most magnetics the load required for the best overall frequency response (particularly at the treble end) is in the order of 47,000 ohms in shunt with 100–200 pF of capacitance reflected from the screened signal leads and amplifier input. It is best to keep shunt capacitance as low as possible. However, as brought out in Chapter 3, the feedback equalisation of the input preamplifier can affect the input impedance, thereby tending (not in all cases of good preamplifier design) to modify slightly the pickup's response at the high-frequency end.

For true constant amplitude response, piezo cartridges need to be loaded with a much higher value of resistance, in the order of megohms, to prevent too early roll-off of the bass. Since the RIAA recording characteristic approximates to constant amplitude, the output from a piezo cartridge is essentially 'flat' over the spectrum, mechanical equalisation sometimes being incorporated to counteract the mild deviation from constant amplitude.

It is possible to achieve an output approximating to 'velocity' from a piezo cartridge by loading with a low value resistor and/or including an 'equalising' network between the cartridge and the preamplifier's input, the RIAA equalisation of the preamplifier then being used, as in the case of magnetic cartridges, to 'flatten' the response. This also causes the output voltage to fall to a value comparable to that of a magnetic cartridge (see page 65). All these aspects of cartridge loading are considered in greater detail in Chapter 3.

It is noteworthy that the output from a piezo cartridge also falls when it is presented with shunt capacitance; which, of course, is because the source is capacitive.

FREQUENCY RESPONSE

The frequency response is affected not only by the electrical loading, but also by mechanical resonances of the pickup system as a whole. At the high-frequency end, good magnetic cartridges are designed so that the falling response resulting from the LCR components (see page 54) is complemented by the rising response resulting from the effective tip mass resonating with the compliance of the record material and, possibly, with the compliance of the stylus coupling elements (i.e. cantilever, etc.).

This is clearly brought out by the Shure diagram in Fig. 8.17, which shows how the falling electrical response of the V15/III is counteracted by the rising output due to mechanical resonance. Since the two curves are complementary, the net effective response is 'flat'.

At the high-frequency end, therefore, the response rolls off after the resonance rather as a low-pass filter characteristic.

The response at the low-frequency end is determined by a high-pass filter characteristic instigated by the effective mass of the pickup (counterweighted arm, headshell and cartridge) resonating with the compliance of the cartridge. To avoid too early bass roll-off, therefore, this resonance must not be too far up the frequency scale. It is, however, of significant importance to other aspects of record reproduction, for if it falls at a very low frequency the stability of low-

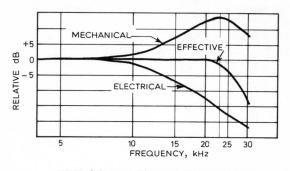

FIG. 8.17. *Curves showing how the electrical response of the Shure V 15/III cartridge is complemented by the mechanical response to provide a flat effective response*

frequency tracking is affected, while if it falls at a frequency corresponding to turntable unit noise and vibrations, these will be amplified unduly, which is often the cause of 'rumble'. Moreover, there may be more than one l.f. resonance due to different values of vertical and lateral compliance and different modes of arm resonance.

DAMPING

If the l.f. and h.f. resonances are poorly damped, the overall response could be as shown by the broken-line curves in Fig. 8.18, while optimum damping would give the response as described by the full-line curves. Top-quality hi-fi magnetic

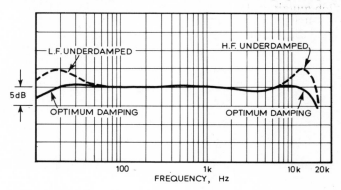

FIG. 8.18. *Inadequate l.f. and h.f. damping (broken-line curves). Optimum l.f. and h.f. damping (full-line curves)*

cartridges incorporate sufficient damping to avoid undue treble peaks, while some arms are equipped with damping to tame peaks at the bass end. The frequency response of the Shure V15/III cartridge when mounted in a high quality arm (such as the SME) is given in Fig. 8.19. The frequency response of a cartridge with a peaky treble resonance is given in Fig. 8.20.

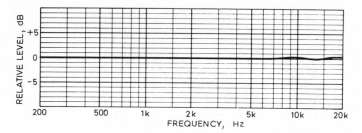

FIG. 8.19. *Frequency response of Shure V15/III cartridge in partnership with high quality arm*

It is noteworthy that many moving-magnet and variable reluctance type cartridges exhibit a mild dip around 5 to 6 kHz (Fig. 8.20). This also results from resonance modes and electromechanical aspects of the design. It is not particularly easy to clear, and even the Shure V15 versions prior to the Mark III were subject to this sort of 'suck out'; but as shown by Fig. 8.19 curve, it has been cleared from the Mark III version.

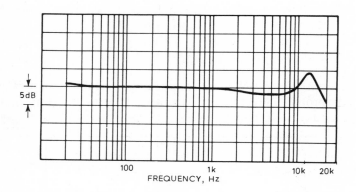

FIG. 8.20. *Showing the treble peak of a cartridge with early and underdamped h.f. resonance*

CARTRIDGE PARAMETERS

Mechanical parameters of a cartridge include compliance, effective tip mass and mechanical resistance (i.e. damping).

COMPLIANCE

Compliance expresses freedom of movement (opposite of stiffness), and is given in terms of deflection (compression, etc.) distance divided by the force in dynes, such that one 'compliance unit' equals 10^{-6} cm/dyne (or 10^{-3} m/N in SI units). Thus, one compliance unit results from one-millionth cm deflection when the force is one dyne.

182

DISC REPRODUCTION

EFFECTIVE TIP MASS

Effective tip mass is that mass reflected to the stylus tip due not only to the mass of the tip itself (diamond), but also to the 'geared-down' mass of the motor coupling to the transducing element.

MECHANICAL RESISTANCE

Mechanical resistance is given in mechanical ohms, and refers to the general damping of the stylus and its coupling system.

Electrical analogues of compliance, mass and mechanical resistance are capacitance, inductance and electrical resistance respectively.

ASPECTS OF TRACKING

The three above mentioned parameters determine the tracking ability of the cartridge. The compliance mostly affects the low-frequency tracking, the effective tip mass the high-frequency tracking and the mechanical resistance the overall tracking, but more particularly that round the middle frequencies, depending on its nature.

Mistracking is said to occur when the stylus tip fails to communicate accurately with the modulation recorded on the walls of the groove. The effect is a sharp rise in harmonic and intermodulation distortion, coupled with disconcerting 'crackling' noises on high-frequency transients. As the tip of the stylus is following the modulation forces of significant magnitude are produced which tend to eject the stylus from the groove. A specific downward force thus needs to be applied (tracking weight) to keep the stylus in the groove. The amount of tracking weight required is a function of the forces generated; the greater the forces, the greater the tracking weight required for stylus/groove communication.

A major force results from the acceleration of the effective tip mass, increasing both with mass M and acceleration g, such that force F equals Mg. For the least record/stylus wear the tracking weight should be as small as possible. Some of the best quality magnetic cartridges track right down to 1 gram or less at all frequencies, even on records of high dynamic range where the accelerations (see expression 7.3, Chapter 7) at high-frequency can be substantial, to say the least! This can only be achieved when the effective tip mass is of a very small order. For example, from $F = Mg$ a force of 1.666 grams can be calculated from an effective tip mass of a mere 1 milligram when g is 1666, corresponding, say, to modulation of 26 cm/s at 10 kHz.

From first principles, therefore, assuming a tip mass of 1 milligram, the tracking weight would need to be at least 1.666 gram for correct tracking of that modulation. To provide tracking at the above mentioned velocity and frequency at 1 gram, then, the effective tip mass would have to be about 0.6 milligram. The tracking, however, is affected also by h.f. resonance and the arm parameters, so the effective tip mass would in practice need to be smaller than this! The Shure V15/III, by way of an example, has an effective tip mass of 0.33 milligram, and is specified as tracking 26 cm/s 10 kHz modulation at a weight of 1 gram in the SME arm.

For tracking the lower frequencies the compliance must be at least as large as that required to accommodate the maximum 0.005 cm amplitude modulations at the specified tracking weight. Compliance C in 10^{-6} cm/dyne is equal to amplitude A in cm divided by force F in dynes (i.e. $C = A/F$). Thus, if the maximum amplitude is taken as 0.005 cm and the tracking force as 1 gram ($= 980$ dynes), then the minimum compliance must be 5.102×10^{-6} cm/dyne, or 5.102 'compliance units' (cu).

In practice, vertical and lateral compliances greater than this are encountered in contemporary cartridges, but the effective value is influenced by mechanical resistance (i.e. damping) while the l.f. tracking, as already noted, can be affected by the compliance/effective arm mass resonance(s). There is also a difference between so-called 'dynamic compliance' (measured via record modulation) and static compliance (an actual measurement of deflection), since the former is essentially low-frequency mechanical impedance.

While the parameters of effective tip mass and compliance may be specified (usually the latter, not very often the former) by the cartridge manufacturer, the mechanical resistance ingredient is never readily available, which is understandable since it is a complex factor.

Tracking ability is now more often expressed in terms of the minimum tracking weight required faithfully to handle specified velocities at stated frequencies without mistracking (particularly by Shure, the firm which coined the term 'trackability'). Tracking ability thus takes account of the compliance, effective tip mass and mechanical resistance; but it must be stressed again that the pickup arm figures significantly in the overall tracking performance (see later).

RESONANCES

A primary h.f. resonance results from the effective tip mass resonating with the compliance of the record material, and from expression 1.27 in Chapter 1 it can be seen that the smaller the mass M and/or compliance C, the higher the resonance frequency f_0. If the compliance of the record material is taken as 3×10^{-8} cm/dyne (3×10^{-5} m/N in SI) (a commonly given value, but it depends on the nature of the material, the tip radius, temperature and tracking weight) and the effective tip mass as 1 milligram, then f_0 will be in the order of 29 kHz. Tip masses greater than 1 milligram will reduce to f_0, but it requires a mass greater than 2 milligrams to bring f_0 into the passband, based on the record compliance given.

Another h.f. resonance which could be of greater in-band significance is that due to the mass at the end of the cantilever remote from the tip resonating with the cantilever compliance. For extended h.f. response, especially as required for playing CD-4 records, such resonances must be well tamed.

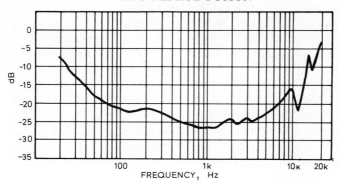

FIG. 8.21. *Magnetic cartridge stereo separation curve, showing how h.f. resonances can affect the h.f. separation*

STEREO SEPARATION

Resonances can also affect the isolation between the two channels of a stereo cartridge, as shown in Fig. 8.21. At middle frequencies, the separation is generally at maximum, not uncommonly between 35 and 20 dB, referred to the speaking channel, but at the frequencies where resonances are troublesome the separation falls swiftly and sometimes exhibits peaks and troughs. For good stereo image placement the separation should not be less than 20 dB over the important part of the spectrum (i.e. from about 100 Hz to 10 kHz), and there should not be great differences in separation referred to either non-speaking channel.

LOW-FREQUENCY RESONANCE

When the pickup arm is adjusted to counterbalance the cartridge/headshell and adjustment made for the required tracking weight, the effective mass of the arm under these conditions is reflected to the tip of the stylus. When the stylus is in contact with the groove the compliance of the cartridge yields a condition of resonance with the effective arm mass, the f_o in this case falling at a low value. For example, an effective mass of 25 grams and a compliance of 30 cu will produce a resonance at 5.812 Hz; f_o will increase to 6.498 Hz when M is reduced to 20 grams and to 7.959 Hz when C is 20 cu and M 20 grams.

When f_o is much below 10 Hz there is a general tendency for unstable tracking since the resonance can be excited by disc ripples and l.f. vibrations, such as may result from the suspension of the motor board or turntable unit.

On the other hand, when f_o falls around 22.5 Hz the resonance can be excited by drive motor 'vibrations', since this frequency corresponds to the 'slip frequency' of certain induction type motors; the result being an aggravation of 'rumble'. If f_o is much higher the bass output will be impaired owing to the high-pass filter effect already mentioned.

Clearly, for the best results the arm/cartridge partnership needs to be chosen with some care. The general rule is that a cartridge of high compliance should be used with an arm of the lowest mass so that f_o falls within the range of about 8 to 18 Hz. The recent SME 3009/II arm with the integrated headshell (which results in a smaller M than when the headshell is detachable, though can be less convenient) has an effective mass of about 6.75 grams when adjusted to track at 1 gram. Including the cartridge, M could rise to 10 or 11 grams, depending on its weight which, with a C of 25 cu, puts f_o at 9.599 or 10 Hz. With a C of 30 cu, f_o falls to 8.762 or 9.19 Hz.

From the l.f. tracking aspect there seems to be little merit in making C unduly large; indeed, a too 'sloppy' suspension will limit the maximum tracking weight owing to suspension 'bottoming'. It will also be appreciated that a low inertia arm is also required with a high compliance cartridge to avoid undue stylus deflection which could result from disc eccentricity.

ARM FEATURES

For optimum tracking the arm must also have very low bearing friction, corresponding to little more (or possibly less) than 20 milligrams at the stylus tip to break the friction both laterally and vertically.

LATERAL TRACKING ERROR CORRECTION

During recording the cutter head takes a true radial path across the disc as shown by the broken line in Fig. 8.22; but when played by a pickup with a

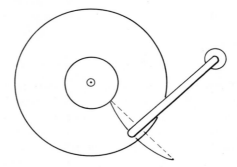

FIG. 8.22. *Showing deviation from true radial cutting and pivoted replay. This deviation results in distortion and is counteracted by offset and overhang (see Fig. 8.23 and text)*

pivoted arm, the stylus follows a curved path as shown by the full line. The deviation is known as the lateral tracking error, and it is responsible for significant distortion.

The error is corrected to a very large degree by the design and adjustment of the arm/cartridge combination. The plan is to achieve near consistent 90 degree angles between the axis of the cartridge and a true disc radius at all positions of the pickup on the disc, and this is arranged by offsetting the axis of the cartridge from that of the arm and adjusting so that the stylus tip overhangs the turntable pivot.

In Fig. 8.23 θ_2 is the offset angle and $d_3 - d_2$ the overhang. The tracking error is thus $90° \pm (\theta_1 + \theta_2)$, which means that there is zero error when $\theta_1 + \theta_2 = 90°$.

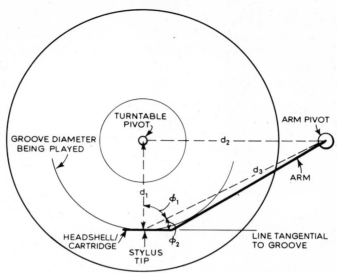

FIG. 8.23. *Illustrating conditions of lateral tracking error. Use in conjunction with expression 8.1* (*see text*)

The following expression, used in conjunction with Fig. 8.23, is useful for calculating the offset angle (θ_2) for zero error, with the overhang $(d_3 - d_2)$ and the effective arm length (d_3) as parameters:

$$\cos x = \frac{d_1^2 - (d_3 - d_2)^2 + 2d_3(d_3 - d_2)}{2d_3 d_1} \tag{8.1}$$

where ϕ_2 for zero tracking error is $90° - x$.

Many combinations of offset and overhang are thus possible for zero lateral tracking error, but pickup designers select that which yields the least error at all arm positions, based on the effective length of the arm. In practice, it is the user's job to adjust the arm or cartridge in the headshell for the least error at the inner groove diameter, using an alignment protractor, for it is here, where the modulation waves are most compressed, that the distortion due to lateral tracking error is highest. With a well designed and adjusted arm the maximum error should not be much greater than 1 to 2 degrees.

There are few record players incorporating virtually true radial tracking, such as those by Bang and Olufsen, Garrard (Zero 100SB), etc.

SIDE-THRUST

Owing to the overhang, the drag of the stylus in the groove gives rise to a force which is displaced from the axis of the arm, as shown in Fig. 8.24 by F_1. This in turn yields torque T_1, and to avoid pressure imbalance of the stylus relative to the two walls of the groove, which can affect both the balance of stereo separation and tracking performance, a counteracting force F_2 is applied by the deliberate introduction of torque T_2. This is applied either magnetically (as patented by Decca and used, for example, on the Decca International arm) or by means of a weight, such as a small weight hanging on a thin thread (as introduced by John Crabbe, Editor of *Hi-Fi News and Record Review*, in the May 1960 issue of *Wireless World*). In both cases the torque resulting from the force biases the arm away from the centre of the record by an adjustable amount.

The amount of bias required is governed by the stylus drag and thus by the frictional properties of the disc, the radius of the stylus, the tracking weight and,

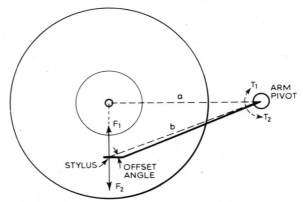

FIG. 8.24. *Showing forces resulting from overhang and the forces required for correction*

of course, by the modulation level of the record. The adjustment, therefore, can only be regarded as a compromise (but certainly a worthwhile one), and is best made under dynamic conditions in conjunction with tracking weight adjustment, aiming for the adjustment which provides optimum tracking of a given band of test modulation at the least tracking weight. A very useful record, carrying such test bands, is that produced by Clement Brown, Editor of *Hi-Fi Sound*, in conjunction with John Wright, the loudspeaker designer. It is called HFS69 and is marketed by *Haymarket Publishing Limited*, Gillow House, 5 Winsley Street, London, W1N 8AP.

It was at one time concluded that T_1 decreased with reducing playing diameter, and as a consequence T_2 is often arranged to reduce as the record plays out; but more recent work* has questioned this.

PICKUP ADJUSTMENTS

To minimise vertical tracking error the cartridge/headshell must be adjusted so that its vertical axis is at right-angles to the surface of the record (Fig. 8.25) and its horizontal axis is parallel with the surface of the record (Fig. 8.26). Undue distortion results from vertical tracking error, as from lateral tracking error. The condition shown in Fig. 8.25 would result in very high distortion and misplaying of CD-4 records.

There is usually a headshell/arm adjustment to cater for condition Fig. 8.25, while condition Fig. 8.26 is achieved by adjusting the height of the arm. It has already been mentioned that records are being made with a 15 degree angle of vertical cut and that cartridges are designed to correlate with this (Fig. 8.27); but

* See R. A. Dean in *Hi-Fi News*, Oct. 1969 and John Wright in *Hi-Fi News*, Oct., Nov. and Dec. 1969.

the latter follows only when condition Fig. 8.26 obtains and when the cartridge is operating within its designed tracking range.*

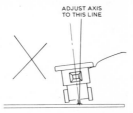

FIG. 8.25. *Align axis of cartridge as shown to reduce vertical tracking error*

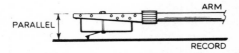

FIG. 8.26. *This is another important adjustment for optimum vertical tracking and to maintain the 15 degree vertical tracking angle*

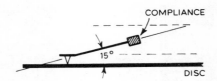

FIG. 8.27. *Illustration of 15 degree vertical tracking angle*

The arm is often counterbalanced (with the cartridge/headshell in situ of course!) by rear weight adjustments, the required tracking weight then being applied either by fine adjustment of the counterbalancing or by adjusting a secondary rider weight. The adjustment is often calibrated in one or half gram intervals. It is noteworthy that the effective mass of the arm is affected by rear weight adjustment, since the inertia is equal to the mass multiplied by the square of its distance from the point about which it acts.

FIG. 8.28. *Measurement of side-thrust correction force by Correx gauge in author's laboratory. Note offset angle of arm as examined in text (also see Fig. 8.23)*

*A new IEC and DIN standard is 20 degrees vertical tracking angle.

As already mentioned, it is desirable to adjust the side-thrust correction with the tracking weight in conjunction with a test record. An absolute measure of corrective force does not help much, though it may be practised during equipment tests, as shown in Fig. 8.28.

TRACKING TESTS

A record for subjective and objective determination of tracking performance is the Shure TTR-103. This contains test bands for h.f., m.f. (medium-frequency) and l.f. tracking. The first is 10.8 kHz sine wave filtered and pulsed at 270 Hz at peak velocities 15, 19, 24 and 30 cm/s for left and right channels. The second is 1 kHz plus 1.5 kHz lateral at peak velocities 20, 25, 31.5 and 40 cm/s. And the third is 400 Hz plus 4 kHz lateral at peak velocities 15, 19, 24 and 30 cm/s.

Oscilloscope analysis of the pickup signals from these bands gives a good impression of the tracking performance. For example, Fig. 8.29 shows at (a) the h.f. 15 cm/s band perfectly handled, and at (b) severe mistracking of the 30 cm/s

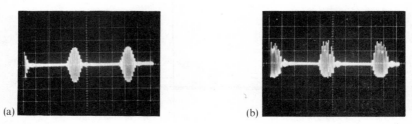

(a)　　　　　　　　　　　　　　　(b)

FIG. 8.29. *High-frequency tracking tests*, (a) *good tracking*, (b) *severe mistracking* (*see text for details*)

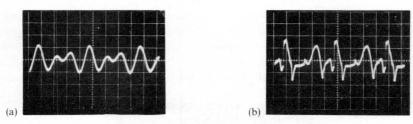

(a)　　　　　　　　　　　　　　　(b)

FIG. 8.30. *Medium-frequency tracking tests*, (a) *good tracking*, (b) *mistracking* (*see text for details*)

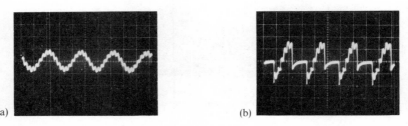

(a)　　　　　　　　　　　　　　　(b)

FIG. 8.31. *Low-frequency tracking tests*, (a) *good tracking*, (b) *severe mistracking* (*see text for details*)

band; Fig. 8.30 shows at (a) good handling of the m.f. 20 cm/s band, and at (b) severe mistracking of the 40 cm/s band; and Fig. 8.31 shows at (a) normal handling of the l.f. 15 cm/s band, and at (b) very severe mistracking of the 30 cm/s band. The pickup in question was tracking at 1.5 grams, and increasing the tracking weight failed to correct the high velocity mistracking. By using the intermediate bands, the tracking performance at the various frequencies can be established at any tracking weight; but the manufacturer's specified maximum should not be exceeded.

TRACKABILITY DEFINED

Shure define 'trackability' thus: 'The term 'trackability' refers to the ability of a phono pickup to reproduce high-level programme material. The trackability limit of a pickup at any given tracking force and frequency is defined as the modulation velocity (measured in cm/s) at which the stylus tip loses contact with one or both of the groove walls. The loss of contact results in severe distortion of the recorded programme material'.

By using a wave analyser, the percentage h.f. distortion (D_{high}) can be evaluated from

$$D_{high} = \frac{\text{voltage at 270 Hz}}{\text{voltage at 10.8 kHz}} \times 100 \qquad (8.2)$$

Similarly, the percentage m.f. distortion can be evaluated from

$$D_{m.f.} = \frac{\text{V at 2.5 kHz} + \text{V at 500 Hz}}{\text{V at 1 kHz} + \text{V at 1.5 kHz}} \times 100 \qquad (8.3)$$

Since the l.f. bands adhere to the SMPTE (Society of Motion Picture and Television Engineers) requirements for IMD analysis, the distortion due to mistracking of these bands is best evaluated this way (see Chapters 2 and 4, and expression 2.4).

Audible determination of mistracking is based on a tonal change at the mistracking threshold when the above mentioned bands are played over the system.

Further information on the Shure trackability tests and record is given by C. Roger Anderson and Paul W. Jenrick in the *Journal of the Audio Engineering Society*, Volume 20, No. 3, April 1972.

OTHER PICKUP DISTORTIONS

Second harmonic distortion arises from normal mis*tracing* of the modulation waveforms, as shown in Fig. 8.32, which obviously increases with frequency and

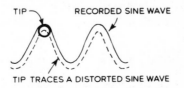

FIG. 8.32. *Illustration of tracing distortion*

recording level. Since the modulation waves compress as the playing diameter decreases, this sort of distortion also increases as the record plays out. However, the smaller the tip radius, the less the distortion, which is where the elliptical stylus has significant merit. High-frequency tracing distortion on the pickup signal is shown in Fig. 8.33, which is the electrical representation of the effect shown in Fig. 8.32. This distortion can rise to very high values at high velocity

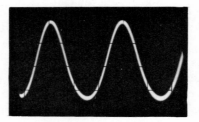

FIG. 8.33. *Electrical representation of tracing distortion (see text)*

and high-frequency, very much greater than produced by the other items of the reproducing chain.

Incorrect adjustment of the lateral and vertical tracking of the pickup can also aggravate distortion; but that resulting from 'normal' errors is generally less than tracing distortion.

PINCH EFFECT

Because the groove is cut by a chisel-shaped tool whose face is at right-angles to the motion of the record, the groove width decreases along the sloping sides

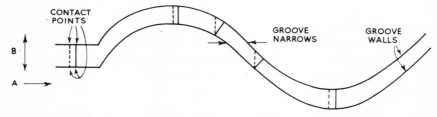

FIG. 8.34. *Illustration of the pinch effect. The full-lines across the groove indicate narrowing and hence a vertical replay component, while the broken-lines indicate the edge of the cutter*

of the waveform, as shown in Fig. 8.34. This, called 'pinch effect', results in vertical oscillation of the replay stylus at a frequency twice that of the modulation and hence in second-harmonic distortion; but owing to cancellation effects, pinch effect is less troublesome on stereo than mono.

SCANNING AND TRANSLATION LOSSES

Further consideration of Fig. 8.32 will make apparent that if the tip radius is too large for high velocity short wavelength (i.e. high-frequency) modulation

192

lack of definition will result with a consequent loss in output. This is called scanning loss.

Translation loss also results in diminishing high-frequency output, but this is generally considered to be caused by deformation of the record material at high accelerations, such that the tip fails fully to respond to the modulation.

CD-4 CARRIER

In the light of the foregoing, the reader may be wondering how the 30 kHz carrier of CD-4 records (with f.m. up to at least 45 kHz) can ever be defined, particularly at the inner diameters. The extra small active radius of the Shibata or Ichikawa stylus helps a lot, of course. Moreover, the carrier is recorded at a level some 19 dB below the L + R modulation (Fig. 7.5), so although the frequency is high the acceleration is low.

Indeed, it is rather surprising just how small the tracing distortion is on the carrier, as shown by the oscillogram of carrier direct from a pickup in Fig. 8.35. The oscillogram in Fig. 8.36 is unique since it shows the whole of the signal 'multiplex' from a pickup playing a CD-4 music record.

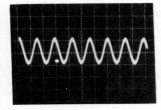

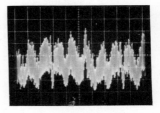

FIG. 8.36. *Unique oscillogram showing complete 'multiplex' from a pickup playing a CD-4 music record*

FIG. 8.35. *30 kHz carrier as obtained from a pickup playing a CD-4 record*

Low capacitance leads between the pickup and the CD-4 demodulator are essential, however, to avoid attenuation of the signal itself.

THE TURNTABLE UNIT

Energy is transmitted to the turntable either by pulleys on the motor drive spindle, via an intermediate 'jockey pulley' assembly (Fig. 8.37), or by the motor shaft, from stepped or 'ratio' pulleys thereon, via a belt (Fig. 8.38).

When the motor is suitably decoupled from the turntable bearing plate (i.e. motor board), the belt drive arrangement generally has the edge on the intermediate drive wheel arrangement in terms of rumble rejection.

RUMBLE

One method of measuring rumble is to establish a readout datum on 10 cm/s 1 kHz modulation from the pickup, via an RIAA-equalised preamplifier, and then compare this level with low-frequency signal from the pickup (after low-

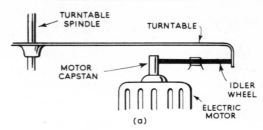

(a)

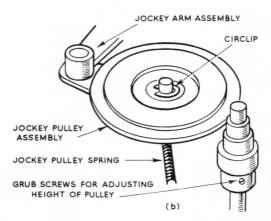

FIG. 8.37. *Turntable drives.* (a) *direct from motor capstan via idler and* (b) *from stepped pulley for speed change, via jockey pulley*

pass filtering to remove groove/stylus noise) when it is tracking an unrecorded groove (i.e. 'silent' groove). The ratio with a good belt-driven unit can be as high as 60 dB. Weighting to DIN, NAB, IEC, etc., is often used.

WOW AND FLUTTER

Wow (speed variations below about 20 Hz) and flutter (speed variations above about 20 Hz) can introduce spurious 'modulation' on the pickup signal, and

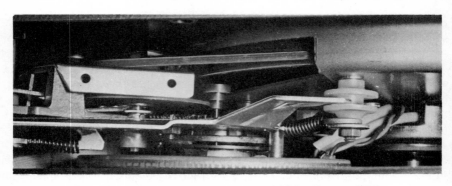

FIG. 8.38. *Belt drive arrangement (Bang and Olufsen Beogram 1000)*

these effects are avoided by careful design and machining of the drive surfaces, bearings, etc.

Speed constancy is provided either by a high mass, dynamically balanced turntable and fairly large, synchronous drive motor operating from a.c. mains supply, or by a lower mass turntable, also accurately balanced, and a smaller motor driven from an electronic circuit. One idea (Thorens TD125 Mk II record player) is based on an oscillator (Wien bridge type in Thorens) which is power amplified to operate the drive motor. Speed change (16, 33 and 45 Thorens) is achieved by frequency change of the oscillator.

With direct mains powering speed change is effected mechanically either by stepped pulleys or by a conical drive whose vertical position on the intermediate drive wheel ('idler') can be adjusted to provide both speed change and fine speed adjustment (Goldring-Lenco). Fine speed adjustment on the type operating from an oscillator merely resolves to a control which provides a small change in oscillator frequency.

ELECTRONIC CONTROL

Electronic systems lend themselves to 'servo' speed control. A small tacho generator (Pye, Ekco and Philips) is sometimes coupled to the drive motor, thereby 'sensing' any tendency for speed variation and introducing suitable correction to the electronics.

The motor control circuit of the record player used in the Ekco ZU8 (similar in the Philips units, etc.) is given in Fig. 8.39, where M is the drive motor and G the tacho generator. M is driven from TS432, which is controlled by TS427 and TS428. The generator output is rectified by the diode bridge and the voltage is fed back to TS427 for control. Now, should the motor speed tend to decrease, owing to an increasing load for example, the tacho output also decreases. This turns on more TS432 current, via the control circuit, to the drive motor, thereby increasing its speed or power to cater for the extra load.

Speed change (33, 45 and 78) is achieved by the switched potentiometer circuits at TS427 base. Variable control on each speed is also provided by the potentiometers.

The control is fast-working and is able to correct both long-term and short-term speed variations, including wow and flutter.

The bottom part of the circuit refers to the start and stop operation which works in conjunction with LDR (light-dependent resistor) 405 and associated transistors. TS430 and TS429 form a bistable circuit which controls TS431. In the off position TS431 is switched off, along with TS429, which removes the motor supply. Operating start switch SK4 changes the bistable mode, which turns on TS429, thereby powering the motor.

Switching off is achieved either by operating off switch SK3, which reverses again the bistable mode, or by moving the arm to the centre of the record (normally done by the play-out groove). This action results from a 'shutter' moving in front of LDR405 and its light source, such that the LDR resistance is increased (see Fig. 8.40). This is sensed by TS431, which communicates this

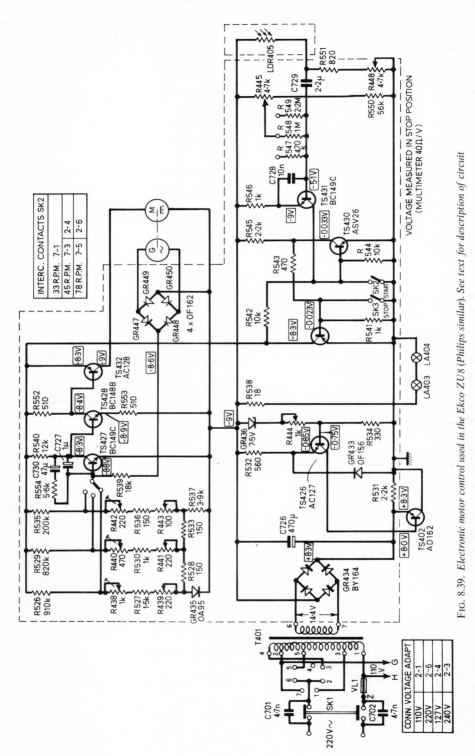

FIG. 8.39. *Electronic motor control used in the Ekco ZU8 (Philips similar). See text for description of circuit*

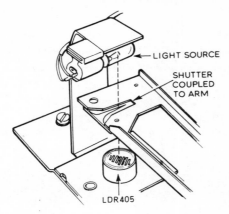

LIGHT SOURCE

SHUTTER COUPLED TO ARM

LDR405

FIG. 8.40. *Principle of Philips electronic automatic switch-off which involves no mechanical loading*

condition to TS430 base. The result is that the bistable mode changes and TS429 is switched off.

As the shutter gradually comes across the light source as the record plays out, the time-constant components on TS431 base prevent the switching action from occurring then. It is only when there is a large change is LDR405 illumination (i.e. on the run-out groove) that the switching action is precipitated.

TS402 and TS426 are concerned with supply stabilisation, via the mains transformer T401 and diode bridge GR434.

A major attribute of the scheme is that automatic switching is achieved without any load whatever being applied to the pickup.

There is a further development of the system (Philips), whereby touch buttons (buttons which 'sense' skin resistance and thus 'trigger' transistor switching circuits by the mere contact of a finger tip) are used for speed change and on/off.

There are other electronic control systems, including one by Goldring-Lenco and an elaborate arrangement by Bang and Olufsen, which incorporates true radial (tangential) tracking and automation (see Fig. 8.41).

Apart from the clockwork and hysteresis-governed units of past ages, the turntable (platter as it is now called) has always received its energy from a separate motor and drive system. This has been necessary because of the relatively high speed drive motor which calls for speed reduction. However, recent application of the Hall effect has made it possible to get the motor shaft to rotate at the selected record speed (33 or 45 r.p.m.), thereby allowing the turntable to be driven directly by the shaft and avoiding the use of ratio mechanical couplings and their attendant shortcomings.

One design (Dual) adopts this principle, such that the top of the motor shaft forms the record spindle. The motor is a d.c. type which is powered from a regulated supply. A pair of Hall effect devices, built into the motor, 'trigger' four switching semiconductors such that a rotating magnetic field is created, and on to this 'locks' the motor's rotor, which thus turns at the speed of the rotating field.

197

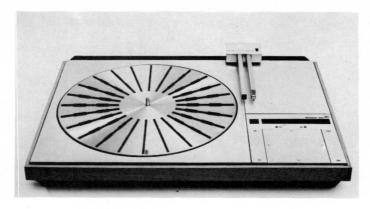

(a)

(b)

FIG. 8.41. *Current record player by Bang and Olufsen (Beogram 4000, Type 5215) with true tangential tracking and full automation (a). The arm is servo-controlled to eliminate imbalance of loading on groove walls, motors are electronically controlled, turntable speed is switched automatically as determined by record size, starting, stopping and cartridge set-down are automatic, a record place cueing indicator is included and it is also possible to cue-in accurately to any place on the record by servocontrol. (b) shows the photoelectric pickup lowering and disc size selection arm (parallel to the cartridge arm). A beam of light from this detector arm is reflected back to a photoelectric cell when there is no record on the turntable, and pulses produced by black ribs on the turntable prevent arm lowering*

198

A feedback control circuit provides instantaneous correction of speed by monitoring any variation and producing an increase or decrease of motor supply current as required. Overlapping of the field windings eliminates motor

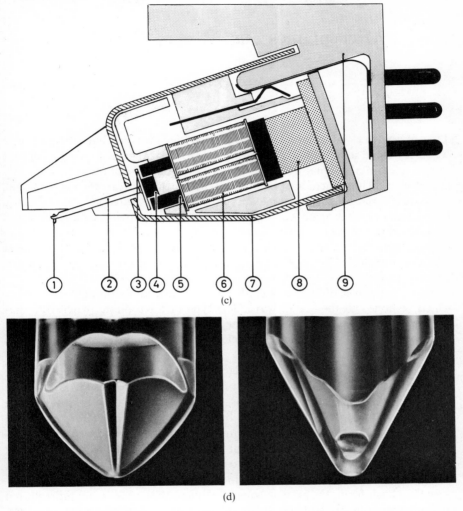

(c)

(d)

FIG. 8.41. (c) *Details of the low tracking weight cartridge used with the player, whose parameters are compatible with those of the arm. The elements shown are: 1 elliptical naked diamond; 2 ultra low-mass aluminium cantilever; 3 moving micro cross; 4 block suspension; 5 four pole pieces; 6 four signal coils; 7 mu-metal screen; 8 Hycomax magnet; 9 $\frac{1}{2}$-in mounting bracket. The last for use in standard headshell. A more recent B & O cartridge of similar design but with a Pramanik stylus for four-channel play is the MMC 6000. (d) shows the geometry of the Pramanik stylus, which is naked diamond with 7 μm horizontal contact and 50 μm vertical contact*

'pulsing' effects, and the motor is so free of vibrations that normal mechanical decoupling is unnecessary. Speed switching is electronic, of course, and each speed has its own fine control which works in conjunction with the circuits controlling the Hall effect devices.

CHAPTER 9

Microphones and Mixers

THE MICROPHONE IS the complementary of the loudspeaker; that is, from sound waves it yields a signal voltage. There are many physical principles which permit the production of a signal which is the electrical analogue of the vibrations in a sound wave. These include contact resistance variation (carbon microphone), resistance variation (strain gauge and glow discharge principle), piezo-electric (crystal and ceramic microphones), electromagnetic (moving coil, ribbon and moving armature microphones) and magnetostriction. All these principles, and others, have been experimented with over the years, but the three most commonly exploited principles are piezo-electric,* electromagnetic and electro-static or capacitive.

All microphones, of course, must have some form of diaphragm or element which responds to the sound wave. The type of microphone where the diaphragm is open to sound waves on one side only is called a *pressure-operated* microphone. Electromagnetic, piezo-electric and capacitor microphones are mostly of this type.

The ribbon microphone (of the electromagnetic family), on the other hand, tends to respond to the particle *velocity* of a sound wave because its diaphragm (ribbon in this case—see later) is exposed to the sound field on both sides. The movement of the ribbon is thus caused by the sound pressure *difference* between the two sides, for which reason it is generally known as a *pressure gradient* microphone. True velocity operation is not possible owing to the inefficiency of coupling of the ribbon to the velocity component of a sound wave, though this term may sometimes be used to describe the ribbon microphone.

In their basic forms the pressure-operated microphone has an omnidirectional response and the pressure gradient microphone a figure-of-eight response. However, these basic polar responses can be modified to yield different directional characteristics; in fact, omnidirectional ribbon microphones have been made, while a cardioid (heart-shaped) polar response can be achieved by combining the principles of pressure and pressure gradient.

PIEZO-ELECTRIC MICROPHONES

One method of piezo-electric microphone construction is shown in Fig. 9.1. The piezo-electric crystal is located at a critical angle between two electrodes so that

*Or electrostrictive (see note on page 175).

the pressure to which it is subjected varies in sympathy with the sound vibrations coupled in from the diaphragm. As already noted (Chapter 8), piezo-electricity is yielded by certain crystalline materials when subjected to stress, strain or pressure. Quartz is a typical natural crystal exhibiting this property; others include Rochelle salt, barium titanate, lead zirconate, ammonium di-

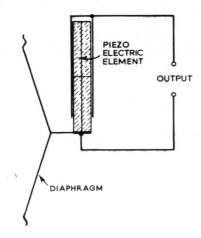

FIG. 9.1. *Elementary impression of piezo-electric microphone*

hydrogen phosphate, etc. Electrically polarised ceramic is another material, which is also used extensively in piezo-electric (ceramic) pickup cartridges.

Choice of crystalline material is referred to environmental, electrical and acoustical requirements. For example, at high temperatures quartz is generally required, though ammonium dihydrogen phosphate is suitable up to about 50 °C. The cheapest and most efficient material is Rochelle salt, but this is humidity sensitive; it will also dissolve in its own liquid of crystallisation at about 50 °C. Electrical output is also dictated by the type of crystal employed and the nature of the acoustical/mechanical coupling.

The simple, inexpensive piezo-electric microphone is not endowed with a very good frequency response, there often being treble peaking followed by roll-off due to upper-frequency resonance and roll-off to bass, depending on the electrical loading. However, some piezo-electric units are designed specifically for wide and smooth frequency response, with response sometimes well into the ultrasonic range. This type, of course, is more expensive and may be based on ammonium dihydrogen phosphate crystal.

There is another construction where the sound pressure acts directly on the crystal, composed of 'bimorph' benders, without the conventional diaphragm. The sound pressure causes bowing of the crystalline plates, wired to yield an additive electrical output. This type of microphone is commonly referred to as a 'sound cell'.

The source of a piezo-electric microphone is capacitive, so electrical coupling is best at high impedance. The input stage can be either a field effect transistor or bipolar transistor arranged for high input impedance, such as by boot-strapping (see Chapter 3, page 64).

(see Chapter 3, page 64)

MOVING-COIL MICROPHONES

Of the electromagnetic family, the moving coil microphone is basically similar in construction to the moving coil loudspeaker, but designed to operate in the converse mode (Fig. 9.2). A small diaphragm is fixed to the coil which is free to operate in a strong magnetic field supplied by circular pole pieces of a permanent magnet. Coil e.m.f. is proportional to the velocity of the coil vibrations.

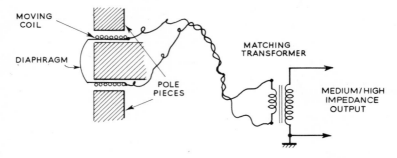

FIG. 9.2. *Moving-coil microphone with step-up impedance matching transformer*

The frequency response of this type of microphone is commonly better than that of the piezo-electric counterpart and resonances in general are more desirably tamed. The diaphragm and coil system exhibit a resonance around 400 Hz, while the *compliance* of the air between the diaphragm and the pole pieces produces a 4–6 kHz resonance in conjunction with the air *mass* in the coil gap. Various artifices are adopted to damp these resonances.

The source, of course, is essentially inductive and the impedance of the coil is of a low order, often around 30 ohms. The output in terms of signal voltage at this impedance is less than that of most piezo-electric microphones, and to achieve the most desirable coupling to the input of an amplifier a step-up transformer is commonly adopted. This, of course, steps up the signal voltage in proportion to the turns ratio and steps up the impedance by the square of the turns ratio. It is possible, however, to design a high-gain solidstate amplifier into which the low-level, low impedance microphone signal can be coupled directly, but noise, then, can represent a problem.

RIBBON MICROPHONES

The ribbon microphone exploits the same principle of signal generation as the moving-coil microphone, the conductor being formed solely by the metallic ribbon instead of by a coil. This means that the output and impedance are lower than with a moving-coil microphone. The ribbon is freely suspended between the pole pieces of a powerful magnet and is arranged so that sound waves can impinge upon both surfaces (Fig. 9.3).

The ribbon is generally made of aluminium foil and corrugated for maximum surface area. Ribbon microphones incorporate a transformer for stepping up the very low impedance to a value comparable with that of the moving-coil

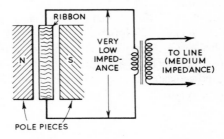

FIG. 9.3. *Basic principle of ribbon microphone with step-up impedance matching transformer*

microphone (30 ohms or so), though the transformers used in some models step up the impedance to a value suitable for direct application to a medium/high impedance amplifier input stage without the need for additional impedance matching.

CAPACITOR MICROPHONES

As implied by its name, this type of microphone is essentially a capacitor. One plate is 'fixed' and the other, consisting of a low mass metallic diaphragm adjacent to the fixed plate, is free to vibrate in sympathy with the sound waves. The capacitance thus varies in accordance with the sound information. A polarising voltage is required, and this is connected in series with the microphone through a high value resistor (Fig. 9.4) which, irrespective of diaphragm

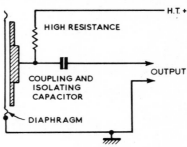

FIG. 9.4. *Elementary impression of capacitor microphone with coupling components*

movement, ensures that the charge remains at a fairly constant value. The voltage also keeps the diaphragm taut by electrostatic forces, since the diaphragm itself has little intrinsic rigidity.

Thus, as the capacitance alters in value the potential across the capacitor varies accordingly since this is equal to the charge divided by the capacitance.

The varying potential constitutes the signal voltage which is applied to a head amplifier with a suitably high input impedance, the output then being at the required impedance for the main amplifier.

The capacitor microphone is a high quality unit and is commonly used for many broadcasting and recording application of the 'professional' class. In somewhat lesser form it is used by amateur tape recordists, but it needs a top-flight recording machine to do full justice to a quality capacitor microphone.

A comparatively recent development of the capacitor microphone is the 'Electret' microphone, which employs a diaphragm composed of a thin polymer film and integrated circuit head amplifier. This type of microphone is used in the less professional sense, and may, in fact, be found as an integral part of the smaller type of tape recorder.

POLAR RESPONSES

As already mentioned, the pressure-operated microphone has an essentially omnidirectional polar response; that is, it is responsive to sounds arriving from all directions within its range. Its polar response thus has 'spherical' distribution. However, at frequencies where the wavelength is comparable with the size of the housing the response tends to veer more towards unidirectional, so that greater sensitivity is exhibited to sounds arriving from the front, as shown in Fig. 9.5.

The pressure-gradient microphone, on the other hand, has a figure-of-eight polar response, as shown in Fig. 9.6. This kind of microphone (i.e. the ribbon)

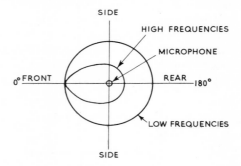

FIG. 9.5. *Omnidirectional response tends towards unidirectional with increasing frequency*

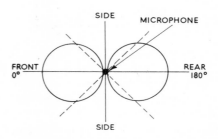

FIG. 9.6. *Figure-of-eight polar response characteristic of ribbon microphone in pressure-gradient mode*

204

responds mostly to sounds arriving at front or rear over an angle of about 100 degrees, depending on frequency. The polar response, however, can often be modified to suit the prevailing acoustical conditions or the requirements by 'closing' the rear by means of an acoustical filter (pad). Operation is then towards pressure and a unidirectional response results.

A cardioid (meaning heart-shaped) response can be achieved by the combination of the pressure and pressure-gradient principles. Combined microphones like this (i.e. cardioid microphones) are often used for broadcasting and recording applications, where rear sound could detract from the required 'sound picture'. The cardioid response is given in Fig. 9.7. Real cardioid microphones

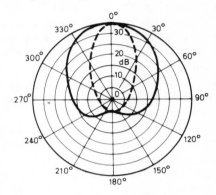

FIG. 9.7. *Cardioid polar response full-line and hypercardioid response broken-line*

are costly and generally outside the pocket of the average enthusiast; they might, nevertheless, be employed by the 'serious' amateur recordist and by organisations operating sound-reinforcement services.

MICROPHONE SENSITIVITY AND OUTPUT

Microphone sensitivity is expressed in decibels relative to 1 V and 1 μb (i.e. 1 dyne/cm² — see Chapter 1). Thus, a microphone specified as having a sensitivity of -80 dB 1 V/μb would yield an output 80 dB below 1 V (i.e. 0.1 mV) when subjected to a sound pressure of 1 μb.

Overall sensitivity, of course, is influenced by the output impedance. For example, a microphone might be specified as having an output of -88 dB at 25 ohms (direct from the coil) and -54 dB at 50 k-ohms (via a step-up transformer).

The output voltage is approximately proportional to the sound pressure, and it is interesting to note that the peak r.m.s. sound pressure at a distance of about 304 mm from a man's mouth is in the order of 10 μb with conversational speech, which means that the output from a microphone of, say, -80 dB sensitivity would be around 1 mV. The sound pressure decreases 6 dB each time the distance is doubled. When speaking with the mouth as close as possible to the microphone, the peak r.m.s. pressure is about 100 μb.

CHOICE OF MICROPHONE

The final choice of microphone always depends on the application as well, of course, as on the depth of one's pocket! No one microphone does everything equally well; the diversity of situations calls for different types of microphone if the end result is to be of the highest order. In this case, considerable knowledge of microphone techniques is essential, and the interested reader would do well to invest in a publication devoted to microphone applications and techniques.

The microphone of greatest general purpose is the moving-coil, and a wide range of this species is available in numerous forms to the enthusiastic amateur at quite reasonable prices nowadays (the *Hi-Fi Year Book*—an IPC Electrical-Electronic Year Books Limited publication—is an excellent source of reference as to what are available and how much). The output from this type of microphone is suitable for the majority of amplifiers, and the impedance can often be matched by transformer switching in the microphone itself—a medium/high impedance, of course, being required when there is no microphone transformer in the amplifier (or tape recorder) itself.

Both omnidirectional and bidirectional (i.e. cardioid) configurations are readily obtainable in moving-coil mode.

The sensitivity of a ribbon microphone (based on a common impedance) does not differ greatly from that of a moving-coil microphone, sensitivities over a range of about -70 to $-80\,dB$ being available in both versions. The ribbon microphone, however, is more suitable for certain applications; for example, in figure-of-eight mode when equal response is required from both front and rear, coupled with least side pick up.

Signal quality from a good ribbon microphone is of a high order, and designs permitting exploitation in cardioid and hypercardioid modes are readily available. The term 'hypercardioid' implies that the acoustics of the design are arranged for enhanced main beam directivity, such that the response to unwanted rear and side sounds is diminished (Fig. 9.7 broken-line response). With this sort of microphone it is possible to discriminate against unwanted pick up off the main axis.

Piezo-electric microphones are of lesser quality than the better class electromagnetic designs, but their electrical output is higher. This sort of microphone is commonly partnered with the inexpensive type of tape recorder, and being of high impedance can be coupled straight into the input (microphone) amplifier without the need for transformer matching. However, a high impedance coupling is incompatible with high impedance, so where long microphone cables are necessary the electromagnetic microphone should be used, so that the signal can be conveyed to the amplifier through a circuit of low impedance. A long cable at high impedance can give rise to hum and microphony problems, and the shunt capacitance of the cable can reduce the output of a piezo-electric microphone.

On long circuits a twin screened cable connected to a balanced input transformer on the amplifier helps to cancel out hum pick up (see Fig. 9.8).

There are more capacitor microphones becoming available at fairly reasonable price; but in general these are designed mostly for true professional applications. A head amplifier (powered usually from a separate unit or battery

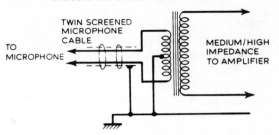

FIG. 9.8. *Balanced input coupling from electromagnetic microphone for hum cancellation over long circuits*

box) is incorporated and this is often built around a field effect transistor. After amplification the output is quite high, sometimes up to 2.6 mV/μb across 1 k-ohms. There are also some pressure-gradient and cardioid capacitor designs.

SPECIAL DIRECTIONAL MICROPHONES

One way of achieving enhanced directivity is by locating the microphone at the focal point of a parabolic reflector which is large with respect to the wavelength of the sound over the frequency range of interest. Thus, the lower the frequency required, the greater the reflector size, and for reasonable efficiency down to about 500 Hz the diameter of the reflector would approach 900 mm. The reflector collects the sound as shown in Fig. 9.9 and concentrates it to the microphone. One disadvantage is that the directivity increases significantly as the frequency is raised, which is overcome by displacing slightly the microphone from the optimum focus point.

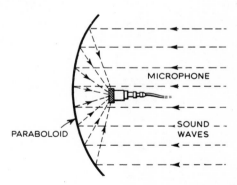

FIG. 9.9. *Enhance directivity and sensitivity in the forward direction is achieved by locating the microphone at the focal point of a paraboloid, as shown*

Another approach is by means of a long tube (sometimes as long as 200 cm, depending on required low-frequency response and directivity) at the end of which the microphone is coupled via a small cavity. Over the years this technique has been refined in various ways by the use of acoustical slits, resistive filters and tube tapering, the idea, as with the reflector, is to concentrate maximum sound energy at the microphone over the frequency range of interest.

207

Tube microphones are used professionally during outside broadcasts to 'isolate' a somewhat distant sound from high-level, local sounds, while the reflector scheme is often favoured by the enthusiast for gathering maximum energy for bird song recordings, etc.

The 'noise-reducing' microphone is another type which, like the directional species, relies on acoustical interference effects (i.e. obtaining discrimination against unwanted sounds due to the difference between the sound wavelength and the acoustical path length). This type, however, is often designed for operation close to the mouth, and a great deal of work has been done by the BBC, for example, in the development of lip microphones of this kind.

Of the three basic types of microphone described, there is a great diversity of designs. There are microphone heads of various types for screwing to a floor or table stand, microphones complete with stands, so-called 'full-vision' microphones, lapel microphones, radio microphones and others.

MICROPHONES FOR STEREO

For two-channel stereo two microphones or microphone systems are required. Many enthusiasts when recording stereo employ two ordinary microphones spaced either side of the sound source, and very good stereo tape recordings have been made with a pair of ribbon microphones suitably spaced and axis orientated relative to the source. However, to minimise rear pickup either moving-coil or ribbon cardioids may be used.

Another approach is by the use of coincident crossed microphones (after Blumlein) as shown in Fig. 9.10 and the polar response (assuming figure-of-eight ribbons) in Fig. 9.11. The coincident crossed technique demands good phase

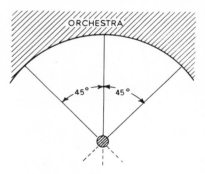

FIG. 9.10. *Crossed coincident microphone system for stereo (after Blumlein)*

and frequency matching and precision of the polar responses over the full frequency range to achieve stability of image placement.

Where dramatic 'motional' effects are required the spaced technique is often adopted, with a spacing between the two microphones of 3 m or more. An alternative to close-spacing is the mounting of the two microphones on an artificial head; but the general opinion seems to favour the cross-microphone technique (Fig. 9.11), though possibly with unidirectional microphones of cardioid polar response. It is intimated that phase cancellations and reinforce-ments are less likely to introduce serious problems with this technique.

Nevertheless, professional recording often demands the featuring of specific instrumentalists, soloists or parts of an orchestra or ensemble, and to this end multiple microphone techniques are used with stereo as with mono.

For the amateur recordist a variety of stereo microphones are becoming available, these generally being of the coincident crossed arrangement designed so that the angle between the two axes of maximum response can be adjusted.

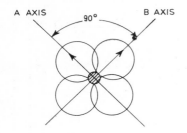

FIG. 9.11. *The axes and polar response of a crossed coincident microphone system, assuming bidirectional microphones*

The microphones are sometimes located one above the other for optimum phase coincidence. Such a microphone by Bang and Olufsen is shown in Fig 9.12. The top section can be unplugged from the bottom section if spaced operation is required, while the plugged-in pair can be turned relative to each other, and the angle between their forward axes is indicated on a calibrated scale.

As already noted, this form of stereo microphone originates from the ideas of Blumlein, dating from about 1929, when it was discovered that the 'stereo effect'

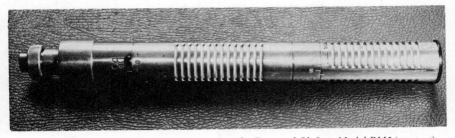

FIG. 9.12. *Crossed coincident stereo microphone by Bang and Olufsen, Model BM5 (see text)*

is related to the difference in time of arrival (phase) and relative strength of the sound at the two ears of the listener. Originally, two close-spaced microphones separated by a dummy head were adopted; but later it was found that the same phase effects could be achieved by the use of a stacked microphone system with right-angled axes, as described. In effect, the phase difference between the sounds arriving at the two microphones is translated to amplitude difference by the microphone pair, which is one of the factors contributing to stereo reproduction. Very dramatic stereo, however, has been achieved by Sennheiser's (W. Germany) recent dummy head and Triaxial MKE 2002 stereo microphone with an element located in the cavity of each ear.

The phase relationships between the left and right signals can be displayed

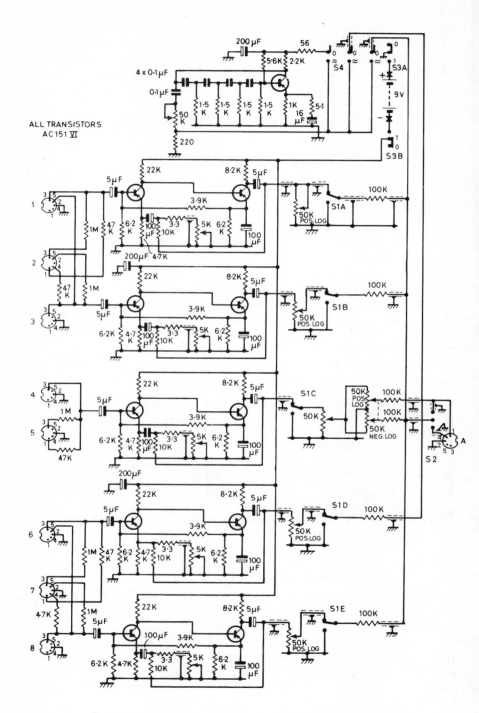

FIG. 9.13. *Circuit diagram of Uher stereo mixer, Model A121 (see text)*

on the screen of an oscilloscope by connecting the signals of one channel to the Y amplifier and the signals of the other channel to the X amplifier (timebase switched off of course). In-phase components of equal amplitude produce a line trace at an angle of 45 degrees while differing-phase and amplitude components result in the trace deviating from the nominal (also see under 'Phase Response' in Chapter 5, page 113).

MICROPHONES FOR QUADRAPHONY

For quadraphony or four-channel stereo four microphones are required, and good results have been obtained with two crossed and coincident systems, one pair responding to the front information and the other pair responding to the back information. Four-channel stereo, however, lends itself to significant experimentation with microphone techniques, and new techniques are being developed with regard to matrix systems (see Chapters 7 and 12) to help with 360 degree image placement and to help combat the reduced channel separation of the matrix systems, in conjunction with phasing and 'logic switching' artifices.

There is still a great deal yet to be learnt about four-channel recording and microphone techniques, and care has to be taken to preserve the best mono and stereo compatibility of four-channel records, for example.

MICROPHONE MIXERS

Microphones can be connected in parallel and then to a common microphone input socket of an amplifier or tape recorder, but this is not a practice to be recommended. It is much better technically to use a microphone mixer so as to maintain the best matching of each microphone to the input, while at the same time having full control of the gain of each channel.

The circuit of the Uher Stereo Mixer, Model A121, is given in Fig. 9.13, and its presentation in Fig. 9.14. This has five mixer (fader) controls, which are sliders located at the output of the mixer sections to ensure the best signal/noise ratio. Inputs 1 and 3 and 6 and 8 are in pairs, which makes it possible to use

FIG. 9.14. *External appearance of Uher Model A121 Stereo Mixer (see Fig. 9.13)*

two pairs (i.e. 1 and 3 and 6 and 8) for stereo. So that the control pairs can be operated together, a plastics coupler is provided to mechanically gang the controls of each pair. Thus, fader control of channel 1 can be ganged with that of channel 3, and likewise with the faders of channels 6 and 8.

Each channel is switchable by S1/A/B/etc., which are separate 'rocker'-type low-noise switches on the mixer panel. Switch S2 selects either mono or stereo mode, while preset level controls located between the two transistor stages of each channel allow the gains to be 'normalised' to the levels of the input signals.

The mixer is powered from a small internal 9 V battery pack, this being under the control of on/off switch S3A/B. The transistor stage at the top of the circuit is a tone generator, switchable by S4, which allows the mono or stereo recording level control(s) (on the recorder) to be adjusted for the correct modulation, after which the programme signal levels can be controlled within the set dynamic range by the panel faders.

Inputs and outputs are via DIN sockets. The output emanates from socket A, and inputs 1 and 6 cater for levels of 1 to 27 mV across about 3 k-ohms. The same conditions apply to inputs 3, 4 and 8, but input 5 is engineered to accept medium-level signals from around 70 mV to 10 V across 1 M. Thus, there are five mono inputs (1, 3, 4 or 5, 6 and 8) and two stereo inputs (2 and 7 or 1 and 3) *plus* a mono input (4 or 5).

Mixers for professional applications are more complex than this relatively simple example, which is directed essentially to the amateur tape recordist. Nevertheless, the general idea is the same, the philosophy being to secure the best signal/noise ratio at each input (mono or stereo) with complete gain control over each channel.

CHAPTER 10

Tape Recording

ALTHOUGH THERE have been numerous advances in the field of tape recording during recent years the basic principle remains. That is, the audio information is implanted in magnetic terms on a magnetic material which forms the coating on one side of a thin plastics ribbon tape.

The amplifier used for making the recording produces in the winding of the recording head an e.m.f. which varies in accordance with the audio signal. This yields a corresponding changing magnetic field across a very small gap formed in the pole pieces of the head, and from here the audio information is trans-ferred to the coated tape, which is passing the gap at a constant velocity, as 'magnetic patterns'.

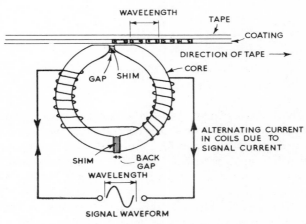

FIG. 10.1. *Elementary impression of magnetic tape recording (see text)*

An elementary impression of the scheme is given in Fig. 10.1. From first principles, the tape coating can be regarded as a continuous chain of miniature magnetic elements of varying length and intensity, related respectively to the frequency and amplitude of the audio signal. The actual length of a magnetic element of given signal frequency depends, of course, on the velocity at which

213

the tape passes the gap. A full signal cycle yields two magnetic elements, as shown in Fig. 10.1.

During replay the recorded tape passes the gap of a similar head, and it is the changing magnetic flux coupled through the pole pieces of this which produces a signal e.m.f. in the associated winding of a character similar to the original recording e.m.f. The resulting signal voltage is equalised and amplified for loudspeaker reproduction.

CYCLE OF MAGNETISATION

The cycle of magnetisation is shown graphically in Fig. 10.2, where H is the magnetising field strength and B the intensity of the induced magnetism. When the ferrous material being magnetised is 'magnetically neutral' and H is

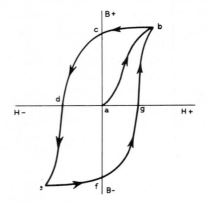

FIG. 10.2. *Cycle of magnetisation (see text for details)*

gradually increased in the positive direction, B will increase in the manner described by curve ab. If now H is decreased (i.e. made less positive) B will not follow the same curve back to a, but will trace line bc, so that even at zero H there will be an appreciable value of B, which corresponds to the strength of the magnetism induced into the ferrous material (i.e. the magnetic coating on the tape).

When H is increased from zero in a negative direction, B will decrease in the manner described by curve cd, where at d the material is once again in the 'magnetically neutral' state. When H is further increased in the negative direction, B also increases negatively as described by curve de, where at point e the material is once again full magnetised, but this time in the opposite polarity. At point f H is again zero, and as H is increased once more in a positive direction so B falls, first along curve fg and then finally from zero B to $+B$, along curve gb.

There are four primary aspects of the cycle of magnetisation, or hysteresis curve as it is sometimes called.

TAPE RECORDING

SATURATION

The first is that magnetic *saturation* of the material is indicated when an increase in H fails to result in any further increase in B; that is, when the material being magnetised is incapable of taking on any more magnetism.

NON-LINEARITY

The second is the *non-linearity* of the cycle of magnetisation; that is, equal increments in magnetising field fail to produce equal increments in residual magnetism in the material being magnetised when the field is removed.

REMANENT INDUCTION

The third is the amount of induction that the material will accept, called *remanent induction* (B_r); that is, the flux (ϕ) remaining in the material when a field of any value is removed. An associated term is *remanence* ($Br_{\text{sat.}}$), which refers to the flux remaining when a field of *saturating* intensity is removed.

COERCIVITY

The fourth refers to the ability of the material being magnetised to retain its magnetism when the field is removed or when its polarity is changed. For example, *coercive force* (H_c) is the *de*magnetising force required to reduce the remanent flux to zero. It thus depends on the strength of the initial magnetisation. *Coercivity* refers to the value of coercive force required to reduce the remanence to zero.

The magnetic material on the tape, therefore, must have a high remanence to provide a high recording level and a high coercivity to reduce losses due to demagnetisation, particularly at h.f. when the lengths of the magnetic elements are small. It should not saturate too early since this would encourage peak distortion due to non-linearity at high recording levels.

The intrinsic non-linearity is one of the biggest problems in tape recording, since this can be responsible for significant harmonic distortion unless something is done about it. One way of combating the curvature of the transfer characteristic is to introduce a standing flux to the tape as it is being recorded. However, this has the effect merely of shifting the operating point to a more linear part of the *BH* transfer characteristic; but this is not the best of solutions since the standing magnetism impairs the signal/noise ratio, reduces the 'sensitivity', since only half the characteristic is used, and tends to aggravate peak overload into saturation.

H.F. BIAS

The contemporary method of overcoming the non-linearity is by superimposing the audio signal on a signal of constant frequency which is well above the highest audio-frequency signal to be handled. This, called h.f. bias, may range from around 30 kHz to 100 kHz or more, depending on the machine. The h.f.

215

bias signal is applied along with the audio signal current to the winding of the recording head.

Fig. 10.3 shows the remanence curve or transfer characteristic of the tape and the distortion to which the recorded signal is subjected due to the non-linearity without any form of correcting bias. Fig. 10.4 shows how the non-linearity is overcome by the application of a h.f. bias. The effect is rather as though the remanence is 'sampled' over the more linear middle parts of the positive and negative curves.

It will be appreciated, of course, that the h.f. bias avoids the induction of residual magnetism on the tape; but in order for this to happen the bias signal

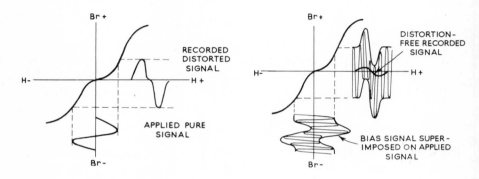

FIG. 10.3. *Recorded signal is badly distorted due to intrinsic non-linearity of BH character-istic when there is no bias*

FIG. 10.4. *Showing how h.f. bias reduces the distortion of the recorded signal*

must be free from even harmonic distortion. No tape remanence occurs due to the bias because as any point on the tape approaches and passes the gap it is subjected to a h.f. magnetic field of increasing and then decreasing strength. Thus, the only tape remanence is that corresponding to the audio information, so the tape is free from redundant remanence, which is not the case when d.c. biasing is used.

Remanence due to d.c. will occur, however, if the h.f. bias carries significant even harmonic distortion, which is exposed as a marked decrease in signal/ noise ratio. To avoid this, good tape recorders are equipped with push-pull oscillators which eliminate even harmonic distortion.

CROSS-FIELD BIASING

A system of two heads, one for the audio signal and the other for the h.f. bias, has been developed by the Akai Company of Japan for reducing the effect that the h.f. bias has on h.f. audio signal components, being of particular value at low tape velocities.

TAPE RECORDING

The basic system is shown in Fig. 10.5. The signal and bias heads are mounted opposite each other and are slightly displaced. The tape is thus effectively 'biased' between points A and C before it is subjected to the recording field across gap B. On some designs the bias head retracts during replay.

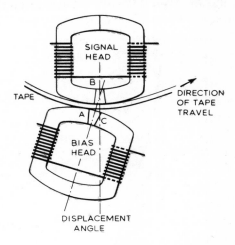

FIG. 10.5. *The cross-field biasing system*

BIASING AND RECORDING LEVELS

For the best results, different tapes require different values of h.f. biasing field for a given recording level. For a given recording level, an initial increase in h.f. bias current (through the head) results in a reduction in distortion and an increase in recording level. Further bias increase, however, encourages peak non-linearity distortion and a reduction in recording level, particularly of the h.f. audio components.

Based on the conventional method of h.f. biasing (i.e. not cross-field), the curves in Fig. 10.6 show how the output at 1 kHz, 5 kHz and 15 kHz and the third harmonic distortion at 1 kHz vary with changes in h.f. bias current. These curves refer to a signal current of 0.63 mA, a Philips recording head of 7 mH and a Philips playback head of 75 mH, where 0 dB ≃ 1.85 mV.

The curves in Fig. 10.7 show how the output and third harmonic distortion vary with changes in signal current through the recording head), the parameters being the same as those for Fig. 10.6.

In SI units tape (magnetic) flux is expressed in nanowebers per metre (nWb/m). It was formerly expressed in millimaxwells per millimetre (mM/mm). For conversion, 1 weber equals 10^8 maxwells, corresponding to 10^8 lines (i.e. 1 mM/mm = 10 nWb/m). A flux of 1 weber linking a circuit of 1 turn produces an e.m.f. of 1 volt as it is reduced to zero at a uniform rate in 1 second.

The flux across a recorded track is a function of its width. For example, if a $\frac{1}{4}$ in (6.35 mm) tape is recorded across its entire width and the recorded level corresponds, say, to 250 nWb/m, then the flux across its width would be

217

1.587 nWb (i.e. $250 \times 6.35 \times 10^{-3}$). It is this flux which would yield the e.m.f. in a full-track playback head.

A half track on $\frac{1}{4}$ in tape (taking into account guard lanes) is approximately 2.5 mm wide, so when this is recorded to the above mentioned level (250 nWb/m) it would have a flux of about 0.625 nWb. Thus, assuming similar head sensitivities, the half-track head would yield an e.m.f. about 0.393 times less than the

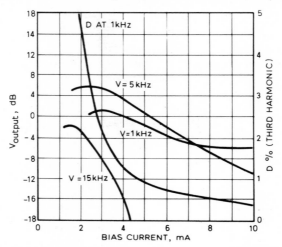

FIG. 10.6. *Third harmonic distortion at 1 kHz and output at 1 kHz, 5 kHz and 15 kHz versus h.f. bias current*

full-track head playing the full-track tape; that is, the output would be approximately 7 to 8 dB down. Thus, the narrower the track referred to a given recorded flux, the smaller the output from a playback head of given sensitivity. This is one of the reasons why the signal/noise ratio falls when the track width is reduced. Test tapes are available (Table 10.1) with specified recorded fluxes and equalisation characteristics (see later).

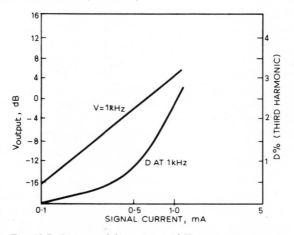

FIG. 10.7. *Output and distortion at 1 kHz versus signal current*

Table 10.1

BASF (UK) Ltd., Knightsbridge House, London SW7

Head Alignment Tape
5.6–16 kHz (noise), full-track, track 3 erased; 45 nWb/m.

DIN Calibration Tapes
31.5 Hz–18 kHz; 320 nWb/m; 70 μsec.
31.5 Hz–18 kHz; 320 nWb/m; 50/3180 μsec.
31.5 Hz–16 kHz; 250 nWb/m; 90/3180 μsec.
31.5 Hz–10 kHz; 250 nWb/m; 120/3180 μsec.

Calibration Compact Cassettes
DIN 45 513/6 (Fe) 4,75/3,81
DIN 45 513 (Cr) 4,75/3,81
BASF Speed Test 4,75/3,81 50 Hz
Flutter Test 4,75/3,81 3150 Hz
Flutter Test 4,75/3,81 3000 Hz
Service Cassette 4,75/3,81 (Fe)
Dolby B Testing 4,75/3,81.

Grundig (GB) Ltd., Newlands Park, London SE26

Alignment Tapes
100 Hz, 3 kHz, 3.15 kHz; speed, wow and flutter at 4.75,
9.5 and 19 cm/sec.
1 kHz and 8 kHz; general purpose adjustment.

Calibration Tape
Azimuth 8 kHz; 333 Hz ref. at 250 nWb/m ± 0.5 dB and
less than 2% distortion. Also for DIN 45 513 frequency
response (replay) at 1 kHz, 40 Hz, 333 Hz, 8 kHz and
12.5 kHz; blank section for record adjustment.

PLAYBACK

The gap length of the playback head has considerable bearing on the h.f. response since flux changes in the pole pieces are cancelled when the recorded wavelength (see Fig. 10.1) corresponds to the *effective* (see later) gap length, the output then being zero at the so-called *extinction frequency*. Recorded wavelength is given by

$$\lambda = \frac{v}{f} \tag{10.1}$$

where λ is the wavelength in μm, v tape velocity is μm/s and f the frequency in Hz. Thus, with an effective gap length of 15 μm and a velocity of 19 cm/s the extinction frequency falls at 12.6 kHz. The -3 dB point occurs at about half this frequency or at about 6.3 kHz in the example. The equalisation is referred to this, so it is not the highest frequency that can be reproduced with such a head, because recording and playback boost can be applied to the higher frequency signals.

To consider the output from the playback head over the spectrum we must take account of the nature of the recording. A constant-current feed from the recording amplifier might be adopted, which means that the signal current is essentially constant for any given amplitude, irrespective of frequency. Excluding recording losses (but see later) and based on a steady-state (i.e. sine wave) signal, therefore, the flux induced on to the tape would tend to hold constant over the frequency range.

Now, if a tape so recorded with a gliding tone is played back, the signal from the playback head will have a characteristic similar to that shown in Fig. 10.8. The initial 6 dB/octave rate of rise occurs due to the increasing *rate* of flux

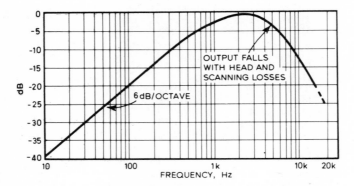

FIG. 10.8. *Playback head output for constant current recording*

change with increasing frequency. Since this is a linear relationship, the head signal doubles each time the frequency doubles.

If there were no head losses the output would continue to rise at this rate. However, at a certain high frequency the output ceases to rise and then starts to fall. This is where the head and scanning losses come into play. The 'turn-over frequency', as it is sometimes called, increases with decrease in gap length and increase in tape velocity, and decreases with diminishing intimacy of the coated side of the tape with the gap pole pieces (i.e. as may result from oxide, etc. build up round the gap).

The nature of the tape also comes into the equation in terms of self-demagnetisation at increasing frequency, since the smaller the length of the recorded 'magnets', the closer their terminal poles and hence the greater the chance of demagnetisation, depending on tape coercivity. Clearly, de-magnetisation will occur at a lower frequency when a tape is recorded at, say, 4.75 cm/s than at 19 cm/s or higher.

This is not the end of the matter, however, for in spite of the constant-current recording the flux on the tape is not constant over the entire spectrum. Re-cording losses also result from head effects, lack of intimacy of tape to head and 'depth loss' owing to the high-frequency short-wavelength signals confining their magnetism more to the surface of the coating, which means that the deeper layers contribute progressively less to playback signal of increasing frequency.

EQUALISATION

Equalisation is thus essential to secure a 'flat' output. Low-frequency boost is often introduced in the head preamplifier for playback by frequency-dependent negative feedback, such that the feedback progressively decreases with falling frequency, thereby causing the gain of the preamplifier to rise at the rate of 6 dB/octave with falling frequency. The 6 dB/octave rate is achieved by a loop RC network. This technique is fully explained in Chapter 3, particularly with regard to magnetic pickup equalisation—the principle being exactly the same for tape replay equalisation, but with different time-constants of course (also see Figs. 10.22 and 10.25).

Passive equalisation networks may also be used, which in basic form resolve to a simple RC network. That shown in Fig. 10.9 is a single-pole network giving bass boost or treble cut. Simple circuits like this are commonly referred to a time-constant T which is numerically equal to the product of C and R. Thus

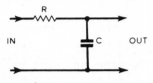

FIG. 10.9. *Simple single-pole bass-lift or treble-cut network, where RC is the time-constant (see expression 10.2)*

$T = CR$, where T is in seconds, C in farads and R in ohms. T in this case refers to the time it takes the p.d. to rise to 0.632 of its final value or fall to 0.368 of its original value.

The requirement is for a playback response which is the complement of the head output response from a tape recorded to a specific standard (see Table 10.1), and because the turnover frequency is related to tape velocity, the equalisation must also refer to this.

Although the curve in Fig. 10.8 implies that the rise in output is exactly 6 dB/octave, starting at a very low frequency, this is not strictly true, because the long wavelengths of low frequencies tend to reduce the amount of flux coupling into the pole pieces, which can precipitate a fall in bass output starting at 12 dB/octave and ultimately increasing to 18 dB/octave. This is sometimes equalised by mild bass boost during recording.

The treble roll-off following the turnover frequency is equalised by treble boost either during recording (pre-emphasis) and playback or during playback only, and recording and playback curves taking all these factors into account are given in Figs. 10.10 and 10.11. The precise equalisation, of course, depends on the tape velocity, and various standards have been evolved, some of which are given in Table 10.2.

At the time of writing new standards are being formulated and proposed, particularly with respect to cassette recorders (tape velocity 4.75 cm/s) using chromium dioxide tape, one proposal being for a change in playback time-constant from 120 μs to 70 μs (IEC, Document 60A-Sec 25-December, 1970). Thus, a recorder correctly equalised to a specific standard will have a 'flat' response from a tape of complementary characteristics; or a recorder adjusted for a 'flat' overall recording/playback response with reference to an equalisation

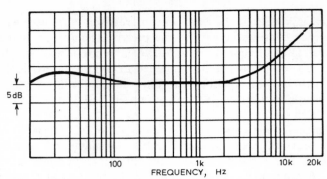

FIG. 10.10. *Recording equalisation characteristic, showing bass and treble boost*

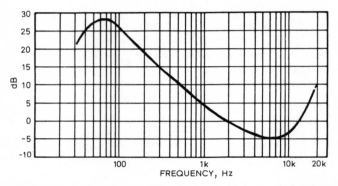

FIG. 10.11. *Replay equalisation characteristic, showing treble boost which helps to offset h.f. head losses*

standard will make a tape recording suitable for 'flat' playback of any other machine of corresponding standard, the standards thereby facilitating interchange of recordings.

Professional machines operating at 38 or 76 cm/s m..y adopt essentially constant-current recording over the primary bandwidth, with possibly a playback time-constant of 35 μs. The l.f. and h.f. time-constants in Table 10.2 refer

Table 10.2

Standard	4.75 cm/s*		9.5 cm/s		19 cm/s	
	l.f.	h.f.	l.f.	h.f.	l.f.	h.f
IEC94, BS1568 (1970)	—	120†				
IEC94, BS1568 (1970)	1590	120				
IEC94 (Europe)			3180	140		
IEC94 (Europe)			—	90		
IEC94 (GB), BS1568 (1970)			3180	90		
CCIR	—	280	—	140		
IEC (France)					—	50
NAB, IEC (USA)					3180	50
CCIR/DIN, IEC94 (GB), BS1568 (1970)					—	70

* Recent 'standards' are 3180/120 and 3180/70 for high energy and CrO_2 tapes.
† Figures refer to time-constants in μs.

in essence to the 'starting frequencies' of the equalisation, such that

$$f_{3\,dB} = \frac{1}{2\pi T} \tag{10.2}$$

where $f_{3\,dB}$ is the frequency in Hz at the response 3 dB point and T is the time-constant in seconds. $f_{3\,dB}$ is commonly referred to as the turnover frequency, so using expression 10.2 and taking the time-constants in Table 10.2 we can obtain the turnover frequencies given in Table 10.3.

Table 10.3

Time-constant μs	Turnover frequency Hz
50	3183.098
70	2273.641
90	1768.388
120	1326.291
140	1136.820
280	568.410
1590	100.097
3180	50.048

The turnover frequencies corresponding to some other commonly used time-constants are given in Table 10.4.

Table 10.4

Time-constant μs	Turnover frequency Hz
200	795.774
100	1591.549
35	4547.283

As already noted, the h.f. frequency response of some machines is enhanced by the application of treble boost in the relay amplifier (by reducing feedback at h.f.); but this is not always the case. The curves in Fig. 10.12, for example, show replay characteristics at three tape speeds *without* treble boost and with mild bass-cut. The complementary recording characteristics in Fig. 10.13 show treble boost (pre-emphasis) and also bass-cut. It should be noted that although the pre-emphasis is greater at the lower tape speeds, this occurs only because the turnover frequency is lower (i.e. greater value time-constant). The slope of a single pole RC network always ultimately assumes a rate close to 6 dB/octave. The turnover frequencies of the curves thus depend on tape speed, and the time-constants corresponding to the curves in Figs. 10.12 and 10.13 can easily be discovered from expression 10.2.

Not all standards provide for l.f. equalisation, and the standards given in Table 10.2 refer in essence to gamma ferric oxide (γFe_2O_3) tape. The proposed reduced h.f. playback time-constant for chromium dioxide (CrO_2) tape (when used in cassette machines operating at 4.75 cm/s) allows maximum advantage to be taken of the improved h.f. performance of this tape (i.e. the equalisation takes effect at a higher frequency, see Fig. 10.20).

For maximum dynamic range not only must the equalisation be optimised for the type of tape employed, but it must not encourage head or tape saturation distortion. The h.f. bias and the type and nature of the tape also have a bearing on dynamic range.

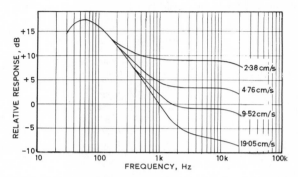

FIG. 10.12. *Replay characteristics at three tape speeds, showing bass cut*

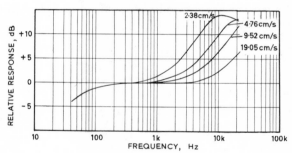

FIG. 10.13. *Recording characteristics at three tape speeds (the complement of the replay characteristics in Fig. 10.12)*

Audio properties of tape can be determined by establishing a reference bias such that the maximum output level (MOL) at 8 kHz is 10 dB below that at 315 or 333 Hz, the first corresponding to the level where the intermodulation distortion is 20% (about 2 dB signal compression) and the second to the level where the third harmonic distortion is 5%. Tests of dynamic range and sensitivity can then be made; it also being possible to evaluate tape signal/noise ratios.

HEADS

Many domestic-based machines have a single head for recording and replay; few have a head for each function. There is always an additional head for erasure, energised from the h.f. oscillator. The basic tape transport and head positions are shown in Fig. 10.14, which indicates, of course, that the tape passes the erase head before arriving at the recording/replay head. The erasure signal is active only during recording.

All heads are electromagnets, the coupling electronics suiting the winding impedance. When a separate head is used for recording, the gap is generally

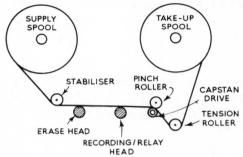

FIG. 10.14. *Basic tape transport, showing head positions*

greater than that of the replay head, since the latter is more critical from the 'scanning' point of view, while the former results in lower mid-frequency distortion when the length of the gap is approximately equal to the depth of the coating on the tape. A composite record/replay head is thus of necessity a compromise. The gap in the erase head may be as much as 30 μm.

The rear gap shown in Fig. 10.1 introduces high reluctance and constant permeability into the magnetic circuit. This gap is greater than the active gap, and without it a closed magnetic circuit would be formed by the tape coating. This would be undesirable owing to the resulting decrease in effective permeability (B/H ratio) of iron with increase in recording frequency.

Pole pieces are still sometimes made of laminated permalloy half-rings, with spacers forming the gaps. More recent heads, however, are made of crystal ferrite set in glass, the design concentrating the active field into a narrow oblong for maximum definition (i.e. focused field, Akai). This assists the engineering of the very small gaps required for the 4.75 cm/s cassette tape velocity.

EFFECTIVE GAP

The effective gap is larger than the physical gap owing to 'spreading' of the field and lack of perfect intimacy between pole pieces and spacer. At the low cassette

Table 10.5

Tape speeds		Spool sizes	
cm/s*	in/s	cm*	in
2.38	$\frac{15}{16}$	7.62	3
4.75	$1\frac{7}{8}$	10.16	4
9.52	$3\frac{3}{4}$	12.70	5
19.05	$7\frac{1}{2}$	14.60	$5\frac{3}{4}$
38.10	15	17.78	7
76.20	30		

* These are generally rounded off.

speed (see Table 10.5), the effective gap can only be a few μm for reasonable h.f. performance. For example, the -3 dB response with an effective gap just under $4\,\mu$m is only 6 kHz at the cassette speed (see page 219), hence the need for the fairly large h.f. time-constant and treble replay boosting. Tape losses are also higher at these very small wavelengths.

TAPE SPEEDS

Cassette speed is now essentially standardised at 4.75 cm/s, and the engineering of the heads, tape and electronics is such that, with a noise reduction system, good fidelity of music reproduction is feasible. The lower speeds of reel-to-reel machines are confined to speech, 9.5 and 19 cm/s being used for music. Only professional machines use 38 and 72 cm/s. Tape cartridges operate at 9.5 cm/s.

TAPE TRACKS

Two or four tracks can be laid on cassette tape whose width is close to 3.7 mm. These give mono or two-channel stereo on each half of the tape. Mono compatibility is provided since a mono head scans the two stereo tracks simultaneously (Fig. 10.15). Guard bands separate the two stereo tracks (left and right) and the two pairs of stereo tracks.

Reel-to-reel tape is about 6.35 mm wide, and this can be recorded full-track (rarely practised in domestic circles), with two tracks (giving mono on each half of the tape or stereo with the two tracks together) or with four tracks (giving

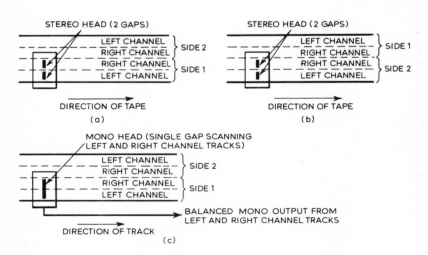

Fig. 10.15. *The four tracks (each approximately 0.6 mm separated by 0.3 mm guard tracks) of a cassette tape give two-channel stereo on one pair of tracks (a) and the same on the other pair of tracks by inverting the cartridge (b). Mono compatibility is provided by a mono head scanning either stereo pair (c). A mono recorder lays one track on each half of the tape, the track then having approximately the width of two quarter tracks*

mono on four tracks or two-channel stereo on each half of the tape by using pairs simultaneously (Fig. 10.16)). Guard bands again separate the tracks.

Cartridges also use 6.35 mm tape, and sometimes up to eight tracks are available with this system, with a guard band between each track. Cartridge

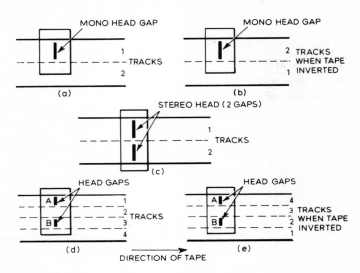

FIG. 10.16. *Two mono tracks each of approximately 2.3 mm separated by 1.65 mm guard track (a) and (b). Pair of stereo tracks each of approximately 2 mm separated by 2.25 mm guard track (c). Four tracks (d) and (e), which can be used for mono (each) or stereo (pairs); each track is approximately 1 mm wide separated by 0.75 mm guard tracks*

systems are providing four-channel stereo (quadraphony); but four-channel has not (at the time of writing) been standardised for reel-to-reel or cassette machines. However, cassettes have been recorded with eight tracks, giving four discrete channels on each half-width of the tape (a four-channel eight-track cassette machine has been made by JVC and H-K). A suggestion for stan-dardisation,* with complete mono and stereo compatibility, is illustrated in Fig. 10.17. Four-channel matrix would also be feasible by utilising the existing two pairs of tracks on a stereo cassette.

RECORDING TAPE

Many tapes to date are based on gamma ferric oxide, and since the advent of this medium significant improvements have occurred with regard to particle size and acicularity (i.e. the particles have increased length/width ratio and are more acicular or needle-like). This, along with improved processing and surface finishes, has resulted in better h.f. response, noise performance and hence dynamic range.

* 'Musicassette Quadrasonic: Tape Record Compatibility', E. R. Hanson (N. American Philips Corporation) *J. Audio Eng. Soc.*, Jan. 1971, Vol. 19, No. 1.

A more recent happening is chromium dioxide tape, the magnetic material of which is a black, conductive ferromagnetic oxide (CrO_2). This is sometimes called Crolyn (which is the trademark of the E. I. du Pont de Nemours and Company—a large chemical firm which holds the patents). Fig. 10.18 compares the *BH* curves of the two types of tape, this showing the higher retentivity (1600

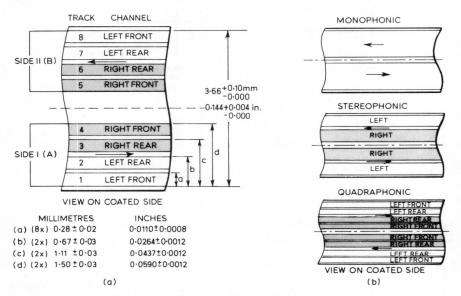

FIG. 10.17. *Suggestion for compatible four-channel (quadraphonic) tape cassette.* (a) *giving dimensions and* (b) *track positioning.*

against 1100 gauss), the higher coercivity (500 against 300 oersted) and the increased squareness (0.9 against 0.75) of CrO_2 with respect to 'standard' gamma ferric oxide (γFe_2O_3). These factors, in addition to high smoothness of coating and large length/width ratio of the particles, endow CrO_2 with desirable features, particularly with regard to cassette tape.

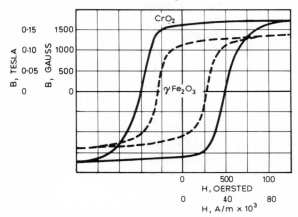

FIG. 10.18. *BH curves of chromium dioxide and conventional gamma ferric oxide tapes compared*

228

The curves in Fig. 10.19 (BASF) show maximum recording levels at 333 Hz and 8 kHz of cassette BASF low-noise (LN) tape and BASF CrO_2 tape. At an operating bias of $+3$ dB for CrO_2 the 333 Hz performance of both types is similar, but at 8 kHz CrO_2 has a dramatically better performance. Compared with conventional $\gamma Fe_2 O_3$ tape, therefore, CrO_2 exhibits higher output at the

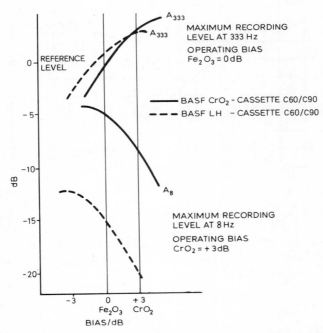

FIG. 10.19. *Maximum recording levels of BASF cassette low-noise and CrO_2 tapes compared*

shorter wavelengths, leading to better signal/noise ratios and hence dynamic range; it accepts a signal more readily and holds it better, and over the range 30 Hz to 15 kHz is capable of 55 dB signal/noise ratio.

'STANDARD' FOR CHROMIUM DIOXIDE TAPE

As already noted, optimum CrO_2 performance requires an equalisation change, the suggested time-constants being 3180 μs (as existing) and 70 μs (from 120 μs). The curves in Fig. 10.20 show these, along with the recording characteristic. Bias and recording level should also be increased about $+3$ or $+4$ dB above the level for conventional $\gamma Fe_2 O_3$ tape. Some recent cassette machines are equipped with equalisation and bias switching—and this may be automatic by the insertion of a CrO_2 cassette into the machine—allowing the best results to be obtained from both types of tape.

Cobalt ferrite ($Co\gamma Fe_2 O_3$) is another tape material, but information on this to date suggests that the h.f. performance, though being better than $\gamma Fe_2 O_3$, falls short of that of CrO_2; it also appears that it may possess some lack of magnetic stability. Nevertheless, encouraging results with regard to some aspects and parameters have been noted, and work on this and various other 'mixes' is proceeding. Moreover, the improving performance of some of the more recent γFe_2O_3 tapes must not be overlooked. A new two-layer tape has recently been

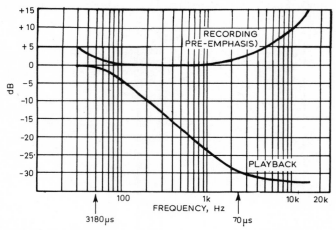

FIG. 10.20. *Recording and playback characteristics for CrO$_2$ tape, showing time constants*

announced using composite ferric oxide and CrO_2 closest to the base film and a thinner top layer of CrO_2, a technique leading to the optimisation of bias and high-frequency conditions.

ERASURE

The oscillator providing the h.f. bias is also connected to the erase head during recording, and this head is matched to the oscillator for maximum h.f. power and hence maximum erase field across the gap. The greater coercivity of CrO_2 tape sometimes calls for a greater erase field than may be generated by a machine designed essentially for γFe_2O_3 tape, so unless the erase field can be increased 'ghost' sounds may plague re-recorded tape of this kind—one solution would be to subject the tape first to bulk erasure.

TAPE RECORDER CIRCUITS

The 'domestic' tape machine—reel-to-reel or cassette—contains three departments. These are preamplification for the microphone or source signal, which is switched for playback head preamplification during playback, power amplification for loudspeaker drive and h.f. bias and erase signal generation. In addition, of course, there is also the power supply.

Machines designed for use with a separate amplifier (i.e. a hi-fi outfit) are without power amplification, since the signals for playback are delivered at a level suitable for the tape recorder input circuits of the parent amplifier. Also, as explained in Chapter 3, the hi-fi amplifier will invariably include outputs suitable for the recording preamplifiers of the tape machine.

With integrated recorders, the power amplification is similar in design to that used in conventional audio amplifiers (Chapter 4), though the power yield may be less and, perhaps, the distortion greater, along with other less exacting parameters. On the other hand, some tape machines are designed deliberately with hi-fi-quality pre- and power-amplification, such that the amplifier can be adopted as the 'heart' of a hi-fi system.

The block diagram of a simple integrated machine is given in Fig. 10.21. Playback head equalisation is sometimes achieved by frequency-dependent negative

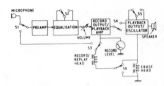

FIG. 10.21. *Block diagram of integrated tape recorder*

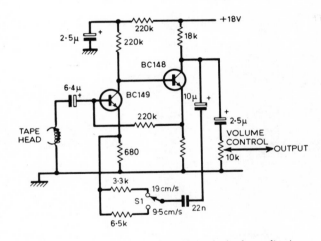

FIG. 10.22. *Negative feedback dependent playback equalisation*

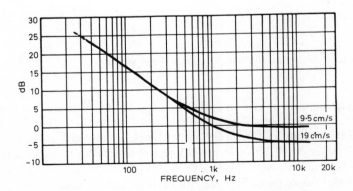

FIG. 10.23. *Equalisation characteristics of the circuit in Fig. 10.22*

231

feedback, as shown in Fig. 10.22. The equalisation characteristics for the two tape speeds are given in Fig. 10.23. This is a straightforward circuit with time-constant switching by S1.

Another scheme for obtaining equalisation is shown in Fig. 10.24, which relies on the changing inductive reactance of the head with frequency. As the frequency increases, so the head reactance increases, which results in increasing feedback.

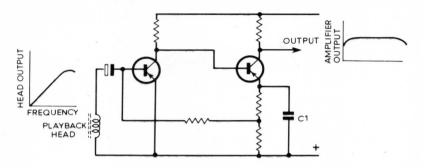

FIG. 10.24. *The inductance of the head working in conjunction with feedback for playback equalisation*

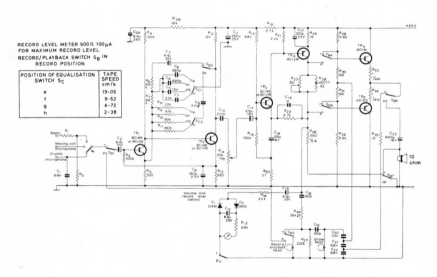

FIG. 10.25. *Tape recorder circuit by Mullard*

An interesting circuit by Mullard (described in the Mullard book entitled *Transistor Audio and Radio Circuits*) is given in Fig. 10.25. In the record mode TR1 and TR2 operate in a preamplifier feedback circuit, with the loop via C3, R6 and R7. Since R6/R7 junction is connected to chassis through one of the capacitors selected by SC1 the feedback reduces with increasing frequency, which provides treble recording pre-emphasis (see the curves in Fig. 10.13 for details). In the playback mode the main feedback loop is via time-constant C8 and the resistor selected by SC2, which increases the feedback with increasing frequency, thereby providing the equalisation, to which the curves in Fig. 10.12 refer.

During playback TR5 and TR6 form a complementary push-pull class B output stage, yielding 4 watts, while during recording the stage serves as an oscillator (switching by SB4/5), which energises the erase head and supplies h.f. bias via C19/R27 to the recording head (which seconds as the replay head in the playback mode).

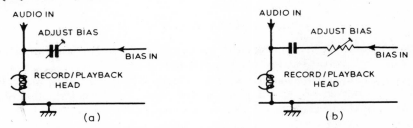

FIG. 10.26. *Methods for adjusting the h.f. bias applied to the recording head*

The meter in circuit with D1/D2, etc. gives a reading in proportion to the pk-pk voltage at TR4 collector, corresponding to 95 μA through the meter and 110 μA through the head.

Constant-current recording is provided by the recording head feed resistor R24, and the record/playback head is a quarter-track Marriott Type X/RPS/36 of 70 mH inductance measured at 1 kHz and 2.54 μm gap length. The erase head is a Marriott Type X/ES/11. Heads of different inductance would not operate successfully with this circuit.

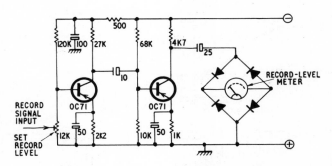

FIG. 10.27. *Amplified recording level meter circuit*

Methods for adjusting the h.f. bias are given in Fig. 10.26, while Fig. 10.27 gives a recording level meter circuit. It is necessary, of course, to be able to monitor the recording current for optimum dynamic range level setting. For example, a too high level would evoke heavy distortion owing to the onset of tape saturation, while a too low level would call for greater playback gain, which would be reflected as impairment in signal/noise ratio.

NOISE REDUCING TECHNIQUES

Various artifices have been developed to reduce noise, particularly in the field of recording, and more especially in recent years in relation to cassette tape recording. A notable scheme is that due to Dr. Ray Dolby, designer of the 'Dolby' noise reduction system. This was first developed for professional studio use, and in this application is known as 'Dolby A'. Less elaborate, though nevertheless still dramatic in effect, is 'Dolby B', which is engineered more towards the 'domestic end of the spectrum'.

'DOLBY B' NOISE REDUCTION SYSTEM

Basic principles are that during playback all low-level h.f. signals are attenuated while during recording all low-level signals undergo a similar boost, so that the overall signal integrity is maintained while the noise is reduced, as shown in Fig. 10.28. The degree of recording boost and hence playback attenuation is governed by the level of the h.f. signals, as shown in Fig. 10.29.

A block diagram on the scheme is given in Fig. 10.30, the top section showing the composition of the blocks denoted 'network'. The input signal is split into two paths. The main path is through the adder to the recorder, and the subsidiary path is through the 'network', where the dynamic processing occurs, and thence to the adder. The recorder thus receives the main signals plus the processed signals.

Now, as the level of the side chain signals increases the cutoff frequency of the variable high-pass filter moves upwards so that the side chain output

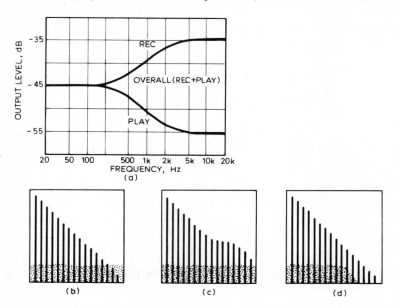

FIG. 10.28. *Basic principles of 'Dolby B'. All low-level h.f. signals are boosted during recording and attenuated during playback, giving an overall 'flat' output (a). Diagram (b) shows how low-level signals would be masked by noise. (c) shows the boosting of the low-level signals and (d) shows how the level of the signals is restored during playback, while the noise is reduced*

234

decreases, which means that a decreasing level signal is added to the main signal. During playback a complementary characteristic is achieved by the side chain 'network' being located in a negative feedback loop. The variable high-pass filter is operated by a field effect transistor, and full-wave rectification is adopted for control voltage production—both in the interests of low distortion. The technique avoids tape overload distortion, etc., which could prove troublesome with simple recording pre-emphasis and playback de-emphasis.

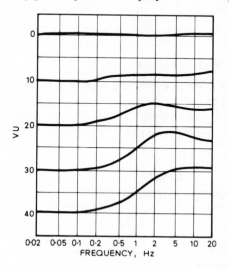

FIG. 10.29. *The degree of boosting and hence playback attenuation depends on the signal level, as shown by these curves. A maximum boost of 10 dB occurs on the lowest level signals*

The circuit includes calibration presets to relate circuit signal levels to a specific tape flux to achieve a 'zero level' condition. The playback preset is adjusted for the correct reference voltage at the input when a tape of standard flux level is played back, after which the recording preset is adjusted so that

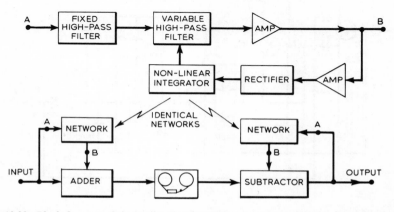

FIG. 10.30. *Block diagram of the 'Dolby B' system. The upper section of the diagram refers to the composition of the blocks denoted 'network'.*

the standard flux level is recorded on a tape when a signal of reference level is applied at the input. The so-called 'Dolby reference level' is 200 nWb/m for cassettes and 180 nWb/m for 6.35 mm tape.

'Dolby B' noise reduction is around 10 dB which, with CrO_2 cassettes, makes possible a dynamic range approaching that of a good disc record. Musicassettes are recorded to 'Dolby B', though are playable by a machine without Dolby by turning down the treble for frequency balance. A decoder is required, of course, for optimum results. A Dolby i.c. is now available.

PHILIPS DYNAMIC NOISE LIMITER

The block diagram of the Philips dynamic noise limiter (DNL) is given in Fig. 10.31. This differs from Dolby in that it is effective during playback only. The playback signal is split into two paths, V_1 going to an adder at the output and V_2 going through a processing side chain before arriving at the adder, where V_1 and V_2 are in phase opposition.

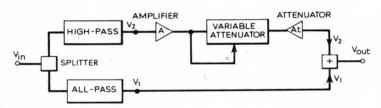

FIG. 10.31. *Block diagram of the Philips dynamic noise limiter (DNL)*

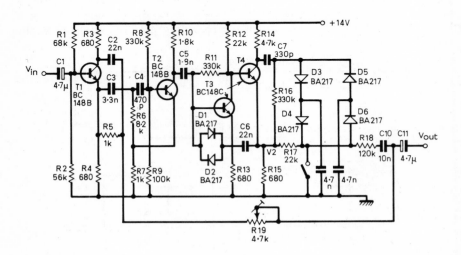

FIG. 10.32. *Circuit of Philips DNL*

236

TAPE RECORDING

The high pass filter operates at about 4 kHz, and signals from this are communicated to the variable attenuator whose attenuation falls with decreasing signal level, so that the h.f. signals are effectively boosted in relation to their level. After passing through the fixed attenuator, V_2 is added to V_1, and owing to the phase opposition here cancellation of h.f. signals, including noise, occurs. Frequency balance is restored, of course, by the side chain boosting, which is a function of the signal level.

The circuit is given in Fig. 10.32. All-pass filtering is by T1/C2/R5, and high-pass filtering by T2/C3/C4/R6/R8/R9, in conjunction with the feedback loop through R7. Intermediate amplification is by T3, with symmetrical clipping by D1/D2. Variable attenuation is by D4/D6, while D3/D5 are peak detectors controlled by T4. The fixed attenuation is by R17/R18, while a high-pass characteristic to the detector diodes is provided by coupling C7/R16.

Since the system operates only during playback it is not so effective as Dolby; unweighted signal/noise ratio improvements are stated as around 10 dB at 6 kHz and 20 dB at 10 kHz. Some cassette machines feature DNL *and* Dolby.

Of recent years other noise reducing systems have been proposed or evolved, including the automatic noise reduction system (ANRS) by JVC-Nivico (used also in conjunction with CD-4 disc production, Chapters 7 and 12) which, in some ways is similar to Dolby, but with a different turnover frequency, the Burwen dynamic noise filter and others.

AUTOMATIC RECORDING LEVEL CONTROL

This control automatically regulates the level of the recording signal so as to avoid overloading due to r.m.s. signal peaks; but is not a limiter as such. Time-constant circuits are employed to retain the overall dynamic range, the auto control doing, in effect, what an operator would do manually during a recording to avoid overload.

Various circuits are in use, but the basic principle is shown in Fig. 10.33. The controlled amplifier in the recording channel is adjusted in gain by rectified signal from a control amplifier fed from the recording amplifier. The control voltage goes via a delay (i.e. time-constant) circuit which is optimised for the type of signal (music or speech) being recorded.

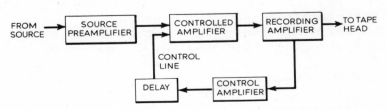

FIG. 10.33. *Block diagram expressing basic features of automatic recording level control*

237

TAPE RECORDING

When manual recording level control is used it is necessary to know the level of signal being applied to the recording head, and this is indicated (sometimes in relative terms) by a meter, 'magic-eye', etc. dB or VU (volume unit) calibrated meters are used with more advanced machines, and with stereo or four-channel machines there is a meter for each channel. There is generally clear indication as to when the signal level is exceeding that for least distortion within the dynamic range capability of the design. Some meters also operate on the replay signal, this allowing the actual output from a given recorded level to be monitored. Test tapes are available—with specified flux levels—for evaluating the accuracy of such meters and for setting the 'Dolby' reference level (200 nWb/m cassettes and 180 nWb/m reel-to-reel tape).

It is noteworthy that signal peaks of up to 10 dB above the meter reading can occur, and to check for this a 'peak level indicator' lamp may also be used (i.e. on the TEAC A450 cassette deck, JVC and others).

TAPE MECHANISMS

It is not possible within the compass of this Chapter—or, indeed, book—to explore the large number of tape mechanisms now current. In any case, the mechanics of these change so often with improvements, etc.

Sophisticated tape transport mechanisms have been developed for the more advanced cassette machine—some with 'servo' control (i.e. Goodmans SCD-100); and having in mind the relatively low cassette tape velocity, extremely low wow and flutter figures are achieved, sometimes better than 0.1% weighted with top-flight designs. The mechanical design of the cassettes themselves, however, can affect the wow and flutter figures; but these too have received detailed attention during recent times (the BASF 'Special Mechanics'—SM—cassette, for example).

Although updated, reel-to-reel transports have not altered much, the wow and flutter parameters tending to improve with the higher tape velocities.

Cartridge decks are essentially for playback of prerecorded music cartridges, though one or two new models are appearing with recording facilities. The cartridge is arranged as an 'endless' tape loop, the tape issuing from the inside of the spool and rewinding on to the outside.

Some tape decks are equipped with a 'third' head which makes it possible, via a suitably equalised preamplifier, to monitor a recording while it is being made, and the 'source/monitor' switch, now fitted to most hi-fi amplifiers, facilitates immediate comparison between the source signal and the recorded signal when a machine with a monitor head is used.

Information on tape transports, general mechanics and serving can be obtained from such publications as the *Tape Recorder Servicing Manual*, by H. W. Hellyer, and from the author's *Radio and Audio Servicing Manual*, both by the publisher of this book.

CHAPTER 11

F. M. Radio

THE AUTHOR'S BOOK entitled *F.M. Radio Servicing Handbook*, by the publishers of this book, deals with the f.m. system of broadcasting and with f.m. tuners and receivers in general, including stereo, as well as with topics of a 'servicing' nature. It was nevertheless decided to include a complementary chapter on the subject in this audio book, not only for the sake of completeness, but also as a means of reflecting some of the more recent trends and test procedures associated with f.m. radio as a hi-fi audio signal programme source.

The f.m. system is capable of providing stereo audio signals of the highest possible quality from a top-flight tuner/aerial partnership. Indeed, from a 'live' transmission conveyed from studio centre to transmitter via the recent pulse-code modulation links of the BBC the quality of the audio signals delivered by a state-of-art tuner receiving a 'clean' aerial signal can be in advance of that provided by even the best gramophone record or tape recording. Recorded f.m. programmes, of course, are no better than can be obtained from the same source at home in terms of quality, that is, assuming that the quality of the replay equipment is comparable to that of the broadcasting authority.

Intrinsic overall distortion of the f.m. system—from microphone to tuner output is low. For example, the distortion produced by a well designed tuner is rarely greater than 1% on stereo (typically less than 0.5% on mono) for 100% modulation. To satisfy the hi-fi requirement, however, the tuner must be endowed with certain *minimum* parameters which, in the present state of the art, are as shown in Table 11.1, but these are often well exceeded.

These parameters are given in the approximate order of importance, but there are others (see below). The front-end selectivity figure of merit (coupled with the large-signal handling capability of the front-end) is becoming of increasing importance as Band II is called upon to carry more and more transmissions. The 'commercial' f.m. stations, for example, may not be co-sited with the BBC stations, with the result that some tuners may receive a powerful signal from a commercial station yet signals of only moderate level from the BBC stations. Under such a condition, therefore, the tuner should be capable of handling the powerful signal without the need for aerial input attenuation since this could detract from the signal/noise ratio, particularly on stereo where a greater signal input is required than for mono for a given signal/noise ratio.

Table 11.1

Parameter	Minimum value
1. Front-end selectivity (figure of merit)	30 dB*
2. Alt. channel selectivity	30 dB
3. Capture ratio	3 dB
4. Ultimate hum and noise†	− 55 dB (ref. 100% mod.)
5. Ultimate S/N ratio†	− 60 dB (ref. 100% mod.)
6. AM rejection ratio	38 dB
7. Full limiting	10 μV (p.d. 75 ohms)
8. 30 dB S/N ratio†	3 μV (p.d. 75 ohms)
9. IHF usable sensitivity†	5 μV (p.d. 75 ohms)
10. Audio output	1 V r.m.s. per channel for 100% mod. max.
11. Frequency response	40 Hz − 15 kHz ± 1 dB ref. 50 μs de-emphasis
12. Distortion factor	1% stereo 100% mod.

* Tested as explained in text.   † Mono mode.

A very strong signal can push the front-end into severe non-linearity (depending on the signal handling capability of the input transistors), which in turn can give rise to intermodulation and spurious responses.

FRONT-END SELECTIVITY FIGURE OF MERIT

How well the front-end discriminates against unwanted signals at different frequencies from the frequency tuned is a function of its selectivity, and the figure of merit refers to a test devised by the author, the setup of which is given in Fig. 11.1. Generator 1 is tuned to frequency f_1 at the low-frequency end of the band (around 88 MHz) at an initial level which produces 50 mV (p.d.) across the aerial terminals of the tuner from the matching 'T' pad, which is essentially a simple 'star' network (Fig. 11.2).

Generator 2 (unmodulated) is adjusted to yield a signal of higher frequency f_2, such that $f_2 - f_1$ equals the intermediate-frequency. The standard f.m. i.f. is 10.7 MHz, so f_2 would be 98.7 MHz when f_1 is 88 MHz. Generator 1 is modulated 100% at 1 kHz or 400 Hz, whichever is the most convenient, and its attenuator adjusted for 50 mV (p.d.) at the tuner.

With the tuner adjusted for maximum gain, the modulation resulting from the intermodulation product $f_2 - f_1$ is detected on Y1 beam of the oscilloscope (it may be necessary to adjust f_1 or f_2 slightly to achieve response of $f_1 - f_2$ via the i.f. channel). Care should be taken to ensure that the tuner is not adjusted to f_1 of course. The tuner should be adjusted to $f_1 + 400$ kHz (or near to this frequency as possible to avoid 'blocking' or interference from f_1).

The resulting modulation on $f_2 - f_1$ is then passed through the distortion factor unit, where the modulation is removed by the notch filter therein. The remainder of the test then follows the procedure as detailed under *IHF Usable Sensitivity*. This is achieved by gradually reducing the output of generator 1, the front-end selectivity figure of merit, expressed in decibels, being the difference between the attenuator setting for the figure of merit test and the IHF usable sensitivity test.

240

F.M. RADIO

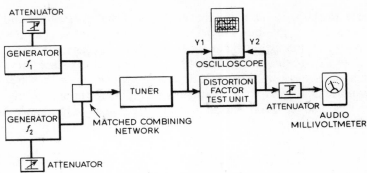

FIG. 11.1. *Instrument setup for measuring front-end selectivity figure of merit, etc. (see text)*

Thus, if the tuner has an IHF usable sensitivity of, say $2\,\mu V$ while the input required for the figure of merit is $2\,mV$, the ratio would be 1,000:1, which is 60 dB. The attenuators are often calibrated in decibels, so if the setting is 12 dB for the IHF usable sensitivity and 72 dB for the figure of merit test, the ratio again is 60 dB (i.e. $72 - 12\,dB$).

Depending on the 'quality' factors of the front-end selectivity, a simple tuner with a solitary variable tuned circuit preceding the mixer will have a figure little better than 20 dB; two variable tuned circuits tend to increase the ratio to 30 dB or more, while three such circuits can give a figure of 60 dB or more. Higher figures result from more than three pre-mixer variable-tuned circuits (excluding the oscillator variable tuning of course).

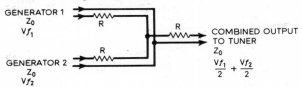

FIG. 11.2. *Simple 'star' network for signal combining. When impedances Z_0 are equal R has the same value in each leg, such that $R = Z_0(n-1)/n+1$, where n is the number of inputs (or outputs). When the inputs are V_{f1} and V_{f2} the outputs are $V_{f1}/2$ and $V_{f2}/2$ (i.e., each is 6 dB down from the input)*

A figure of 60 dB or more may be necessary under difficult reception conditions where a 'local' station is producing a very high signal field in competition with weaker wanted stations. A figure of 30 dB is generally sufficient for normal reception conditions, but tuners with figures much below this rarely fall in the 'hi-fi' category.

Since the figure is a function of the front-end selectivity, it follows that a tuner with a high figure will also have high image (a response twice the i.f. from a powerful signal), repeat spot (a response half the i.f. from a powerful signal) and i.f. (a response at the i.f.) rejection ratios, whose minimum 'hi-fi' values should be around 45 dB, 60 dB and 70 dB respectively.

Spurious responses resulting from inadequate front-end selectivity and possibly poor large-signal handling performance of the input transistors can be reduced by adopting aerial attenuation. Frequency-selective attenuation, however, may be required to avoid undue attenuation of weak, wanted signals.

241

Clearly, the large-signal handling capability of the r.f. amplifier and possibly mixer also affects the input dynamic range, and more attention is being directed towards this aspect of f.m. tuner design. Field effect transistors are often used to reduce intermodulation and third-order products since these have an essentially square-law transfer characteristic, for which reason they are also ideal for low-noise mixing. However, bipolar r.f. amplifiers running at high emitter current can also be arranged to handle large signal inputs with minimal non-linearity.*

ALTERNATE CHANNEL SELECTIVITY

Prime selectivity is provided by tuned couplings or filters in the i.f. channel. The recent ceramic filters help significantly with their steep skirts. Low distortion stereo reception requires an i.f. passband around 250 kHz (-6 dB points), Fig. 11.3, but to avoid adjacent and alternate channel interference the -6 dB passband should not be greater than 250 kHz. The benefit to stereo quality arising from the use of a greater passband is often overstated, though there is a

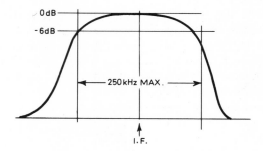

FIG. 11.3. *Practical ideal i.f. passband characteristic*

definite need for optimum phase linearity over the passband to cater for the large modulation index with the least harmonic distortion (Fig. 11.4).

The width of an f.m. channel is 200 kHz, which means that a well controlled i.f. response characteristic is essential for minimum adjacent channel interference.

The response attenuation at the alternate channel when the wanted signal is applied at a level of 100 μV is the IHF expression of rated alternate channel selectivity (new IHF standards proposals require a test also of adjacent channel selectivity, see page 255). Two generators are used and their signals are combined to a common output for matched application to the tuner (Fig. 11.2). The generators simulating the in-channel wanted signal (f_w) is applied to the tuner at a level of 100 μV (p.d.), unmodulated, at a standard IHF test frequency (90, 98 and 109 MHz; 98 MHz being adopted when a test at only one frequency is made), and the alternate unwanted signal (f_u) is applied at a frequency of $f_w + 400$ kHz or $f_w - 400$ kHz, modulated to 100% (i.e. ± 75 kHz deviation) at

* see *Mullard Technical Communications*, Vol. 12, No. 119, July 1973, which is also issued as an Application Note TP1395.

400 Hz (or 1 kHz if more convenient). For evaluation of response symmetry the test needs to be made at both frequencies.

Initially, f_u is switched off and f_w is modulated to 100% at the adopted modulation frequency and applied at a higher level than 100 μV in order to achieve a 0 dB datum on an audio millivoltmeter with switched attenuator connected to the tuner output. When this condition has been established, the two generators are then adjusted as previously described.

The signal at f_u is increased in level until the audio millivoltmeter gives a reading which is *30 dB below* the 0 dB datum, which is most conveniently

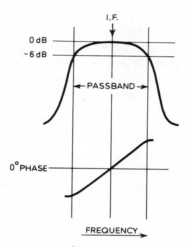

FIG. 11.4. *Practical ideal passband/phase characteristic*

obtained by decreasing the meter attenuation by 30 dB and referring to the 0 dB datum on the scale. The rated alternate channel selectivity is the difference between the levels of f_u and f_w, expressed in decibels.

Tuners with three or so transformer bandpass couplings generally have an alternate channel selectivity around 30 dB, while those equipped with piezo-electric filters often yield values of 50 dB or more, depending on the number of such filters used and the general design of the i.f. channel. Multiple and lattice filters provide the required i.f. bandwidth; but it is noteworthy that significant differences in selectivity between $f_w + 400$ kHz and $f_w - 400$ kHz are sometimes observed due to poor response symmetry, resulting from poor filter matching.

Owing to the very steep skirts provided by piezo-electric filters, the 400 kHz offset needs to be very accurately applied for meaningful results; and in the interests of accuracy a digital frequency counter should be used to establish the alternate channel frequency.

CAPTURE RATIO

The ability of an f.m. tuner to respond in essence only to the stronger of two signals in the same channel is intrinsic to the f.m. system. It results from the *capture effect*, which is explained in the author's *F.M. Radio Servicing Handbook*. The effect, however, can be influenced by the design of the i.f. channel and its amplitude limiting characteristics and by the design of the f.m. detector, which should have a wide and linear frequency characteristic.

The effect is measured in terms of the *capture ratio*, which is another IHF parameter. The test setup is similar to that explained for alternate channel selectivity, but this time it is f_w which is modulated to 100% and both f_u and f_w are applied at exactly the same standard test frequency.

The *rated* capture ratio requires f_w to be applied to the tuner at a level of 1,000 μV. The level of unmodulated f_u is then adjusted (up from zero) until the output millivoltmeter, previously adjusted for 0 dB datum on the modulated f_w, falls by 1 dB. The f_u signal level required for this condition is noted.

The level of f_u signal is further advanced until the audio millivoltmeter gives a reading *30 dB below* the 0 dB datum which, again, is most conveniently obtained by decreasing the meter attenuation by 30 dB and referring to the 0 dB datum on the scale. The f_u signal level required for this condition is also noted.

The ratio of the two levels noted is translated to decibels and then divided by 2, the result being the rated capture ratio for 100% modulation.

The smaller the dB number, the better the ability of the tuner to suppress an unwanted co-channel signal. The test thus evaluates the inherent effects of the f.m. detector, the amplitude limiting and the automatic gain control (a.g.c.).

State-of-art tuners based on i.c. i.f. channels, piezo-electric filtering and wideband f.m. detectors, coupled with good amplitude limiting, can have a capture ratio of 1 dB or less, while with less sophisticated designs the figure may be 3 dB or higher.

A.M. REJECTION RATIO

The ability of an f.m. tuner to suppress amplitude modulated (a.m.) signals also depends on the efficiency of the amplitude limiting and the linearity and symmetry of the f.m. detector. The BSI (British Standards Institution) test for this is based on 30% modulation.

A 0 dB datum is established on an audio millivoltmeter at the tuner output from an input signal of specified level applied at a standard test frequency (the BSI standard test frequencies are 88, 94 and 100 MHz, 94 MHz being used when the test is made at one frequency only) and modulated to 30%.

The generator is then switched to a.m. and the attenuation of the audio millivoltmeter reduced to obtain the 0 dB datum reading. The amount of attenuation switched out is a direct measure of the 30% a.m. rejection ratio.

This test needs accuracy of tuning, to avoid assymmetry of f.m. detector response which will result in a.m. demodulation, and a generator which yields very minimal spurious f.m. on a.m. The test is best made at a number of inputs from the usable sensitivity level up to 1 mV (p.d.) or more.

Reasonable tuners should exhibit a ratio of at least 35 dB. Top-flight tuners have a ratio virtually limited by noise.

F.M. RADIO

ULTIMATE HUM AND NOISE

An input signal for this test is applied at a relatively high level (between about 1 and 10 mV, depending on the sensitivity of the tuner) and modulated to 100% (any different modulation level must be *clearly* specified as it will affect the ratio). A 0 dB datum is then established on an audio millivoltmeter connected at the tuner's output.

The modulation is switched off and the attenuation of the audio millivoltmeter is reduced to obtain the 0 dB datum. The amount of attenuation switched out is a direct measure of the hum and noise with reference to the modulation level (i.e. about 9 dB difference in ratio occurs between 100% and 30% modulation levels).

This test requires a generator of very low hum and noise output, and the test must be conducted to prevent the introduction of earth loops (which could add to the hum components). A battery powered audio millivoltmeter helps in this respect; but at one stage of the test it is desirable to secure radiated coupling from the generator to the tuner to ensure that a hum loop is not occurring via the generator signal connections via the tuner.

An oscilloscope connected to monitor the tuner output is useful for detecting hum components when switched for a sweep of about 10 ms/cm and 100 μV/cm Y gain. The trace will also show h.f. noise, of course.

A good tuner should not exhibit a ratio much worse than 55 dB (ref. 100% modulation); a smaller ratio would probably indicate excessive hum component (see next section).

ULTIMATE SIGNAL/NOISE RATIO

This test is the same as for ultimate hum and noise, but filtering is provided in the audio millivoltmeter circuit to eliminate the hum components. A high-pass filter with a turnover frequency around 250 Hz and 12 dB/octave rate of roll-off is suitable.

The difference between ultimate hum and noise ratio and S/N ratio should be minimal when design attention has been directed for a very low hum component output.

Weighting is sometimes applied to the S/N ratio (see the filter in Fig. 5.2 and the weighting values in Table 5.1, Chapter 5), this effectively eliminating the hum components while also reducing the amplitude of h.f. noise components.

FULL LIMITING

Owing to the amplitude limiting built into the i.f. channel, the audio output signal fails to increase in level with increase in f.m. aerial signal level beyond a certain input voltage, called the full limiting voltage (also see Fig. 11.5).

The lower the voltage at which the tuner goes into full limiting, the better from the point of view of reception of weak signals. Some very sensitive tuners with i.c. limiters in the i.f. channel may reach full limiting at a signal level as low as 2 μV (p.d.), while less exotic designs may require as much as 100 μV (p.d.) for the same condition.

Because the rise in output immediately prior to full limiting is not very fast, the aerial input voltage for − 3 dB full limiting may be specified. This, of course, refers to the input signal voltage where the audio output voltage is 3 dB below the ultimate maximum.

30 dB S/N RATIO

The sensitivity of a tuner is expressed in terms of aerial input signal voltage required for a 30 dB difference between the noise present when the input signal is unmodulated and the audio output when the input signal is modulated to a specified value (usually 100% or 30%). It will be apparent, of course, that the output signal will contain noise as well as the modulation frequency, so a measure of the *true* S/N ratio requires the audio signal to be passed through a very narrow-band bandpass filter prior to application to the audio milli-voltmeter. An audio wave analyser (see Chapter 5) tuned accurately to the modulation frequency will pass only the modulation while significantly reducing the noise power bandwidth.

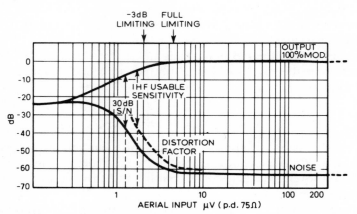

FIG. 11.5. *Curves showing −3 dB limiting, full limiting, 30 dB S/N ratio and IHF usable sensitivity, mono mode*

However, under practical conditions, the noise on the modulated signal when the S/N ratio is in advance of about 15 dB detracts very little from the accuracy of measurement when a narrow-band bandbass filter is *not* used.

The noise decreases as the aerial signal voltage is increased, as shown in Fig. 11.5. The top curve also reveals the − 3 dB and full limiting input voltages.

DIFFERENCE BETWEEN μV (p.d.) AND μV (e.m.f.)

The input voltage in Fig. 11.5 is given in terms of μV (p.d.), which is the potential difference actually existing across the aerial terminals of the tuner. However, as some signal generators have their attenuators calibrated in μV (e.m.f.), which is the intrinsic generator electromotive force, the distinction between p.d. and e.m.f. so far as tuner sensitivity is concerned must be fully understood.

The generator source impedance is always known, and this impedance must match, or be arranged to match, the aerial input impedance of the tuner. Thus we achieve a matched coupling from generator to tuner. Now, if the generator output is given at the attenuator in μV (e.m.f.), the p.d. across the tuner aerial terminals will be exactly half this value, as explained by Fig. 11.6. The

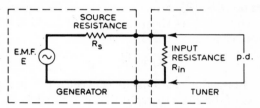

FIG. 11.6. *Showing the difference between e.m.f. (i.e. open circuit voltage from generator) and p.d. In a matched coupling $R_{in} = R_s$, so p.d. = e.m.f./2*

IHF tests require the input to be stated in μV (p.d.), while BSI tends to favour μV (e.m.f.) or available power at the particular load impedance, expressed in $dB (\mu V)$ or $dB (mW)$ respectively, where the bracketed symbol gives the dB reference (i.e. $60\,dB (\mu V)$ corresponds to $1\,mV$—the BSI standard input signal level—which is the e.m.f. or equivalent *open circuit* voltage).

EFFECT OF TUNER INPUT IMPEDANCE ON SENSITIVITY

Tuners made in or destined for the UK have a standard 75 ohms unbalanced input impedance, suitable for connecting aerial feeder, while tuners made in or designed for the American market have a 300 ohms balanced input impedance suitable for connecting to 300-ohm twin balanced aerial feeder. Some Continental tuners have a 240-ohm balanced input impedance (i.e. DIN standard).

The generator must, of course, be connected so that a correct match is applied to the tuner, as shown at (*a*) in Fig. 11.7. Assuming that R_{in} is substantially resistive, which is generally reasonably true (if not, then the reactive component of the load should be taken into account for accurate results), the p.d. across the aerial terminals (i.e. across R_{in}) is given by

$$\text{p.d.} = \text{e.m.f.} \times \frac{R_{in}}{R_s + R_{in}} \qquad (11.1)$$

This shows, of course, that where $R_{in} = R_s$ the p.d. is equal to e.m.f./2, as described in Fig. 11.6.

When R_{in} is less than R_s correct matching to the tuner can be achieved by connecting a resistor R_p across the generator output, as shown at (*b*) in Fig. 11.7. The value for the resistor can be found from

$$R_p = \frac{R_s \times R_{in}}{R_s + R_{in}} \qquad (11.2)$$

247

The relationship between the e.m.f. indicated by the attenuator controls of the generator and that presented to R_{in} is then given by

$$\text{e.m.f.}_{gen} = \text{e.m.f.}_e \times \frac{R_p + R_s}{R_p} \tag{11.3}$$

where e.m.f.$_{gen}$ is the e.m.f. indicated by the generator and e.m.f.$_e$ the effective e.m.f. from R_{in}.

When R_{in} is greater than R_s correct matching to the tuner is achieved by the use of a series resistor R1, as shown at (a) in Fig. 11.7. The value for R1 can be found from

$$R_1 = R_{in} - R_s \tag{11.4}$$

Under this condition the relationship between the e.m.f. indicated by the attenuator controls of the generator and that presented to R_{in} is given by

$$\text{e.m.f.}_{gen} = \text{e.m.f.}_e \tag{11.5}$$

In other words, the effective e.m.f. is the same as the generator e.m.f. as indicated by its controls.

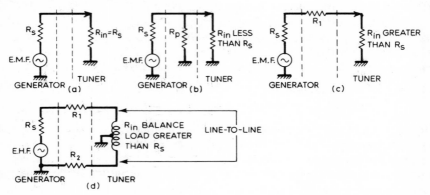

FIG. 11.7. *Various generator/tuner matching arrangements, (a), (b) and (c) unbalanced and (d) balanced. See text for details of component values, etc.*

The matching arrangements given at (a), (b) and (c) in Fig. 11.7 are all based on a generator of unbalanced output. Most generators are of this kind, and some may be supplied with terminating units to provide directly for different load values, so the insertion attenuation (usually 6 dB) of these when used between the generator and the tuner termination must, of course, be taken into account when determining the signal level from the attenuator controls of the generator. Some attenuators, in fact, are calibrated on the assumption that a terminating unit is to be used. Without the unit the signal output is generally 6 dB greater than that shown by the attenuator controls.

It is also possible to include a fixed attenuator of specific value between the generator and the load, and such additional attenuation may be required when testing tuners of very high sensitivity; but the generator must not be responsible for direct radiation from itself or its mains cable.

When R_{in} is a balanced load and greater than R_s correct matching to the tuner is achieved by the use of two series resistors R1 and R2, as shown at (d) in Fig. 11.7. The values for the resistors can be found from

$$R_1 = \frac{R_{in}}{2}$$

$$R_2 = \frac{R_{in}}{2} - R_s$$

(11.6)

where R_{in} in this case is the total line-to-line impedance. Thus, when connection is from a generator of 75 ohms to a balanced 300-ohm tuner aerial input R1 would be 150 ohms and R2 75 ohms.

Table 11.2

R_{in} (ohms)	Approx. m_f (R_s = 75 ohms)
10	0.12
40	0.35
52	0.41
75*	0.50
100	0.57
200	0.73
240	0.76
300	0.80
600	0.89

* i.e. $R_{in} = R_s$

Under this condition the effective line-to-line e.m.f. is equal to the e.m.f. indicated by the attenuator controls of the generator.

As indicated by expression 11.1 multiplying factors can be derived for converting from source e.m.f. to p.d. across the tuner aerial terminals and, relative to an R_s of 75 ohms, Table 11.2 gives such approximate factors m_f for various external load impedances.

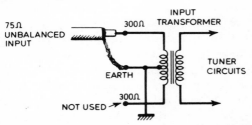

FIG. 11.8. *Showing how a 75-ohm unbalanced input can be obtained by utilising half the 300-ohm input transformer primary winding (see text)*

An alternative method for obtaining a balanced tuner coupling from an unbalanced generator is by the use of a 'balun' transformer. Low-loss (insertion loss less than 1 dB) transformers of this kind are not difficult to obtain or make (see, for example, the author's *The Practical Aerial Handbook*, 2nd Edition, pp. 56–60, by the publishers of this book).

F.M. RADIO

Tuner sensitivity based on μV (p.d.) will obviously appear to be less at R_{in} 300 ohms than at R_{in} 75 ohms. The 4:1 impedance difference implies a voltage ratio of 2:1, which, excluding losses, means that a tuner of $4\,\mu$V (p.d.) sensitivity at 300 ohms will have a $2\,\mu$V (p.d.) sensitivity at 75 ohms (also see Table 11.3).

Many tuners with a 300-ohm balanced aerial input use a centre-tapped input transformer primary winding, which means that a correctly matched coupling will be achieved by utilising half the winding due to the 2:1 ratio auto-transformer effect. This is shown in Fig. 11.8.

IHF USABLE SENSITIVITY

The IHF usable sensitivity is expressed in terms of μV (p.d.) required for a 30 dB ratio between the output for 100% modulation and the output when the modulation is 'notched out'; that is, the 30 dB ratio refers to the difference between the 100% modulation output and the distortion factor. This is shown in Fig. 11.5 which thus compares the 30 dB S/N ratio sensitivity with the IHF usable sensitivity. Since distortion is taken into account with the latter (30 dB $D_f \approx 3.2\%$), the IHF usable sensitivity will always be less than the 30 dB S/N ratio sensitivity (see Table 11.3). However, the difference should be fairly small with a well designed tuner because the f.m. distortion factor at low input signal levels should not be much greater than the noise.

The instrument setup in Fig. 11.1 is suitable for IHF usable sensitivity measurement, and under normal conditions there would only be one signal generator. After tuning and balancing the distortion factor test unit for maximum suppression of the modulation signal, the tuner input signal p.d. is adjusted by the generator's attenuator to the level where the audio milli-voltmeter indicates a difference of 30 dB between the 'set 100%' and 'read' functions of the distortion unit, which of course is the IHF usable sensitivity voltage (μV (p.d.)).

After establishing a 0 dB datum on the scale of the audio millivoltmeter, the audio attenuator can be reduced by 30 dB to allow use of the same 0 dB datum but this time with the distortion unit switched to 'read' (i.e. notch active). The Y1 trace of the oscilloscope will display the modulation signal and the Y2 trace the distortion factor residual.

When the signals of two generators are combined for the front-end selectivity test, generator 1 can be switched off for the sensitivity test. Generator 2 will thus be used which, as described earlier, makes it possible to obtain a front-end selectivity reference to the IHF usable sensitivity, which is a requirement of the test.

The IHS usable sensitivity parameter is more searching of tuner performance than simple S/N ratio since it serves to indicate the relative freedom of the tuner from objectional distortion during periods of maximum modulation as well as from noise during pauses in modulation.

The maximum IHF usable sensitivity of currently available tuners is veering towards the maximum limited by thermal noise produced by the radiation resistance of the aerial within the effective bandwidth. Table 11.3 lists factors involved in the IHF usable sensitivity 'equation' for mono operation and reveals that at 75 ohms aerial impedance the ultimate IHF usable sensitivity at one optimised frequency could be as high as $0.92 \mu V$.

Table 11.3

Noise input 75 ohms 250 kHz bandwidth ($= 0.27 \mu V$ (p.d.))	-11.2 dB, ref. $1 \mu V$
Noise figure	$+ 2.5$ dB
Input S/N for 30 dB output S/N	$+ 5.0$ dB
Extra for IHF usable sensitivity	$+ 3.0$ dB
	$+ 0.7$ dB, ref. $1 \mu V$
	$= 0.92 \mu V$

At 300 ohms the noise input would be about $0.55 \mu V$ (p.d.), which reduces the first dB entry to about -5.2 dB (ref. $1 \mu V$) and the total to $+5.3$ dB which referred to $1 \mu V$, works out to about $1.84 \mu V$ (p.d.), twice that at 75 ohms. In practice, 1 to 2 dB degradation results from front-end tracking compromises and i.f. tilt.

Owing to the multiplexing within ± 75 kHz maximum deviation (i.e. 100% modulation) and the greater bandwidth involved, the noise from a tuner operating in the stereo mode is greater than that produced by the same tuner operating in the mono mode. This, of course, reduces both the 30 dB S/N ratio sensitivity and the IHF usable sensitivity. The noise and distortion factor curves in Fig. 11.5 refer to the mono mode. For the same 30 dB S/N ratio sensitivity and IHF usable sensitivity in the stereo mode the input signal might have to be increased by as much as 20 dB.

AUDIO OUTPUT

This is the r.m.s. voltage at the output at 1 kHz, when the output is correctly terminated, at a stated modulation level. The vast majority of f.m. tuners yield an output which is compatible with the tuner input sensitivity of the amplifier.

FREQUENCY RESPONSE

Pre-emphasis is applied to the modulation signal at the transmitter, which is referred to a time-constant (see expression 10.2 and Fig. 10.9) of $50 \mu s$ for the European system (including the UK) and $75 \mu s$ for the American system. Thus the modulation is subjected to treble emphasis. The response is equalised at the tuner by complementary treble cut based on the corresponding time-constant. This is called de-emphasis. The technique improves the overall S/N ratio.

Measurement of the frequency response of a tuner, therefore, must take account of the de-emphasis, and the best way of catering for this is to apply the appropriate pre-emphasis to the variable-frequency audio signal applied to the f.m. generator for modulation.

Clearly, a tuner with the American $75 \mu s$ de-emphasis operating on the European transmissions will exhibit early treble roll-off, and, conversely, a tuner with 50 μs de-emphasis operating on the American transmissions will exhibit treble lift. It should be noted that the de-emphasis can be affected by excessive shunt capacitance at the output which, for example, may be unwittingly introduced by an abnormally long screened connecting cable from tuner to amplifier.

Modulation is carried up to about 15 kHz, and after this the response should fall swiftly (aided by filters) so that the attenuation is high at the 19 kHz stereo pilot tone and 38 kHz subchannel frequencies.

<h3 style="text-align:center">THE USE OF DOLBY</h3>

The FCC rules permit broadcasting of Dolby-B encoded signals in the US; other countries, too, are experimenting along these lines. With a complementary Dolby decoder at the tuner, coupled with a reduction is pre- and de-emphasis (25 μs has been suggested), the resulting improvement in S/N ratio (12 to 13 dB) can more than double the effective service area of a transmitter, with no increase in transmitter power. Receivers and tuners with Dolby B built in are becoming available at the time of writing; but UK listeners will not benefit from this unless the broadcasting authorities decide to introduce the necessary encoding. Also see page 257.

<h3 style="text-align:center">DISTORTION FACTOR</h3>

Distortion factor at any in-band frequency and modulation level can be measured with an instrument setup such as given in Fig. 11.1. However, the f.m. generator should be capable of accepting an external modulation signal of very low distortion and provide calibrated modulation up to 100% level at minimal distortion.

For measuring stereo distortion a stereo encoder is required at the generator, the net distortion measured then being that produced not only by the tuner i.f. channel and f.m. detector, but also by the stereo decoder and audio circuits in the tuner. A top-flight hi-fi stereo tuner should not produce much more than about 2% harmonic distortion in the subcarrier, though the stereo distortion at 1 kHz should be significantly less than this. It will be appreciated that the de-emphasis time-constant will effect the h.f. distortion, which means that in

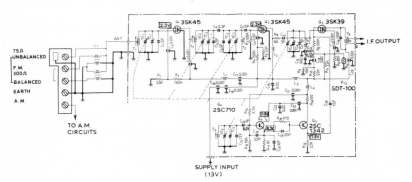

FIG. 11.9. *F.M. front-end section of Pioneer Model TX-9100 tuner (see text for more information)*

general a tuner with $75\,\mu s$ time-constant will exhibit less h.f. distortion than a counterpart with $50\,\mu s$ time-constant.

CURRENT TUNER DESIGN

Tuners at the pinnacle of contemporary design include MOS field effect transistors and the least three tuned circuits in front of the mixer in the front-end. Variable tuning is sometimes achieved by varicaps (i.e. capacitor diodes); but this is by no means a design criterion, as some excellent designs still make use of variable capacitor gangs (see Fig. 11.9).

The i.f. channel is equipped with i.c.s with limiting functions, while 'phase linear' ceramic filters are used for sharp selectivity.

Integrated circuits are also extensively adopted for the stereo decoder, and in this respect the 'phase lock loop' i.c. is becoming popular.

The front-end of the Pioneer TX-9100 tuner (Japanese) is given in Fig. 11.9.

Table 11.4

Parameter	Measured Value (Pioneer TX-9100 Tuner)
1. Front-end selectivity	90 dB* (figure of merit)
2. Alt. channel selectivity	90 dB*
3. Capture ratio	0.8 dB
4. AM rejection ratio	64 dB (to hum and noise)
5. Ultimate hum and noise	-64 dB
6. Ultimate S/N ratio	-75 dB
7. Full limiting	$2\,\mu V$ (p.d. 75 ohms)
8. 30 dB S/N ratio	$0.75\,\mu V$ (p.d. 75 ohms) approx.
9. IHF usable sensitivity	$0.95\,\mu V$ (p.d. 75 ohms)
10. Audio output	0.5 V r.m.s. per channel for 100% modulation†
11. Frequency response	$+\frac{3}{4}$ dB -1.5 dB 20 Hz $-$ 15 kHz, ref. 50 μsec. de-emphasis
12. Distortion factor	0.4% at 1 kHz 100% mod.

* limit of test equipment.
† also a variable output 60 mV $-$ 1.8 V 100% modulation.

This was one of the most advanced tuners available at the time of writing, and the parameters of this with the measured values are given in Table 11.4 for comparison with the minimum values suggested in Table 11.1 at the commencement of this chapter.

These are state-of-art values which at the time of writing only very few tuners could match.

The high front-end selectivity (including large-signal handling ability) and high sensitivity are achieved by the use of MOS (metal oxide semiconductor) dual-gate field effect transistors for r.f. amplification and mixing (two r.f.) and four variable-tuned circuits prior to the mixer in the front-end and four limiting i.c.s in the i.f. channel.

Referring to the circuit in Fig. 11.9, Q1 is the first r.f. transistor whose input gate is tuned by VC1. Q2 is the second r.f. amplifier with a passband coupling from Q1 tuned by VC2 and VC3. Q3 is the mixer whose input is tuned by VC4. The local oscillator is Q4, tuned by VC5, and the output of this is applied to mixer Q3 via emitter-follower oscillator buffer Q5.

The 75-ohm aerial input is applied directly to a tap on the input coil T1, and for 300 ohms balanced input a 'balun' transformer L1 is included. The tuner also features a m.w. a.m. band, but the circuit for this is not shown.

The i.f. channel includes four limiting i.c.s and two pairs of ceramic filters which drives a ratio detector. Filtering is employed to the stereo decoder which is a phase lock loop i.c.

Further information on stereo encoding and decoding can be found in the author's *F.M. Radio Servicing Handbook*, 2nd Edition, by the publishers of this book.

F.M. AERIAL

To conclude this chapter mention must be made of the f.m. aerial which, even in this age of highly sensitive and selective tuners, is equally as important as it ever has been. The full performance of any tuner will only be realised when it

FIG. 11.10. *Eight-element high-gain f.m. aerial suitable for long-distance and fringe area reception. This, the Fuba Uka Stereo 8 (distributed in the UK by Audio Workshops Limited, 29 High Street, Robertsbridge, Sussex), has an average gain of 9 dB, an average front/back ratio of 24 dB, a horizontal acceptance angle of 49 degrees and a vertical acceptance angle of 70 degrees. It includes a matching transformer suitable for either 75-ohm coaxial or 240/300-ohm balanced twin feeder*

receives a 'clean' signal free from reflected signal (which are responsible for so-called 'multipath distortion'). With tuners less selective and more readily overloaded (i.e. limited input dynamic range) the discrimination against unwanted strong signals may have to be provided by aerial directivity; and this applies, too, when distant-station reception, especially of stereo signals, is of interest (see Fig. 11.10).

THIRD-ORDER INTERMODULATION

When the 'local' group of stations is responsible for a strong signal field aerial attenuation may be necessary to avoid 'f.m. birdies'. One cause of this is third-

254

order intermodulation which manifests as the production of an interfering frequency of $f_2 + f_4 - f_3$ from the three frequencies f_2, f_3 and f_4 of Radios 2, 3 and 4. This interfering frequency lies in the f_3 transmission channel and is perturbed by modulation in any of the three channels.

Inadequate selectivity in the i.f. channel can also encourage a 'warbling' type of interference on stereo, which can be aggravated by harmonics of the stereo subchannel components. It can be reduced by the inclusion of a simple 55 kHz low-pass filter between f.m. detector and stereo decoder.

PROPOSALS FOR UPDATING THE IHF TUNER SPECIFICATIONS

Leading to enlarged and partly revised IHF f.m. tuner specifications, proposals for the updating of the original specifications were in the course of study by the membership of the IHF during the time that this book was being published. Since the original IHF standards were published in 1958, provision was not made in them for stereo tuners, so the proposals for enlargement specifically include parameters pertaining to f.m. tuners.

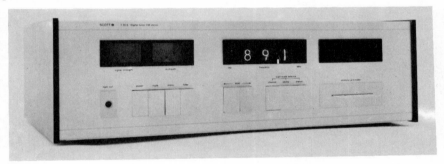

FIG. 11.11. *State-of-art tuner with digital readout of f.m. stations. This is the American Scott Model T33S which has a guaranteed tuning accuracy of 0.001% and 100 kHz channel spacing. This, in conjunction with 1 μV 30 dB s/n ratio sensitivity, 1.8 μV IHF sensitivity, 75 dB IHF selectivity, 1.2 dB capture ratio and 95 dB cross modulation rejection, would be eminently suitable for DX activities as well as for normal reception, particularly in difficult reception areas. It has a phase lock acquisition time of 10 ms, automatic scanning of 5 channels per second (automatic tuning), preselection by punched cards, medium-scale integrated circuits and plug-in modules. The UK Distributor is Photax (London) Limited, Eastbourne, Sussex*

However, some of the proposed revision is appropriate also to mono f.m. tuners or stereo tuners in mono mode. The draft proposals now include ten parameters for 'minimum' performance description and a further eight secondary parameters for 'complete' performance description. The 'minimum' requirements are given in Table 11.5(a) and the additional requirements in Table 11.5(b), from which will be seen that fully to specify the performance of a stereo tuner fourteen parameters relating to mono and ten relating to stereo would be required.

Unchanged are the usable sensitivity, ultimate signal/noise ratio, drift, frequency response, intermodulation distortion, alternate channel selectivity, spurious response rejection and hum.

New parameters proposed are usable sensitivity in the stereo mode with the same 30 dB ratio (signal/distortion factor ratio) as the mono test (see page 250), 50 dB quieting sensitivity for both mono *and* stereo, harmonic distortion for both mono *and* stereo input for 50 dB quieting, ultimate signal/noise ratio in stereo mode, ultimate harmonic distortion in stereo mode, frequency response in stereo mode, stereo separation, subcarrier rejection ratio, SCA rejection ratio (applicable essentially to American-located tuners), adjacent channel selectivity (the existing standards require a test only of *alternate* channel selectivity) and stereo decoder switching threshold.

Table 11.5

Parameter	Mono	Stereo
(a)		
Usable sensitivity	*	**
50 dB quieting sensitivity	**	**
Harm. Dist. at 50 dB quieting sen.	**	**
Ultimate signal/noise ratio	*	**
Ultimate harmonic distortion	***	**
Drift	*	****
Frequency response	*	**
Stereo separation	*****	**
Subcarrier rejection	*****	**
SCA rejection	*****	**
(b)		
Intermodulation distortion	*	*****
Capture ratio	***	*****
Alternate channel selectivity	*	*****
Adjacent channel selectivity	**	*****
Spurious response rejection	*	*****
Stereo threshold	*****	**
Hum	*	*****
AM rejection ratio	***	*****

*	unchanged	****	not required
**	new parameter	*****	not applicable
***	revised parameter		

The revisions refer to ultimate harmonic distortion, where test frequencies of at least 100 Hz, 1 kHz and 7.5 kHz mono and 5 kHz top frequency for stereo are proposed, to capture ratio at an input of 100 μV as well as 1 mV (the existing standards require an input of 1 mV for the *rated* capture ratio) and to a.m. rejection ratio, where the measurement is proposed at both 100 μV *and* that corresponding to the 50 dB quieting sensitivity (the existing standards require this test to be made only at 100 μV input).

At the time of writing other standards are being devised or revised by the various authorities relating to virtually all items of audio and hi-fi equipment in an endeavour meaningfully to appraise the very exacting equipment which is currently being designed, manufactured and sold.

The German DIN is one such authority which is currently updating their standards. The British Standard Institution (BSI) is also very active in this respect, and is currently working on a series of specifications—the 'equivalent' of the DIN 45–500 specifications—for domestic hi-fi equipment, which it is hoped will lead to a long overdue series of 'international' standards in this area.

Organisations participating in the BSI exercise include BREMA, FBA, APAE and RECMF in the form of an Audio Specification Co-ordinating Committee. British activity along these lines commenced some six years ago, and of more recent times a Technical Committee (TLE/26) has been established to correlate the work. A number of draft specifications for hi-fi equipment has already been released, and in order to help precipitate an international standard these are under examination by the International Electrotechnical Commission operating under working group 12 of sub-committee SC29B. It is likely, therefore, that before this book has been on the market for very long a new set of British standards will have evolved.

DOLBY AND F.M.

In America the Federal Communications Commission (FCC) has now authorised the use of Dolby B for f.m. broadcasting combined with a reduction in pre-emphasis from 75 to 25 μs. Dolby B encoding boosts progressively the higher audio frequencies with reducing signal level. Decoding at the receiver is complementary (see page 234), the overall effect being rather like variable pre- and de-emphasis. In America the combination is said to yield acceptable frequency balance with tuners devoid of Dolby B decoding but with 75 μs de-emphasis. Similar compatibility with existing European (and UK) tuners of 50 μs de-emphasis would call for lower than 25 μs pre-emphasis combined with Dolby B (17 μs been suggested). To reap the advantages of the Dolby noise reduction, of course, the tuner would require the addition of a Dolby B decoder and a corresponding reduction in the de-emphasis time-constant. The result would undoubtedly be significantly improved s/n ratio, particularly on stereo in fringe areas (see page 252).

There is no evidence that the scheme will be adopted by the BBC. An attribute of a reduced pre-emphasis time-constant allied with Dolby B encoding is the avoidance of treble overmodulation. However, this is already avoided by the BBC, not by peak clipping, but by the use of variable de-emphasis limiters which automatically and momentarily reduce the pre-emphasis when there is a very large amplitude, high-frequency content in the modulation signal. These are employed at most BBC stations carrying stereo information and are working very well.

CHAPTER 12

Surround Sound and Four-Channel Systems

AS IS NOW FAIRLY well known, stereo reproduction requires the signals of the left and right channels derived from microphones at the sound source to be conveyed in virtual isolation all the way through the recording/transmitting/reproducing system for application to two loudspeakers at the left- and right-hand sides of the sound stage in the listening room. With correct phasing the sounds from the two loudspeakers blend so that a listener some distance from them and approximately equal distance from each experiences an impression of the original sound scene in terms of breadth and spatial relationships of the individual sounding sources. This is a two-channel system.

With reducing channel separation the breadth of the sound stage appears to diminish until eventually, when the separation falls to zero, the mono condition pertains, and the sound then appears to emanate from a point midway between the two loudspeakers. Incorrect phasing results in some confusion of image location and apparent widening of the sound stage outside the boundaries determined by the placement of the two loudspeakers.

A sounding source is located by a listener by differences in intensity and time of arrival of the sound waves at his two ears, the latter being a dominating factor. This can be proved by operating two spaced loudspeakers at exactly the same intensity with corresponding signals but with a small time delay on one signal with respect to the other. Under this condition a listener located at an equal distance from the two loudspeakers will receive the impression that the sound is emanating from the loudspeaker whose signal is *not* subjected to the time delay. This is called the precedence (or Haas) effect. It is quite astonishing, for with a 50 ms delay it requires the intensity of the delayed sound to be increased by 10 dB or more before it appears to emanate from that loudspeaker.

Thus, the stereo effect relies on both the intensity and the timing (or phasing, which is a similar thing) of the sound from the two loudspeakers, which means that the *signals* in the two stereo channels vary both relatively in amplitude and phase.

In the concert hall our ears respond not only to the sounds directly from the various instruments of the orchestra but also to sounds arriving from all other directions due to reflections. The reflected sounds contain the information relating to the acoustical characteristics of the concert hall. It follows, there-

258

fore, that by introducing them in correct perspective in the listening room enhanced realism of the reproduced sound scene would be achieved; in other words, the reflected sounds introduce the ambience, reverberance and spatial relationships that a listener would have experienced at the live performance.

A stereo microphone system obviously responds to some of the reflected sounds so they must contribute to the left and right stereo signals, but with ordinary two-loudspeaker stereo reproduction they arrive from the front and not from the sides, back and ceiling, as well as the front, as they do in reality. A closer approach to the original sound scene can be obtained by 'decoding' the ambience and feeding this to separate loudspeakers placed at the sides or back of the listening room.

The simplest form of four-loudspeaker reproduction is based on this technique. It must be clearly understood that although there are in this arrangement four loudspeakers there still remain only the two stereo channels. The extra loudspeakers are wired so that they are driven essentially by the ambience contained in the signals of the two stereo channels. The scheme can also be used with just one extra speaker placed behind the listener.

NOMENCLATURE

A difficult problem in writing this chapter was deciding on the terminology to adopt. About the only 'four-channel' term that has been recognised internationally is 'quadraphonic' or 'quadraphony', but as mentioned in Chapter 7 this term is barely acceptable in some circles and totally unacceptable in others!

One confusion results from the fact that the number of intermediate channels often differs from the number of speakers employed. Thus if 'quadraphony' refers to four loudspeakers a mono system running four speakers could be called by this name!

There are three primary factors involved in any system which are (i) the number of source-derived signal inputs or channels, (ii) the number of intermediate channels and (iii) the number of loudspeaker channels and/or loudspeakers required for the *intended* use of the system, and a simple shorthand based on these three factors is often used to identify the various systems. Thus we have 1-1-1 for mono, 2-2-2 for stereo and 4-4-4 for full four-channel. In all these examples each input has its own intermediate channel and speaker.

Now, when two extra speakers are wired to respond to the derived ambience we get 2-2-4, which implies that the two stereo speakers plus two extra speakers (intended for ambience) are fed from a two-channel source through two channels. With only one extra speaker for ambience we have 2-2-3. When the source is derived four-channel and this is matrixed to two channels and then matrixed back to four channels for operating four loudspeakers we have 4-2-4.

Variations to this shorthand have been suggested, but to delve into these would add to rather than ease the general confusion. Ambiguities can still arise since the shorthand fails to indicate the nature of the coding and decoding in a 4-2-4 system, for example. Moreover, a system designated 2-2-4 could have the two extra speakers merely connected in parallel with the two for stereo and thus not respond to ambience at all; or with a 2-2-3 configuration the extra

259

speaker could be wired to respond to $\frac{1}{2}(L + R)$, and placed between the left and right speakers to eliminate the 'hole in the middle effect'. Nevertheless, in spite of these possible aberrations the shorthand is useful when interpreted in the intended sense.

Terms often used for the 2-2-4 arrangement are 'ambiophony' and 'ambiphonic'. 'Surround sound' is another term of more neutral nature, but this could be applicable equally to any of the other arrangements. The term has been defined* as any system in which straight lines joining the loudspeakers enclose the space surrounding the listener, and other suggested terms are 'ambisonic' where the listener obtains an acceptable approximation to the impression of directionality and reverberance which he would (or could) experience at the live performance, 'periphonic' where this occurs in three directions, including height, and 'pantophonic' where the ambisonics occur essentially in the horizontal plane.

Although it is true, of course, that the more channels there are available, the greater the scope there is for information coding (essentially in the amplitude sense, for instance, when there is a channel for each signal input and loudspeaker, such as with a 4-4-4 system), totally independent channels all round are not necessary for acceptable results. This is because in practice the signals themselves are not completely independent—common components exist in all channels. Thus there is bound to be some redundancy in a system of totally independent channels, so by taking account of the 'differences'—that is, of the relative amplitudes and phases of the signals—this redundancy can be exploited to reduce the number of channels in a multi-loudspeaker system.

However, microphone techniques and arrays, the nature of the coding and the placement of the speakers in the listening room constitute important factors in the overall equation. The scope is great with regard to microphones, arrays and techniques, and considerable attention is being directed to this area of the craft.

SPEAKER NUMBER AND PLACEMENT

The least number of speakers required for surround-sound is, of course, three; but in the vast majority of cases four are used (from which the deprecated designation 'quadraphonic' was encouraged), one placed approximately at each corner of the listening scene. Six can yield some improvement, but it would appear that only minimal advantage is to be gained from a greater number.

When height is also considered (as in 'periphonic' reproduction) a minimum of four loudspeakers is desirable arranged to occupy the alternate corners of the listening 'cube'. One in each corner (total of eight) is said to be better! However, programme software coded in three directions was not normally available at the time of writing. Most programme software of the so-called 'four-channel' category 'captures' essentially surround-sound in the horizontal plane, but even so some enhancement to the reproduction may be possible by adding height to the loudspeaker formation. The back loudspeakers of a simple 2-2-4

*'Perspectives for Surround-Sound', Fellgett, P. B., *Hi-Fi Sound Annual, 1974.*

SURROUND SOUND AND FOUR-CHANNEL SYSTEMS

technique, for example, may yield improved results when placed above the listener and turned towards the wall to diffuse the ambience.

As we have seen (Chapters 7 and 8), there is a 4-4-4 technique via disc multiplexing, which is the JVC-Nivico CD-4 system. Four independent channels can also be obtained from tape tracks, an example being the JVC CD-4 1680 *cassette* machine, which includes the JVC automatic noise reduction system (ANRS) referred to in Chapter 10 (also see page 271 of this chapter). Four-channel tape cartridge systems are also in use.

RADIO COMPATIBILITY

An advantage of the 4-2-4 techniques is that they do not require any more bandwidth than regular stereo systems, which means that conveyance can be through the existing two channels of an f.m. stereo radio system when the stereo decoder is followed by a suitable decoding matrix.* This aspect of bandwidth saving will probably rank high when a standard for transmission through radio is finally chosen. Clearly, 2-2-4 reproduction is already possible from f.m. stereo radio.

It would also be possible to transmit via three or four channels by an extension of the existing f.m. stereo multiplexing techniques. The additional channel or channels could adopt amplitude/phase subcarrier modulation, possibly similar to the coding of the U and V chroma signals of colour television (see the author's book *Colour Television Servicing*, 2nd edition, by the publishers of this book). Another method (proposed for CD-4) could be an extra subchannel, but the extra channel or channels would need to be arranged to avoid incompatibility with existing stereo reception.

Some four-channel receivers are already equipped with an output direct from the f.m. detector (prior to de-emphasis) in anticipation of three or four channel decoding.

MONO AND STEREO COMPATIBILITY

Records for matrix or multiplex broadcasting must obviously be acceptably reproducible in mono or stereo; that is, in these modes no parts of the recorded programme should be lost or unduly weakened with respect to other parts. Such compatibility is equally as important so far as disc play itself is concerned. CD-4 records, by the nature of the coding, have complete mono and stereo compatibility. However, matrixed records are less accommodating (see Chapter 7), and can suffer from varying degrees of incompatibility, particularly in the mono mode. For example, SQ matrixing results in centre back signal suppression in the mono mode, for which reason soloists are not located at this position during recording. Also with SQ in two-channel mode rear signal images are placed within two speakers, whereas with QS the anti-phase rear signals produce images outside the two speakers. With front crosstalk the overall effect is quite acceptable. However, one cannot really expect four-loudspeaker reproduction to be as acceptable when played mono or stereo as a disc specifically recorded for mono or stereo reproduction. The same applies,

*U.S. broadcasters are already advertising the use of matrix software, and professional matrix encoders are readily available to them.

261

anyway, to a stereo disc when played mono. There is bound to be some loss from, say, 4-2-4 through 4-2-2 to 4-1-1, but new recording techniques are reducing the shortcomings.

Impressions of sound scenes resulting from 4-4-4, 1-1-1 and 2-2-2 reproducing techniques are given in Fig. 12.1 with reference to the original sound scene at (a) where the various symbols represent different sound points. It is obviously the aim of a 4-4-4 or 4-2-4 technique to reconstitute the original sound scene

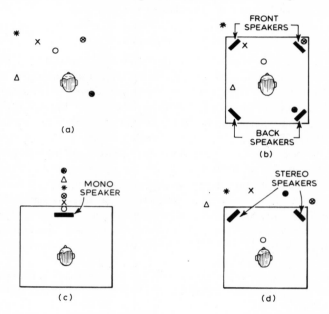

FIG. 12.1. *The symbols at (a) represent point sources as observed by a listener in the original sound scene. (b) shows the location of the point sources when the reproduction is through an ideal four-channel system. (c) gives an impression of the scene reproduced in mono, where there is no localisation at all, while (d) gives an impression of the scene reproduced in stereo*

in the listening room complete with ambience and reverberance round 360 degrees as shown at (b). The mono scene is depicted at (c) where the sound is effectively compressed into a 'tunnel' and is devoid of spatial relationships and complete and natural ambience, while the stereo scene is depicted at (d).

Clearly, the difference between (a) and (d) is dramatic, but the degree of co-incidence of (b) to (a) depends on the effectiveness of the coding and on the number of compromises that the system imposes. Four channels impose fewer compromises than two channels, so it follows that a 4-4-4 technique has greater potential than a 4-2-4 technique. It is somewhat a matter of bandwidth; a four-channel system has twice the audio bandwidth of a two-channel system. However, it does not necessarily follow that more accurate reconstitution of a complex sound scene will result from a 4-4-4 technique. Much depends on how well the extra available bandwidth has been utilised. If there is significant re-dundancy then bandwidth will have been wasted and a 4-2-4 technique would have done almost as well. It has been indicated (see the reference of the footnote on page 260) that, based on systems which use only amplitude to indicate directionality, three channels are needed for pantaphonic sound and four channels for periphonic sound, where height is also included.

As explained in Chapter 7, matrix systems are based on a predetermined matrix equation for combining the four originating source signals of specified angular positions, such as left front (L_F), right front (R_F), left back (L_B) and right back (R_B), into two composite signals left total (L_T) and right total (R_T). This is the coding function.

For reproduction a complementary matrix is used to reconstitute the four originating signals. However, resulting from the nature of a matrix (which is a kind of 'mixing' circuit) the output signals can never be untainted replicas of the input signals because a signal applied to one of the coding inputs will appear in at least three of the decoding outputs. A matrix thus suffers from crosstalk between the outputs.

While crosstalk in a stereo system results in the narrowing of the sound stage, a degree of subjective counteracting of the effect is exhibited in a matrix (i.e. 4-2-4) system owing to the four loudspeakers and the 'timing' or phasing of the signals applied to them. For example, the sounds which are simultaneously emanating from the loudspeakers adjacent to that of the intended angular position tend, as the result of subjective phenomena, to 'relocate' the image so that the listener receives the impression that it is located approximately at the intended angular position.

Matrix systems also use various circuit dodges in an endeavour to improve the quality of localisation. A 'blending' circuit, for example, may be used to add one of the decoded signals to the other at the respective front and back channel pairs, such that the C_F signals are increased while the C_B signals are decreased, which is a technique for improving the C_F to C_B (centre front and centre back respectively) separation. SQ decoding may also use degrees of fixed 'blending', one version being 25% between the front and the back channels and another 10% between the front and 40% between the back channels.

The basic SQ technique has infinite front left-to-right and back left-to-right separation, 3 dB between left and right front-to-back and 3 dB between diagonally opposite outputs. With this system there are phase shifts of +90 degrees at L_B relative to L_F and −90 degrees at R_B relative to R_F. The net result is infinite separation between the front two outputs and the same between the back two outputs, with virtually zero crosstalk in the stereo mode but with centre back signal suppression in the mono mode.

So-called 'gain-riding' and 'logic' control are SQ refinements, which shift the power preferentially to the front and back circuits depending on the signal information (phase and amplitude), thereby giving prominence to the C_F or C_B information yielded by the matrix under the control of the signals.

Logic control includes amplifiers which respond to the signal parameters and which regulate the power distribution of the channels in relation to these. So-called 'wave-matching' is also employed, whereby the balance of power is transferred to the front or back outputs as determined by the presence of front and back corner signals.

Other SQ techniques include 'variable blend logic', 'paramatrix' and, more recently, 'selective logic' (SL). Little information was available on the last

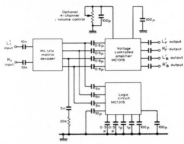

FIG. 12.2. *Schematic diagram of the Motorola SQ i.c. decoder. Notice that the gain control follows the matrix in SQ*

mentioned at the time of writing, but signal cancellation effects figure in para-matrix, where the transfer of signals into one arm of the decoding matrix is cancelled selectively by the signals transferred into the complementary arm, again under 'logic' control.

Integrated circuit decoders are available and in current application. The schematic of the Motorola SQ matrix i.c. with logic is given in Fig. 12.2.

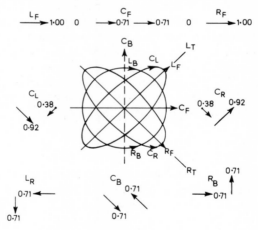

FIG. 12.3. *SQ vectors and position code*

Vectors of the SQ matrix, with position code, are given in Fig. 12.3, where the vectors signify complete front separation.

While the 'balance', etc. of a matrix can be altered, the fundamental properties remain. It is something like squeezing a balloon into different shapes. It remains a balloon whatever is done (unless it bursts!) though it can be given an infinite number of shapes. The balance of the output signals can be altered easily enough, as can the phase of the signals and the distribution of crosstalk between the various outputs.

Gain-riding and 'logic' control circuits can only vary the outputs in different ways; they cannot change a matrix into a true four-channel circuit. Thus the effects provided by such artifices are essentially subjective, for which reason they are sometimes questioned. It is sometimes argued that crosstalk is not necessarily undesirable in surround-sound systems and that of greater importance than localisation are reverberance and ambience yielded by this form of reproduction, which have the effect of enhancing the localisation anyway.

The various matrix artifices endeavour to improve localisation, and the way that they attempt this may not always be aesthetically acceptable. For example, it is not possible for the control circuits to differentiate between all kinds of signals and transients, so there may be displacement of one image so that another can take up its more correct position.

On the other hand, the net result is essentially subjective, so schemes that enhance the illusion, even though not physically accurate, should not be discouraged.

The 4-4-4 technique is troubled less by localisation mishaps; this technique, in fact, exceeds the potentialities of mere surround-sound or 4-2-4 techniques, though how it will develop will depend on the skill directed to the coding.

The QS system is another 4-2-4 configuration, whose coding and complementary decoding arrangements are given respectively at (a) and (b) in Fig. 12.4,

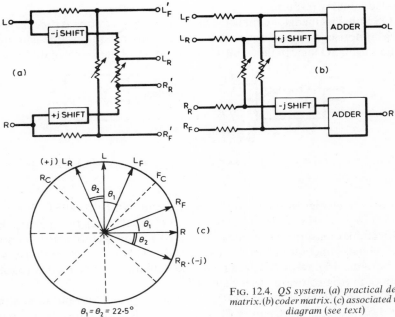

$\theta_1 = \theta_2 = 22 \cdot 5°$

FIG. 12.4. *QS system.* (a) *practical decoder matrix.* (b) *coder matrix.* (c) *associated vector diagram (see text)*

with associated vectors at (*c*). With this system there are phase shifts of -90 degrees at L_B relative to L_F and $+90$ degrees at R_B relative to R_F, and the L_F and L_B modulations are orientated by 22.5 degrees with respect to the left and right axes, which result in a separation of 7.7 dB between front-to-back and side-to-side centres, 3 dB separation from any output to its neighbour and infinite separation between diagonally opposite outputs. Thus, the system has the merit of being symmetrical, for which reason it is sometimes favoured.

Fig. 12.5 shows how the sounds are phased with respect to the four loudspeakers. The out-of-phase sounds tend to enhance localisation accuracy

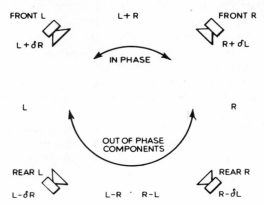

FIG. 12.5. *Sound phasing round the four loudspeakers of the QS system*

because they emanate either side of the loudspeaker corresponding to the intended angular position.

A QS embellishment for enhancing inter-channel separation is the *variomatrix*, which comprises a phase discriminator, phase shifters and variable-gain matrix. It differs from SQ logic in that controlled 'blending' of the four signals is achieved

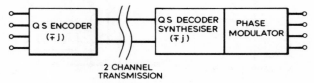

FIG. 12.6. *Block diagram of the QS system, showing decoder synthesiser and phase modulator (see text)*

without gain change of the decoder amplifiers (it will be recalled—Fig. 12.2— that SQ logic works by level-controlling the signals after the matrix). Based on directional masking phenomenon, almost instantaneous matrix control is achieved as a function of the input signals, such that the total relative sound volume of the original field is preserved. The technique also facilitates accommodation of matrix software other than QS.

A block diagram of an earlier QS system with random-phase modulator (now discontinued, see Chapter 7) is given in Fig. 12.6. This shows that the

QS basic matrix will also work as a four-channel synthesiser from two-channel stereo sources, also see under 2-2-3 and 2-2-4 techniques.

Various other matrices have been developed or are in the course of development at the time of writing. Some have been abandoned and others are being demonstrated and evaluated, leading to possible sponsoring by uncommitted record companies.

An interesting system has been devised by Dr. Duane Cooper of the University of Illinois (Cooper-Shiga)* and developed by Nippon Columbia Company Limited whereby the merits of matrix have been combined with those of 'multiplex'. The basic matrix (BMX) is a phasor system which, unlike SQ and QS, provides full mono compatibility because the derived horizontal plane difference signal has a phase shift that lags the mono signal by an amount equal to the relative source angle. On four-loudspeaker playback, distribution is symmetrical over 45 degree angles, which means that unwanted emissions either side of the wanted ones are phased by ± 45 degrees, which tends to enhance localisation.

At the time of writing (1974), launching of the Nippon Columbia UD-4 system has been announced. This combines the matrix with two supplementary channels based on a 30 kHz carrier of *circa* 3 to 4 kHz bandwidth, the deviation being ± 6 kHz at a carrier level of 35.4 mm/sec, thereby giving a maximum frequency of 36 kHz, which is less than that of CD-4. The carrier channels, which need not be exploited unless required, augment the 'directivity' and render listener placement less critical. The scheme is thus highly versatile in that UD-4 software (fifty records are planned for release in 1974) is compatible with mono without directional anomalies, with two-channel stereo, with four-loudspeaker 'surround sound' and with 'discrete' replay utilising the carrier channels. A scheme has also been worked out for f.m. broadcasting.

2-2-3 AND 2-2-4 TECHNIQUES

The ambience contained in the two channels of a regular stereo record takes the form of out-of-phase components which, as explained in Chapter 7, give rise to vertical vibrations of the pickup stylus. The ambience is also present, of course, in the left and right stereo signals from any other source since it has been coded in a somewhat random way by the originating stereo microphone system.

The ambience can be caused to operate an extra pair of loudspeakers placed behind the listener by connecting them across the 'live' terminals of the stereo amplifier's left and right outputs. The back loudspeakers then receive drive whenever the L and R signals deviate from the in-phase condition. Thus with a correctly phased stereo amplifier operating in the mono mode (L + R) there will be no drive to the back loudspeakers when left and right signal levels are equal.

Because the reflected sounds arriving towards the sides and back of the stereo microphone system tends to swing towards L − R, the back loudspeakers will thus deliver sound containing some of the components of the original ambience. Just how well the ambience is reproduced depends to some extent on the nature

* Duane H. Cooper and Takeo Shiga, 'Discrete-Matrix Multichannel Stereo', *J. Audio. Eng. Soc.*, vol. 20, No. 5, p. 346 (June, 1972).

of the microphone system which was used to originate the signals. Experiments indicate that some of the best effects are obtained from recordings and transmissions using a single Blumlein crossed figure-of-eight microphone pair (see Chapter 9).

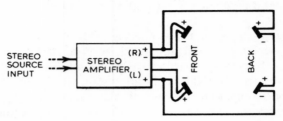

FIG. 12.7. *Simple way of obtaining 2-2-4 reproduction by feeding the 'differential' of the L and R signals to the back loudspeakers. Maximum amplifier loading occurs when the signals swing antiphase (see text)*

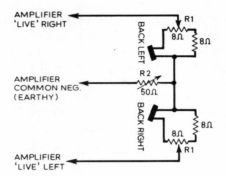

FIG. 12.8. *Development of Fig. 12.7 (see text)*

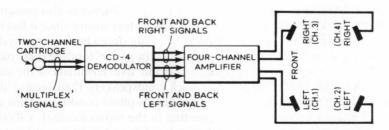

FIG. 12.9. *Functional diagram of the CD-4 four-channel system, showing CD-4 demodulator*

The two back loudspeakers can be connected in series or parallel to suit the sensitivity and impedance, but in phase opposition for the best results, and diffusion sometimes helps by reflecting their emissions from a wall. A system of this kind was described some years ago by a David Hafler, and 2-2-4 setups are often called after his name. Stereo amplifiers are now being made with two

268

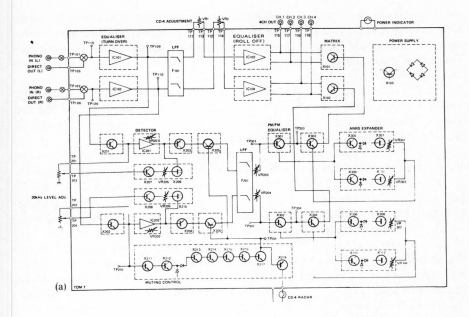

(a)

Fig. 12.10. *Schematic diagram of the CD-4 JVC Model 4DD-5 demodulator, which is described in the text*

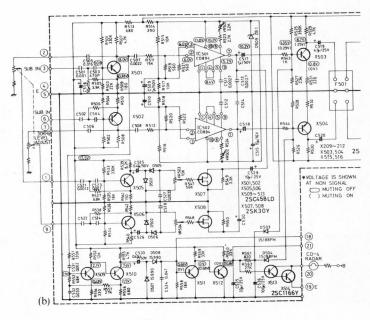

(b)

269

extra loudspeaker outlets to facilitate 2-2-4 reproduction. Switching is sometimes included so that the outlets can provide either ambience or ordinary stereo signals for a second pair of loudspeakers. Some manufacturers also include simple low-pass filtering for the back loudspeakers to improve the reproduction of the ambience.

Fig. 12.7 shows the basic idea, while a development is given in Fig. 12.8 where variable resistors R1 provide for back speaker level adjustments and R2 for L-to-R 'blending', the resulting front crosstalk tending to introduce directionality to the ambience at the expense of front separation.

The stereo amplifier should have a common 'earthy' speaker circuit (most have), and the extra loading seen by each channel due to the back loudspeakers depends on the L and R signal phasing from moment to moment. When $L + R$ pertains there is no extra loading of course, but the extra per-channel loading swings to maximum when the phase difference between L and R is 180 degrees, which rarely (if ever) happens in practice. However, assuming this worst possible condition $1/Z_T = 1/Z_1 + 1/Z_2 + 1/Z_3$, where Z_T is the per-channel load seen by the amplifier, Z_1 the impedance of the left speaker, Z_2 the impedance of the right speaker and Z_3 the total impedance of the back speakers and circuit. Thus in the basic case (Fig. 12.7) when the two front speakers are each 8 ohms and the total impedance of the back speakers also 8 ohms (i.e. two 4-ohm in series or two 16-ohm in parallel) each amplifier output will 'see' 2.6 ohms (a highly improbable phasing condition though).

2-2-4 working is sometimes expressed as 'synthesising', and four-channel equipment with a specific 4-2-4 matrix can usually be switched to such a mode. However, an advantage of the simple schemes of Figs. 12.7 and 12.8 is that additional power amplifiers are not required for the back loudspeakers (or

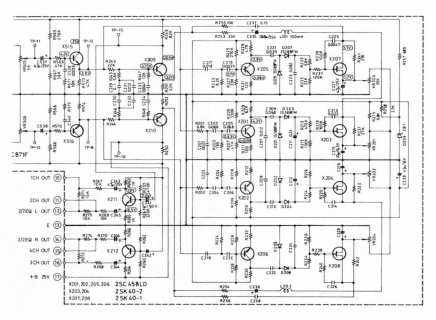

270

loudspeaker in the 2-2-3 mode). When four amplifiers exist in the equipment, then of course an amplifier is used for each loudspeaker and the synthesising is performed before the power amplifiers. A variable control may also be incorporated to adjust the frequency/amplitude characteristics of the back signals for the best effect.

The Sansui QS synthesising function is based on the regular matrix, including the use of the same $\pm j$ shifters and blending co-efficient, and is enhanced by the phase modulator (Fig. 12.6).

CD-4 SYSTEM

A schematic diagram of the JVC CD-4 Disc Demodulator is given in Fig. 12.10(a), while a complete circuit of the demodulator is given at (b). Referring to (a), the complex pickup signals enter the 'turnover' section of the equaliser (IC101/102), whose response is shown by curve 1 in Fig. 12.11(a). After passing through low-pass filter F101, the signals are further equalised by the 'roll-off' section IC103/104, whose response is shown by curve 2 in Fig. 12.11(a). In combination, the equaliser sections match the RIAA requirement, as shown by curve 3 in Fig. 12.11(b).

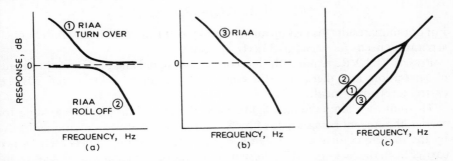

FIG. 12.11. *The RIAA equalisation curve (b) is made up of two curves at 1 and 2 in (a) to facilitate extraction of the modulated difference signal in the JVC 4DD-5 demodulator (see text). The curves at (c) refer to the JVC automatic noise reduction system (ANRS), which is used in the 4DD-5 demodulator (also see Chapter 7)*

The low-pass filter removes the modulated difference signals above 15 kHz so that only the sum signals pass through the full equaliser and hence to the matrix circuits X101/102. Full details of the nature of the sum and difference signals are given in Chapter 7 and in Fig. 7.5.

The modulated difference signals prior to the low-pass filter are applied to the detector IC201/202 through X201/202, and the output from the detector is passed to muting circuit X205/206 through X203/204, which is controlled by X211–X217.

The muting control responds to carrier signal applied to X211 from X202, and the muting is active only when a CD-4 record is being played; that is, when carrier is present on the pickup signal. Under this condition the signal from the output of the detector, which is the difference signal, is applied to the PM/FM compensation circuit X301/302, via low-pass filter F201, which removes the residual carrier. The compensation circuit equalises the difference signal for noise reduction.

The JVC automatic noise reduction system (ANRS) is adopted for the difference signals (Chapter 10), the operation of which is as follows. Curve 2 in Fig. 12.11(c) refers to the CD-4 recording, which reveals that a signal for recording whose level is lower than a predetermined value is boosted. The boost is progressive above 500 Hz. The expander circuit is arranged to provide the complementary function, shown by curve 3 in Fig. 12.11(c). A 'flat' characteristic, curve 1 in Fig. 12.11(c), is thus produced by the compression during recording and the expansion during play.

Expander X303/304 is controlled by two circuits, one dealing with the middle frequencies (X305–308) and the other dealing with the high frequencies (X309–312). The difference signal from the expander is then conveyed to the matrix X101/102, where it is added to or subtracted from the sum signal. The processing is such that

$$L_F = \tfrac{1}{2}[(L_F + L_B) + (L_F - L_B)]$$
$$L_B = \tfrac{1}{2}[(L_F + L_B) - (L_F - L_B)]$$
$$R_F = \tfrac{1}{2}[(R_F + R_B) + (R_F - R_B)]$$
$$R_B = \tfrac{1}{2}[(R_F + R_B) - (R_F - R_B)]$$

For optimum results the pickup must respond to at least 45 kHz and the channel separation needs to extend to 30 kHz upwards.

Presets VR1/VR2 regulate the level of the sum signal and provide adjustment of separation, and there are also controls for channel balance and 30 kHz carrier level adjustment.

The indicator lamp ('radar') lights when the demodulator is responding to carrier, the current being supplied by X218, this being turned on automatically by the muting control circuit. On a regular stereo record, when there is no carrier from the pickup, X205/206 switch off and prevent spurious signals from being fed to the matrix. Under this condition X218 is non-conducting and the indicator lamp is not lit. The indicator is similar in function to that of stereo tuners responding to the pilot tone.

CD-4 PICKUPS

Connections to and from the demodulator are shown in Fig. 12.12, and as explained in Chapter 8 the cartridge must have a response extending to 45 kHz. It should also be free from undamped resonances; a bad resonance around 30 kHz, for example, could unbalance the difference signals and cause distortion. The 30 kHz preset can correct for this, adjustment being made in conjunction with a test record of 400 Hz tone for maximum stability and least distortion.

Improved h.f. tracing can be achieved by a Shibata, Pramanik or Ichikawa stylus (see Chapter 8), but almost any good magnetic cartridge which tracks at 1.5 grams or less equipped with elliptical stylus is capable of CD-4 reproduction. Shunt capacitance must be minimised by the use of low-capacitance leads,

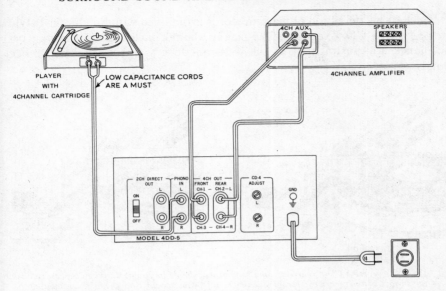

FIG. 12.12. *Showing how the JVC 4DD-5 demodulator is connected between the pickup and four-channel amplifier*

and the cartridge needs to be carefully adjusted in the arm as shown at (*a*) in Fig. 12.13. Maladjustment as at (*b*) could result in poor quality.

CD-4 channel coding is given in Table 12.1 and the colour codes in Table 12.2

Table 12.1

Channel	Channel Number
Front left	1
Back left	2
Front right	3
Back right	4

Table 12.2

Channel Number	Colour
1	Brown
2	Red
3	Orange
4	Yellow
PU left	White
PU right	Red

It is desirable when playing CD-4 records mono or stereo to ensure that the cartridge is of reasonable quality and free from 30 kHz resonance, since this could emphasise the carrier signal fed to the amplifier which, if responsive to 30 kHz, as many are, will cause the signal to appear across the speakers. Although outside the passband, it is not desirable for the amplifier to pass relatively large amplitude 30 kHz signal.

273

The best h.f. definition of matrix records is obtained with an elliptical stylus or one of the CD-4 versions. The pickup should have a good tracking performance, for mistracking in the 4-2-4 mode is emphasised by the back loudspeakers.

(a)   (b)

FIG. 12.13. *For correct CD-4 reproduction the cartridge should be mounted in the arm perpendicular to the surface of the record (a). Unsatisfactory results would result from the angled mounting (b)*

FOUR-LOUDSPEAKER SYSTEMS

At the time of writing one of the best schemes appears to be a system whereby the chosen matrix or decoder can be plugged into the parent four-channel amplifier or receiver as a separate unit, and some four-channel equipment is designed along these lines. As an example, the four-channel (Quadradial) Marantz amplifiers and receivers accept a pluggable matrix underneath. Without the matrix, however, the equipment will still reproduce through four loudspeakers when switched to the 2-2-4 mode; and coded records can also be played in this mode.

REPRODUCING MODE

Fig. 12.14 shows the various four-loudspeaker modes of the Marantz Model 1115 Quadradial Four Receiver. The mono mode is shown at (a), where all four speakers are driven (via separate amplifiers) by the same sum signals. The two-channel mode is shown at (b), where the left front and left back signals are summed. The so-called 'discrete' mode is shown at (c), where each speaker is driven only by its appropriate signal, and the 'synthesised' mode is shown at (d), where the left front and right front signals feed the corresponding speakers (as in stereo), while the back speakers are driven by signals derived from the two front channels, as already explained.

Any four-channel (meaning four amplifier channels and speakers) equipment, even when equipped with a decoder, can be switched to the 'discrete' mode for 4-4-4 reproduction from CD-4 disc or tape. Four-channel amplifiers and receivers (i.e. JVC) are now available with switched matrix decoding and CD-4 demodulation.

FROM 2-2-2 TO 4-2-4 OR 4-4-4 OPERATION

A 2-2-2 stereo technique can be developed into a 4-2-4 or 4-4-4 technique by the addition of two loudspeakers, a two-channel amplifier and matrix decoder or CD-4 demodulator, as shown in Fig. 12.15, (a) for matrix and (b) for CD-4 or four-channel tape without the demodulator.

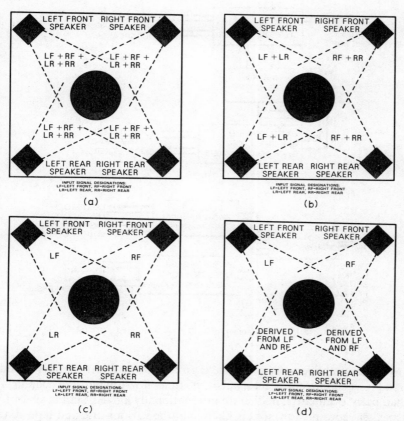

FIG. 12.14. *Four-loudspeaker reproduction.* (a) *mono*; (b) *stereo,* (c) *4-4-4 and* (d) *derived rear channel*
(see text)

The two input signals required for the matrix (a) can be obtained from the L and R recording outputs of the front amplifier, and by switching this amplifier to tape monitoring the front left and right matrix outputs can be fed back to the power amplifiers of the front amplifier by way of the L and R tape monitoring or replay sockets. In the monitoring position, the preamplifiers and power amplifiers are disconnected and so can be operated independently.

Some stereo amplifiers incorporate a switch which disconnects the pre-amplifiers from the power amplifiers, with preamplifier outputs and power amplifier inputs, which amounts to the same thing.

The L and R back outputs of the matrix are then connected to the appropriate channels of the extra amplifier for driving the two back loudspeakers.

For 'discrete' operation there are fewer complications as will be appreciated from diagram (b).

Two-channel amplifiers complete with decoding matrix facilities are also available. The principle is the same as already noted, but the wiring is less complicated. Matrix discs can be recorded on a stereo tape machine and replayed through a four-channel system via a corresponding decoding matrix.

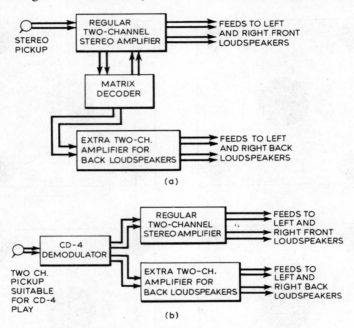

FIG. 12.15. *Development of 2-2-2 to 4-2-4 (a) and 4-4-4 (b)*

F.M. tuner-amplifiers may also have provision for multi-channel decoding from radio when the time comes, but at the time of writing no UK standard for this had been formulated; neither an internationally agreed 'standard' for four-loudspeaker reproduction, so it is likely that the various disc and tape systems will co-exist for some time yet to come. Equipment is, in fact, being manufactured with easy switching to any of the three predominating systems, namely CD-4, QS and SQ, with a synthesising mode, some of the JVC equipment, for example, being equipped with both matrix switching and CD-4 demodulating.

To summarise, then, as with stereo, there must be reliance on psycho-acoustical principles for four-loudspeaker illusion of directionality, reverberance and ambience, but as more information is made available to the listener through more loudspeakers and signal channels, so the need for the ear/brain to 'synthesise' to make good the lack of information is reduced, the reproduction then having greater accuracy potential to the original, depending on the recording techniques, etc.

The 'image localising' artifices of some of the matrix systems are included in an endeavour to obtain from two intermediate signal channels the effects that

276

are more easily provided by four, especially in terms of directionality. Matrix systems, or even sometimes simple synthesising, are preferred by some listeners, while others veer strongly in favour of four full or partially restricted bandwidth channels.

It is noteworthy that during the time this book was being published proposals for a British system for 'all-round' ambisonic sound (see the reference on page 260) were announced. This is aimed at giving the listener the experience not only of the special disposition of the performers, but also of the directional qualities of the reverberant sound that adds significantly to the realism and enjoyment of the actual performance.

Called the NRDC (after the *National Research Development Corporation*, its sponsors) Ambisonic System, it was researched at the Department of Applied Physical Sciences, Cybernetics Division, University of Reading in collaboration with the British IMF Company and Professor Peter B. Fellgett. Subjected to patents, the system is basically of phasor 'matrix' configuration and is compatible with conventional stereo playback.

Professor Fellgett's research has shown that while it is possible for two channels to carry full information about the direction of sound, an extension of the NRDC Ambisonic System could, nevertheless, be aligned to four-channel media (such as CD-4 and Nippon-Columbia Cooper-Shiga UD4), thereby allowing optimum exploitation in the 'periphonic' mode of the full four-channel capacity (see page 260).

CONCLUSIONS

As stated in the opening pages, a great deal has happened in the world of audio and hi-fi since the book from which this new one was born was written. Much is still taking place, but special pains have been taken to ensure that this book gives a fairly up-to-date reflection of the existing state of the art.

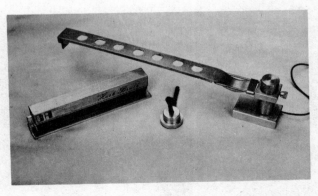

FIG. 12.16. *Novel cleaning devices by Chelston Audiocraft Limited. These employ multitudinous very fine conductive fibres which not only seek deeply into the groove spiral for extracting deep-seated dust but also tend towards discharge of the static on the surface of a disc, thereby inhibiting further dust attraction. The pivoted brush for trailing on a rotating disc is biased magnetically for self-parking and for correcting side-thrust; it also incorporates a wire for 'earthing' the conducting fibres. The small brush is for stylus cleaning and the large brush for hand-cleaning a record, also by Decca*

In conclusion, just a word or two about gramophone records. To avoid undue background noises, particularly with respect to four-loudspeaker reproduction, records should be kept free from dust. This is not easy since small particles are violently attracted to their surfaces by static electricity which is generated by friction—for example, by merely extracting a record from its sleeve. Various devices have been developed over the years to clear the dust, etc. from the grooves while at the same time helping to discharge the static. Some recent devices of this kind by Decca and Chelston Audiocraft Limited have brushes composed of a large number of very fine carbon fibres which seek well into the bottom of the grooves while the conduction discharges the static. Some of the first Audiocraft wares are shown in Fig. 12.16, which are a magnetically biased brush for trailing on a rotating disc, a hand brush and stylus cleaning brush.

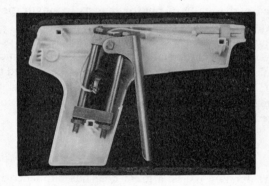

FIG. 12.17. *These photographs (with Donald Aldous) show the Zerostat Pistol in action and the inside piezoelectric ceramic element and trigger mechanism*

278

Another very interesting static removing device is shown in Fig. 12.17. This works on the piezoelectric principle and is called the Zerostat Pistol. When the trigger is drawn back the piezoelectric ceramic element is stressed and a high electric charge develops on a pin electrode located in the muzzle. In operation, the 'pistol' is 'fired' at a record and any electric charge on it, such as produced by its withdraw from the sleeve, is effectively neutralised by the piezoelectric charge. It is necessary, of course, to remove the dust from the record by more conventional means, but when the record is free from static this is a relatively simple matter.

Designed by the University of North Wales at Bangor under the direction of Dr. Secker, the Zerostat Pistol is manufactured and marketed by Cambridge Electro Sciences at Cambridge.

FIG. 12.18. *Hi-fi housing by Calyx Shelving Limited, showing the record storage section (see text)*

Still on records, Fig. 12.18 shows a good way of storing these. This is the bottom section of a hi-fi cabinet by Calyx Shelving Systems Limited. The top section (not visible) is designed to accommodate the amplifier, tuner, record playing unit, tape machine, etc. The records are firmly held flat and vertically between two spring-tensioned wooden surfaces.

Index

281

INDEX

INDEX

INDEX